Praise for *The Glass Castle*

The autobiographer is faced with the daunting challenge of . . . attempting to understand, forgive and even love the witch. . . . Readers will marvel at the intelligence and resilience of the Walls kids."
                              —Francine Prose, *The New York Times Book Review*

"A pull-yourself-up-by-the-bootstraps, thoroughly American story."
                              —*Kirkus Reviews*

"Charles Dickens has nothing on Jeannette Walls, author of *The Glass Castle,* the unflinching story about her grueling, nomadic childhood. Dickens' scenes of poverty and hardship are no more audacious and no more provocative than those in the pages of this stunning memoir."
                              —*The Atlanta Journal-Constitution*

"An excellent book. . . . Walls has a fantastic storytelling knack."
                              —*Publishers Weekly*

"*The Glass Castle* will at times exhaust you, occasionally fill you with fury, and finally leave you in slack-jawed wonderment."
                              —*National Review Online*

"Jeannette Walls has decided to tell all, and the result is this riveting memoir."

                              —*Glamour*

"You'll root for the Walls family."

                              —*Newsweek*

"*The Glass Castle* is the kind of story that keeps you awake long after the rest of the house has fallen asleep."

                              —*Vogue*

"Walls writes with clarity and feeling; it's her deep respect that infuses this astonishing story with grace."

—*Tampa Tribune*

"A beautiful, brave, transformative book."

—Rosie O'Donnell

"Jeannette Walls has carved a story with precision and grace out of one of the most chaotic, heartbreaking childhoods ever to be set down on the page. This deeply affecting memoir is a triumph in every possible way, and it does what all good books should: it affirms our faith in the human spirit."

—Dani Shapiro, author of *Family History*

"*The Glass Castle* is the saga of the restless, indomitable Walls family, led by a grand eccentric and his tempestuous artist wife. Jeannette Walls has survived poverty, fires, and near starvation to triumph. She has written this amazing tale with honesty and love."

—Patricia Bosworth, author of *Anything Your Little Heart Desires* and *Diane Arbus: A Biography*

"Just read the first pages of *The Glass Castle* by Jeannette Walls, and I defy you not to go on. It's funny and sad and quirky and loving. I was incredibly touched by it."

—Dominick Dunne, author of *The Way We Lived Then: Recollections of a Well-Known Name Dropper*

My parents, Rose Mary and Rex Walls,
on their wedding day, 1956

THE
GLASS CASTLE

a memoir

Jeannette Walls

SCRIBNER

New York   London   Toronto   Sydney   New Delhi

SCRIBNER
An Imprint of Simon & Schuster, Inc.
Avenue of the Americas
New York, NY 10020

The names and identifying details of some characters
in this book have been changed.

This Scribner trade paperback edition July 2017

SCRIBNER and design are registered trademarks of
The Gale Group, Inc., used under license
by Simon & Schuster, the publisher of this work.

For information about special discounts for bulk purchases,
please contact Simon & Schuster Special Sales at
1-800-506-1949 or business@simonandschuster.com.

The Simon & Schuster Speakers Bureau can bring authors to your live event.
For more information or to book an event contact the Simon & Schuster Speakers
Bureau at 1-866-248-3049 or visit our website at www.simonspeakers.com.

INTERIOR DESIGN BY KYOKO WATANABE
Text set in Minion

Manufactured in the United States of America

1   3   5   7   9   10   8   6   4   2

Library of Congress Cataloging-in-Publication Data
Walls, Jeannette.
The glass castle : a memoir / Jeannette Walls.
p. cm.
1. Walls, Jeannette. 2. Children of alcoholics—United States—Biography.
3. Children of alcoholics—West Virginia—Biography.
4. Problem families—United States—Case studies.
5. Problem families—West Virginia—Welch—Case studies.
6. Poor—West Virginia—Welch—Biography.
7. Homeless persons—New York (State)—New York—Family relationships.
I. Title.
HV5132.W35 2005
362.82'092—dc22
[B]   2004058907

ISBN 978-1-5011-7158-1 (pbk)
ISBN 978-1-4165-5060-0 (eBook)

To John,
for convincing me that everyone who is
interesting has a past

Acknowledgments

I'd like to thank my brother, Brian, for standing by me when we were growing up and while I wrote this. I'm also grateful to my mother for believing in art and truth and for supporting the idea of the book; to my brilliant and talented older sister, Lori, for coming around to it; and to my younger sister, Maureen, whom I will always love. And to my father, Rex S. Walls, for dreaming all those big dreams.

Very special thanks also to my agent, Jennifer Rudolph Walsh, for her compassion, wit, tenacity, and enthusiastic support; to my editor, Nan Graham, for her keen sense of how much is enough and for caring so deeply; and to Alexis Gargagliano for her thoughtful and sensitive readings.

My gratitude for their early and constant support goes to Jay and Betsy Taylor, Laurie Peck, Cynthia and David Young, Amy and Jim Scully, Ashley Pearson, Dan Mathews, Susan Watson, and Jessica Taylor and Alex Guerrios.

I can never adequately thank my husband, John Taylor, who persuaded me it was time to tell my story and then pulled it out of me.

Dark is a way and light is a place,
Heaven that never was
Nor will be ever is always true

—*Dylan Thomas,*
"Poem on His Birthday"

I

A Woman
on the Street

I WAS SITTING IN a taxi, wondering if I had overdressed for the evening, when I looked out the window and saw Mom rooting through a Dumpster. It was just after dark. A blustery March wind whipped the steam coming out of the manholes, and people hurried along the sidewalks with their collars turned up. I was stuck in traffic two blocks from the party where I was heading.

Mom stood fifteen feet away. She had tied rags around her shoulders to keep out the spring chill and was picking through the trash while her dog, a black-and-white terrier mix, played at her feet. Mom's gestures were all familiar—the way she tilted her head and thrust out her lower lip when studying items of potential value that she'd hoisted out of the Dumpster, the way her eyes widened with childish glee when she found something she liked. Her long hair was streaked with gray, tangled and matted, and her eyes had sunk deep into their sockets, but still she reminded me of the mom she'd been when I was a kid, swan-diving off cliffs and painting in the desert and reading Shakespeare aloud. Her cheekbones were still high and strong, but the skin was parched and ruddy from all those winters and summers exposed to the elements. To the people walking by, she probably looked like any of the thousands of homeless people in New York City.

It had been months since I laid eyes on Mom, and when she looked up, I was overcome with panic that she'd see me and call out my name, and that someone on the way to the same party would spot us together and Mom would introduce herself and my secret would be out.

I slid down in the seat and asked the driver to turn around and take me home to Park Avenue.

The taxi pulled up in front of my building, the doorman held the door for me, and the elevator man took me up to my floor. My husband was working late, as he did most nights, and the apartment was silent except for the click of my heels on the polished wood floor. I was still rattled from seeing Mom, the unexpectedness of coming across her, the sight of her rooting happily through the Dumpster. I put some Vivaldi on, hoping the music would settle me down.

I looked around the room. There were the turn-of-the-century bronze-and-silver vases and the old books with worn leather spines that I'd collected at flea markets. There were the Georgian maps I'd had framed, the Persian rugs, and the overstuffed leather armchair I liked to sink into at the end of the day. I'd tried to make a home for myself here, tried to turn the apartment into the sort of place where the person I wanted to be would live. But I could never enjoy the room without worrying about Mom and Dad huddled on a sidewalk grate somewhere. I fretted about them, but I was embarrassed by them, too, and ashamed of myself for wearing pearls and living on Park Avenue while my parents were busy keeping warm and finding something to eat.

What could I do? I'd tried to help them countless times, but Dad would insist they didn't need anything, and Mom would ask for something silly, like a perfume atomizer or a membership in a health club. They said that they were living the way they wanted to.

After ducking down in the taxi so Mom wouldn't see me, I hated myself—hated my antiques, my clothes, and my apartment. I had to do something, so I called a friend of Mom's and left a message. It was our system of staying in touch. It always took Mom a few days to get back to me, but when I heard from her, she sounded, as always, cheerful and casual, as though we'd had lunch the day before. I told her I wanted to see her and suggested she drop by the apartment, but she wanted to go to a restaurant. She loved eating out, so we agreed to meet for lunch at her favorite Chinese restaurant.

Mom was sitting at a booth, studying the menu, when I arrived. She'd made an effort to fix herself up. She wore a bulky gray sweater with only a few light stains, and black leather men's shoes. She'd washed her face, but her neck and temples were still dark with grime.

She waved enthusiastically when she saw me. "It's my baby girl!" she called out. I kissed her cheek. Mom had dumped all the plastic packets of soy sauce and duck sauce and hot-and-spicy mustard from the table into her purse. Now she emptied a wooden bowl of dried noodles into it as well. "A little snack for later on," she explained.

We ordered. Mom chose the Seafood Delight. "You know how I love my seafood," she said.

She started talking about Picasso. She'd seen a retrospective of his work and decided he was hugely overrated. All the cubist stuff was gimmicky, as far as she was concerned. He hadn't really done anything worthwhile after his Rose Period.

"I'm worried about you," I said. "Tell me what I can do to help."

Her smile faded. "What makes you think I need your help?"

"I'm not rich," I said. "But I have some money. Tell me what it is you need."

She thought for a moment. "I could use an electrolysis treatment."

"Be serious."

"I am serious. If a woman looks good, she feels good."

"Come on, Mom." I felt my shoulders tightening up, the way they invariably did during these conversations. "I'm talking about something that could help you change your life, make it better."

"You want to help me change my life?" Mom asked. "I'm fine. You're the one who needs help. Your values are all confused."

"Mom, I saw you picking through trash in the East Village a few days ago."

"Well, people in this country are too wasteful. It's my way of recycling." She took a bite of her Seafood Delight. "Why didn't you say hello?"

"I was too ashamed, Mom. I hid."

Mom pointed her chopsticks at me. "You see?" she said. "Right there. That's exactly what I'm saying. You're way too easily embarrassed. Your father and I are who we are. Accept it."

"And what am I supposed to tell people about my parents?"

"Just tell the truth," Mom said. "That's simple enough."

II

THE DESERT

I WAS ON FIRE.

It's my earliest memory. I was three years old, and we were living in a trailer park in a southern Arizona town whose name I never knew. I was standing on a chair in front of the stove, wearing a pink dress my grandmother had bought for me. Pink was my favorite color. The dress's skirt stuck out like a tutu, and I liked to spin around in front of the mirror, thinking I looked like a ballerina. But at that moment, I was wearing the dress to cook hot dogs, watching them swell and bob in the boiling water as the late-morning sunlight filtered in through the trailer's small kitchenette window.

I could hear Mom in the next room singing while she worked on one of her paintings. Juju, our black mutt, was watching me. I stabbed one of the hot dogs with a fork and bent over and offered it to him. The wiener was hot, so Juju licked at it tentatively, but when I stood up and started stirring the hot dogs again, I felt a blaze of heat on my right side. I turned to see where it was coming from and realized my dress was on fire. Frozen with fear, I watched the yellow-white flames make a ragged brown line up the pink fabric of my skirt and climb my stomach. Then the flames leaped up, reaching my face.

I screamed. I smelled the burning and heard a horrible crackling as the fire singed my hair and eyelashes. Juju was barking. I screamed again.

Mom ran into the room.

"Mommy, help me!" I shrieked. I was still standing on the chair, swatting at the fire with the fork I had been using to stir the hot dogs.

Mom ran out of the room and came back with one of the army-surplus blankets I hated because the wool was so scratchy. She threw the blanket around me to smother the flames. Dad had gone off in the car, so Mom grabbed me and my younger brother, Brian, and hurried over to the trailer next to ours. The woman who lived there was hanging her laundry on the clothesline. She had clothespins in her mouth. Mom, in an unnaturally calm voice, explained what had happened and asked if we could please have a ride to the hospital. The woman dropped her clothes-pins and laundry right there in the dirt and, without saying anything, ran for her car.

When we got to the hospital, nurses put me on a stretcher. They talked in loud, worried whispers while they cut off what was left of my fancy pink dress with a pair of shiny scissors. Then they picked me up, laid me flat on a big metal bed piled with ice cubes, and spread some of the ice over my body. A doctor with silver hair and black-rimmed glasses led my mother out of the room. As they left, I heard him telling her that it was very serious. The nurses remained behind, hovering over me. I could tell I was causing a big fuss, and I stayed quiet. One of them squeezed my hand and told me I was going to be okay.

"I know," I said, "but if I'm not, that's okay, too."

The nurse squeezed my hand again and bit her lower lip.

The room was small and white, with bright lights and metal cabinets. I stared for a while at the rows of tiny dots in the ceiling panels. Ice cubes covered my stomach and ribs and pressed up against my cheeks. Out of the corner of my eye, I saw a small, grimy hand reach up a few inches from my face and grab a handful of cubes. I heard a loud crunching sound and looked down. It was Brian, eating the ice.

The doctors said I was lucky to be alive. They took patches of skin from my upper thigh and put them over the most badly burned parts of my stomach, ribs, and chest. They said it was called a skin graft. When they were finished, they wrapped my entire right side in bandages.

"Look, I'm a half-mummy," I said to one of the nurses. She smiled and put my right arm in a sling and attached it to the headboard so I couldn't move it.

The nurses and doctors kept asking me questions: How did you get burned? Have your parents ever hurt you? Why do you have all these bruises and cuts? My parents never hurt me, I said. I got the cuts and bruises playing outside and the burns from cooking hot dogs. They asked what I was doing cooking hot dogs by myself at the age of three. It was easy, I said. You just put the hot dogs in the water and boil them. It wasn't like there was some complicated recipe that you had to be old enough to follow. The pan was too heavy for me to lift when it was full of water, so I'd put a chair next to the sink, climb up and fill a glass, then stand on a chair by the stove and pour the water into the pan. I did that over and over again until the pan held enough water. Then I'd turn on the stove, and when the water was boiling, I'd drop in the hot dogs. "Mom says I'm mature for my age," I told them, "and she lets me cook for myself a lot."

Two nurses looked at each other, and one of them wrote something down on a clipboard. I asked what was wrong. Nothing, they said, nothing.

Every couple of days, the nurses changed the bandages. They would put the used bandage off to the side, wadded and covered with smears of blood and yellow stuff and little pieces of burned skin. Then they'd apply another bandage, a big gauzy cloth, to the burns. At night I would run my left hand over the rough, scabby surface of the skin that wasn't covered by the bandage. Sometimes I'd peel off scabs. The nurses had told me not to, but I couldn't resist pulling on them real slow to see how big a scab I could get loose. Once I had a couple of them free, I'd pretend they were talking to each other in cheeping voices.

The hospital was clean and shiny. Everything was white—the walls and sheets and nurses' uniforms—or silver—the beds and trays and medical instruments. Everyone spoke in polite, calm voices. It was so hushed you could hear the nurses' rubber-soled shoes squeaking all the way down the hall. I wasn't used to quiet and order, and I liked it.

I also liked it that I had my own room, since in the trailer I shared one with my brother and my sister. My hospital room even had its very own television set up on the wall. We didn't have a TV at home, so I watched it a lot. Red Buttons and Lucille Ball were my favorites.

The nurses and doctors always asked how I was feeling and if I was hungry or needed anything. The nurses brought me delicious meals three times a day, with fruit cocktail or Jell-O for dessert, and changed the sheets even if they still looked clean. Sometimes I read to them, and they told me I was very smart and could read as well as a six-year-old.

One day a nurse with wavy yellow hair and blue eye makeup was chewing on something. I asked her what it was, and she told me it was chewing gum. I had never heard of chewing gum, so she went out and got me a whole pack. I pulled out a stick, took off the white paper and the shiny silver foil under it, and studied the powdery, putty-colored gum. I put it in my mouth and was stunned by the sharp sweetness. "It's really good!" I said.

"Chew on it, but don't swallow it," the nurse said with a laugh. She smiled real big and brought in other nurses so they could watch me chew my first-ever piece of gum. When she brought me lunch, she told me I had to take out my chewing gum, but she said not to worry because I could have a new stick after eating. If I finished the pack, she would buy me another. That was the thing about the hospital. You never had to worry about running out of stuff like food or ice or even chewing gum. I would have been happy staying in that hospital forever.

When my family came to visit, their arguing and laughing and singing and shouting echoed through the quiet halls. The nurses made shushing noises, and Mom and Dad and Lori and Brian lowered their voices for a few minutes, then they slowly grew loud again. Everyone always turned and stared at Dad. I couldn't figure out whether it was because he was so handsome or because he called people "pardner" and "goomba" and threw his head back when he laughed.

One day Dad leaned over my bed and asked if the nurses and doctors were treating me okay. If they were not, he said, he would kick some asses. I told Dad how nice and friendly everyone was. "Well, of course they are," he said. "They know you're Rex Walls's daughter."

When Mom wanted to know what it was the doctors and nurses were doing that was so nice, I told her about the chewing gum.

"Ugh," she said. She disapproved of chewing gum, she went on. It was a disgusting low-class habit, and the nurse should have consulted her before encouraging me in such vulgar behavior. She said she was going to give that woman a piece of her mind, by golly. "After all," Mom said, "I am your mother, and I should have a say in how you're raised."

"Do you guys miss me?" I asked my older sister, Lori, during one visit.

"Not really," she said. "Too much has been happening."

"Like what?"

"Just the normal stuff."

"Lori may not miss you, honey bunch, but I sure do," Dad said. "You shouldn't be in this antiseptic joint."

He sat down on my bed and started telling me the story about the time Lori got stung by a poisonous scorpion. I'd heard it a dozen times, but I still liked the way Dad told it. Mom and Dad were out exploring in the desert when Lori, who was four, turned over a rock and the scorpion hiding under it stung her leg. She had gone into convulsions, and her body had become stiff and wet with sweat. But Dad didn't trust hospitals, so he took her to a Navajo witch doctor who cut open the wound and put a dark brown paste on it and said some chants and pretty soon Lori was as good as new. "Your mother should have taken you to that witch doctor the day you got burned," Dad said, "not to these heads-up-their-asses med-school quacks."

The next time they visited, Brian's head was wrapped in a dirty white bandage with dried bloodstains. Mom said he had fallen off the back of the couch and cracked his head open on the floor, but she and Dad had decided not to take him to the hospital.

"There was blood everywhere," Mom said, "but one kid in the hospital at a time is enough."

"Besides," Dad said, "Brian's head is so hard, I think the floor took more damage than he did."

Brian thought that was hilarious and just laughed and laughed.

Mom told me she had entered my name in a raffle at a fair, and I'd won a helicopter ride. I was thrilled. I had never been in a helicopter or a plane.

"When do I get to go on the ride?" I asked.

"Oh, we already did that," Mom said. "It was fun."

Then Dad got into an argument with the doctor. It started because Dad thought I shouldn't be wearing bandages. "Burns need to breathe," he told the doctor.

The doctor said bandages were necessary to prevent infection. Dad stared at the doctor. "To hell with infection," he said. He told the doctor that I was going to be scarred for life because of him, but, by God, I wasn't the only one who was going to walk out of there scarred.

Dad pulled back his fist as if to hit the doctor, who raised his hands and backed away. Before anything could happen, a guard in a uniform appeared and told Mom and Dad and Lori and Brian that they would have to leave.

Afterward, a nurse asked me if I was okay. "Of course," I said. I told her I didn't care if I had some silly old scar. That was good, she said, because from the look of it, I had other things to worry about.

A few days later, when I had been at the hospital for about six weeks, Dad appeared alone in the doorway of my room. He told me we were going to check out, Rex Walls–style.

"Are you sure this is okay?" I asked.

"You just trust your old man," Dad said.

He unhooked my right arm from the sling over my head. As he held me close, I breathed in his familiar smell of Vitalis, whiskey, and cigarette smoke. It reminded me of home.

Dad hurried down the hall with me in his arms. A nurse yelled for us to stop, but Dad broke into a run. He pushed open an emergency-exit door and sprinted down the stairs and out to the street. Our car, a beat-up Plymouth we called the Blue Goose, was parked around the corner, the engine idling. Mom was up front, Lori and Brian in the back with Juju. Dad slid me across the seat next to Mom and took the wheel.

"You don't have to worry anymore, baby," Dad said. "You're safe now."

A FEW DAYS AFTER Mom and Dad brought me home, I cooked myself some hot dogs. I was hungry, Mom was at work on a painting, and no one else was there to fix them for me.

"Good for you," Mom said when she saw me cooking. "You've got to get right back in the saddle. You can't live in fear of something as basic as fire."

I didn't. Instead, I became fascinated with it. Dad also thought I should face down my enemy, and he showed me how to pass my finger through a candle flame. I did it over and over, slowing my finger with each pass, watching the way it seemed to cut the flame in half, testing to see how much my finger could endure without actually getting burned. I was always on the lookout for bigger fires. Whenever neighbors burned trash, I ran over and watched the blaze trying to escape the garbage can. I'd inch closer and closer, feeling the heat against my face until I got so near that it became unbearable, and then I'd back away just enough to be able to stand it.

The neighbor lady who had driven me to the hospital was surprised that I didn't run in the opposite direction from any fire I saw. "Why the hell would she?" Dad bellowed with a proud grin. "She already fought the fire once and won."

I started stealing matches from Dad. I'd go behind the trailer and light them. I loved the scratching sound of the match against the sandpapery brown strip when I struck it, and the way the flame leaped out of the red-coated tip with a pop and a hiss. I'd feel its heat near my fingertips, then wave it out triumphantly. I lit pieces of paper and little piles of brush and held my breath until the moment when they seemed about to blaze up out of control. Then I'd stomp on the flames and call out the curse words Dad used, like "Dumb-ass sonofabitch!" and "Cocksucker!"

One time I went out back with my favorite toy, a plastic Tinkerbell figurine. She was two inches tall, with yellow hair pulled up in a high ponytail and her hands on her hips in a confident, cocky way that I admired. I lit a match and held it close to Tinkerbell's face to show her how it felt. She looked even more beautiful in the flame's glow. When that match went out, I lit another one, and this time I held it really close to Tinkerbell's face. Suddenly, her eyes grew wide, as if with fear; I realized, to my horror, that her face was starting to melt. I put out the match, but it was too late. Tinkerbell's once perfect little nose had completely disappeared, and her saucy red lips had been replaced with an ugly, lopsided smear. I tried to smooth her features back to the way they had been, but I made them even worse. Almost immediately, her face cooled and hardened again. I put bandages on it. I wished I could perform a skin graft on Tinkerbell, but that would have meant cutting her into pieces. Even though her face was melted, she was still my favorite toy.

DAD CAME HOME IN the middle of the night a few months later and roused all of us from bed.

"Time to pull up stakes and leave this shit-hole behind," he hollered.

We had fifteen minutes to gather whatever we needed and pile into the car.

"Is everything okay, Dad?" I asked. "Is someone after us?"

"Don't you worry," Dad said. "You leave that to me. Don't I always take care of you?"

"'Course you do," I said.

"That's my girl!" Dad said with a hug, then barked orders at us all to speed things up. He took the essentials—a big black cast-iron skillet and the Dutch oven, some army-surplus tin plates, a few knives, his pistol, and Mom's archery set—and packed them in the trunk of the Blue Goose. He said we shouldn't take much else, just what we needed to survive. Mom hurried out to the yard and started digging holes by the light of the moon, looking for our jar of cash. She had forgotten where she'd buried it.

An hour passed before we finally tied Mom's paintings on the top of the car, shoved whatever would fit into the trunk, and piled the overflow on the backseat and the car floor. Dad steered the Blue Goose through the dark, driving slowly so as not to alert anyone in the trailer park that we were, as Dad liked to put it, doing the skedaddle. He was grumbling that he couldn't understand why the hell it took so long to grab what we needed and haul our asses into the car.

"Dad!" I said. "I forgot Tinkerbell!"

"Tinkerbell can make it on her own," Dad said. "She's like my brave little girl. You *are* brave and ready for adventure, right?"

"I guess," I said. I hoped whoever found Tinkerbell would love her despite her melted face. For comfort, I tried to cradle Quixote, our gray and white cat who was missing an ear, but he growled and scratched at my face. "Quiet, Quixote!" I said.

"Cats don't like to travel," Mom explained.

Anyone who didn't like to travel wasn't invited on our adventure, Dad said. He stopped the car, grabbed Quixote by the scruff of the neck, and tossed him out the window. Quixote landed with a screeching meow and a thud, Dad accelerated up the road, and I burst into tears.

"Don't be so sentimental," Mom said. She told me we could always get another cat, and now Quixote was going to be a wild cat, which was much more fun than being a house cat. Brian, afraid that Dad might toss Juju out the window as well, held the dog tight.

To distract us kids, Mom got us singing songs like "Don't Fence Me In" and "This Land Is Your Land," and Dad led us in rousing renditions of "Old Man River" and his favorite, "Swing Low, Sweet Chariot." After a while, I forgot about Quixote and Tinkerbell and the friends I'd left behind in the trailer park. Dad started telling us about all the exciting things we were going to do and how we were going to get rich once we reached the new place where we were going to live.

"Where are we going, Dad?" I asked.

"Wherever we end up," he said.

Later that night, Dad stopped the car out in the middle of the desert, and we slept under the stars. We had no pillows, but Dad said that was part of his plan. He was teaching us to have good posture. The Indians didn't use pillows, either, he explained, and look how straight they stood. We did have our scratchy army-surplus blankets, so we spread them out and lay there, looking up at the field of stars. I told Lori how lucky we were to be sleeping out under the sky like Indians.

"We could live like this forever," I said.

"I think we're going to," she said.

WE WERE ALWAYS DOING the skedaddle, usually in the middle of the night. I sometimes heard Mom and Dad discussing the people who were after us. Dad called them henchmen, bloodsuckers, and the gestapo. Sometimes he would make mysterious references to executives from Standard Oil who were trying to steal the Texas land that Mom's family owned, and FBI agents who were after Dad for some dark episode that he never told us about because he didn't want to put us in danger, too.

Dad was so sure a posse of federal investigators was on our trail that he smoked his unfiltered cigarettes from the wrong end. That way, he explained, he burned up the brand name, and if the people who were tracking us looked in his ashtray, they'd find unidentifiable butts instead of Pall Malls that could be traced to him. Mom, however, told us that the FBI wasn't really after Dad; he just liked to say they were because it was more fun having the FBI on your tail than bill collectors.

We moved around like nomads. We lived in dusty little mining towns in Nevada, Arizona, and California. They were usually nothing but a tiny cluster of sad, sunken shacks, a gas station, a dry-goods store, and a bar or two. They had names like Needles and Bouse, Pie, Goffs, and Why, and they were near places like the Superstition Mountains, the dried-up Soda Lake, and the Old Woman Mountain. The more desolate and isolated a place was, the better Mom and Dad liked it.

Dad would get a job as an electrician or engineer in a gypsum or copper mine. Mom liked to say that Dad could talk a blue streak, spinning tales of jobs he'd never had and college degrees he'd never earned. He could get about any job he wanted, he just didn't like keeping it for long. Sometimes he made money gambling or doing odd jobs. When he got bored or was fired or the unpaid bills piled up too high or the lineman from the electrical company found out he had hot-wired our trailer to the utility poles—or the FBI was closing in—we packed up in the middle of the night and took off, driving until Mom and Dad found another small town that caught their eye. Then we'd circle around, looking for houses with for-rent signs stuck in the front yard.

Every now and then, we'd go stay with Grandma Smith, Mom's mom, who lived in a big white house in Phoenix. Grandma Smith was a West Texas flapper who loved dancing and cussing and horses. She was known for being able to break the wildest broncs and had helped Grandpa run the ranch up near Fish Creek Canyon, Arizona, which was west of Bullhead City, not too far from the Grand Canyon. I thought Grandma Smith was great. But after a few weeks, she and Dad would always get into some nasty hollering match. It might start with Mom mentioning how short we were on cash. Then Grandma would make a snide comment about Dad being shiftless. Dad would say something about selfish old crones with more money than they knew what to do with, and soon enough they'd be face-to-face in what amounted to a full-fledged cussing contest.

"You flea-bitten drunk!" Grandma would scream.

"You goddamned flint-faced hag!" Dad would shout back.

"You no-good two-bit pud-sucking bastard!"

"You scaly castrating banshee bitch!"

Dad had the more inventive vocabulary, but Grandma Smith could outshout him; plus, she had the home-court advantage. A time would come when Dad had had enough and he'd tell us kids to get in the car. Grandma would yell at Mom not to let that worthless horse's ass take her grandchildren. Mom would shrug and say there was nothing she could do about it, he was her husband. Off we'd go, heading out into the desert in search of another house for rent in another little mining town.

Some of the people who lived in those towns had been there for years. Others were rootless, like us—just passing through. They were gamblers or ex-cons or war veterans or what Mom called loose women. There were old prospectors, their faces wrinkled and brown from the sun, like dried-up apples. The kids were lean and hard, with calluses on their hands and feet. We'd make friends with them, but not close friends, because we knew we'd be moving on sooner or later.

We might enroll in school, but not always. Mom and Dad did most of our teaching. Mom had us all reading books without pictures by the time we were five, and Dad taught us math. He also taught us the things that were really important and useful, like how to tap out Morse code and how we should never eat the liver of a polar bear because all the vitamin

A in it could kill us. He showed us how to aim and fire his pistol, how to shoot Mom's bow and arrows, and how to throw a knife by the blade so that it landed in the middle of a target with a satisfying thwock. By the time I was four, I was pretty good with Dad's pistol, a big black six-shot revolver, and could hit five out of six beer bottles at thirty paces. I'd hold the gun with both hands, sight down the barrel, and squeeze the trigger slowly and smoothly until, with a loud clap, the gun kicked and the bottle exploded. It was fun. Dad said my sharpshooting would come in handy if the feds ever surrounded us.

Mom had grown up in the desert. She loved the dry, crackling heat, the way the sky at sunset looked like a sheet of fire, and the overwhelming emptiness and severity of all that open land that had once been a huge ocean bed. Most people had trouble surviving in the desert, but Mom thrived there. She knew how to get by on next to nothing. She showed us which plants were edible and which were toxic. She was able to find water when no one else could, and she knew how little of it you really needed. She taught us that you could wash yourself up pretty clean with just a cup of water. She said it was good for you to drink unpurified water, even ditch water, as long as animals were drinking from it. Chlorinated city water was for namby-pambies, she said. Water from the wild helped build up your antibodies. She also thought toothpaste was for namby-pambies. At bedtime we'd shake a little baking soda into the palm of one hand, mix in a dash of hydrogen peroxide, then use our fingers to clean our teeth with the fizzing paste.

I loved the desert, too. When the sun was in the sky, the sand would be so hot that it would burn your feet if you were the kind of kid who wore shoes, but since we always went barefoot, our soles were as tough and thick as cowhide. We'd catch scorpions and snakes and horny toads. We'd search for gold, and when we couldn't find it, we'd collect other valuable rocks, like turquoise and garnets. There'd be a cool spell come sundown, when the mosquitoes would fly in so thick that the air would grow dark with them, then at nightfall, it turned so cold that we usually needed blankets.

There were fierce sandstorms. Sometimes they hit without warning, and other times you knew one was coming when you saw batches of dust devils swirling and dancing their way across the desert. Once the wind started whipping up the sand, you could only see a foot in front of your face. If you couldn't find a house or a car or a shed to hide in when the sandstorm started, you had to squat down and close your eyes and mouth real tight and cover your ears and bury your face in your lap until it passed, or else your body cavities would fill with sand. A big tumbleweed might hit you, but they were light and bouncy and didn't hurt. If the sandstorm was really strong, it knocked you over, and you rolled around like you were a tumbleweed.

When the rains finally came, the skies darkened and the air became heavy. Raindrops the size of marbles came pelting out of the sky. Some parents worried that their kids might get hit by lighting, but Mom and Dad never did, and they let us go out and play in the warm, driving water. We splashed and sang and danced. Great bolts of lightning cracked from the low-hanging clouds, and thunder shook the ground. We gasped over the most spectacular bolts, as if we were all watching a fireworks show. After the storm, Dad took us to the arroyos, and we watched the flash floods come roaring through. The next day the saguaros and prickly pears were fat from drinking as much as they could, because they knew it might be a long, long time until the next rain.

We were sort of like the cactus. We ate irregularly, and when we did, we'd gorge ourselves. Once when we were living in Nevada, a train full of cantaloupes heading east jumped the track. I had never eaten a cantaloupe before, but Dad brought home crates and crates of them. We had fresh cantaloupe, stewed cantaloupe, even fried cantaloupe. One time in California, the grape pickers went on strike. The vineyard owners let people come pick their own grapes for a nickel a pound. We drove about a hundred miles to the vineyards, where the grapes were so ripe they were about to burst on the vine in bunches bigger than my head. We filled our entire car full of green grapes—the trunk, even the glove compartment, and Dad piled stacks in our laps so high we could barely see over the top. For weeks afterward, we ate green grapes for breakfast, lunch, and dinner.

All this running around and moving was temporary, Dad explained. He had a plan. He was going to find gold.

Everybody said Dad was a genius. He could build or fix anything. One time when a neighbor's TV set broke, Dad opened the back and used a macaroni noodle to insulate some crossed wires. The neighbor couldn't get over it. He went around telling everyone in town that Dad sure knew how to use his noodle. Dad was an expert in math and physics and electricity. He read books on calculus and logarithmic algebra and loved what he called the poetry and symmetry of math. He told us about the magic qualities every number has and how numbers unlock the secrets of the universe. But Dad's main interest was energy: thermal energy, nuclear energy, solar energy, electrical energy, and energy from the wind. He said there were so many untapped sources of energy in the world that it was ridiculous to be burning all that fossil fuel.

Dad was always inventing things, too. One of his most important inventions was a complicated contraption he called the Prospector. It was going to help us find gold. The Prospector had a big flat surface about four feet high and six feet wide, and it rose up in the air at an angle. The surface was covered with horizontal strips of wood separated by gaps. The Prospector would scoop up dirt and rocks and sift them through the maze of wooden strips. It could figure out whether a rock was gold by the weight. It would throw out the worthless stuff and deposit the gold nuggets in a pile, so whenever we needed groceries, we could go out back and grab ourselves a nugget. At least that was what it would be able to do once Dad finished building it.

Dad let Brian and me help him work on the Prospector. We'd go out behind the house, and I'd hold the nails while Dad hit them. Sometimes he let me start the nails, and then he'd drive them in with one hard blow from the hammer. The air would be filled with sawdust and the smell of freshly cut wood, and the sound of hammering and whistling, because Dad always whistled while he worked.

In my mind, Dad was perfect, although he did have what Mom called a little bit of a drinking situation. There was what Mom called Dad's "beer phase." We could all handle that. Dad drove fast and sang really loud, and locks of his hair fell into his face and life was a little bit scary but still a lot of fun. But when Dad pulled out a bottle of what Mom called "the hard stuff," she got kind of frantic, because after working on the bottle for a while, Dad turned into an angry-eyed stranger who threw around furniture and threatened to beat up Mom or anyone else who got in his way. When he'd had his fill of cussing and hollering and smashing things up, he'd collapse. But Dad drank hard liquor only when we had money, which wasn't often, so life was mostly good in those days.

Every night when Lori, Brian, and I were about to go to sleep, Dad told us bedtime stories. They were always about him. We'd be tucked in our beds or lying under blankets in the desert, the world dark except for the orange glow from his cigarette. When he took a long draw, it lit up just enough for us to see his face.

"Tell us a story about yourself, Dad!" we'd beg him.

"Awww. You don't want to hear another story about me," he'd say.

"Yes, we do! We do!" we'd insist.

"Well, okay," he'd say. He'd pause and chuckle at some memory. "There's many a damned foolhardy thing that your old man has done, but this one was harebrained even for a crazy sonofabitch like Rex Walls."

And then he'd tell us about how, when he was in the air force and his plane's engine conked out, he made an emergency landing in a cattle pasture and saved himself and his crew. Or about the time he wrestled a pack of wild dogs that had surrounded a lame mustang. Then there was the time he fixed a broken sluice gate on the Hoover Dam and saved the lives of thousands of people who would have drowned if the dam had burst. There was also the time he went AWOL in the air force to get some beer, and while he was at the bar, he caught a lunatic who was planning to blow up the air base, which went to show that occasionally, it paid to break the rules.

Dad was a dramatic storyteller. He always started out slow, with lots of pauses. "Go on! What happened next?" we'd ask, even if we'd already heard that story before. Mom giggled or rolled her eyes when Dad told his stories, and he glared at her. If someone interrupted his storytelling, he got mad, and we had to beg him to continue and promise that no one would interrupt again.

Dad always fought harder, flew faster, and gambled smarter than everyone else in his stories. Along the way, he rescued women and children and even men who weren't as strong and clever. Dad taught us the secrets of his heroics—he showed us how to straddle a wild dog and break his neck, and where to hit a man in the throat so you could kill him with one powerful jab. But he assured us that as long as he was around, we wouldn't have to defend ourselves, because, by God, anyone who so much as laid a finger on any of Rex Walls's children was going to get their butts kicked so hard that you could read Dad's shoe size on their ass cheeks.

When Dad wasn't telling us about all the amazing things he had already done, he was telling us about the wondrous things he was going to do. Like build the Glass Castle. All of Dad's engineering skills and mathematical genius were coming together in one special project: a great big house he was going to build for us in the desert. It would have a glass ceiling and thick glass walls and even a glass staircase. The Glass Castle would have solar cells on the top that would catch the sun's rays and convert them into electricity for heating and cooling and running all the appliances. It would even have its own water-purification system. Dad had worked out the architecture and the floor plans and most of the mathematical calculations. He carried around the blueprints for the Glass Castle wherever we went, and sometimes he'd pull them out and let us work on the design for our rooms.

All we had to do was find gold, Dad said, and we were on the verge of that. Once he finished the Prospector and we struck it rich, he'd start work on our Glass Castle.

As much as Dad liked to tell stories about himself, it was almost impossible to get him to talk about his parents or where he was born. We knew he came from a town called Welch, in West Virginia, where a lot of coal was mined, and that his father had worked as a clerk for the railroad, sitting every day in a little station house, writing messages on pieces of paper that he held up on a stick for the passing train engineers. Dad had no interest in a life like that, so he left Welch when he was seventeen to join the air force and become a pilot.

One of his favorite stories, which he must have told us a hundred times, was about how he met and fell in love with Mom. Dad was in the air force, and Mom was in the USO, but when they met, she was on leave visiting her parents at their cattle ranch near Fish Creek Canyon.

Dad and some of his air force buddies were on a cliff of the canyon, trying to work up the nerve to dive into the lake forty feet below, when Mom and a friend drove up. Mom was wearing a white bathing suit that showed off her figure and her skin, which was dark from the Arizona sun. She had light brown hair that turned blond in the summer, and she never wore any makeup except deep red lipstick. She looked just like a movie star, Dad always said, but hell, he'd met lots of beautiful women before, and none of them had ever made him weak in the knees. Mom was different. He saw right away that she had true spirit. He fell in love with her the split second he laid eyes on her.

Mom walked up to the air force men and told them that diving off the cliff was no big deal, she'd been doing it since she was little. The men didn't believe her, so Mom went right to the edge of the cliff and did a perfect swan dive into the water below.

Dad jumped in after her. No way in hell, he'd say, was he letting a fine broad like that get away from him.

"What kind of dive did you do, Dad?" I asked whenever he told the story.

"A parachute dive. Without a parachute," he always answered.

Dad swam after Mom, and right there in the water, he told her he was going to marry her. Twenty-three men had already proposed to her, Mom told Dad, and she had turned them all down. "What makes you think I'd accept your proposal?" she asked.

"I didn't propose to you," Dad said. "I told you I was going to marry you."

Six months later, they got married. I always thought it was the most romantic story I'd ever heard, but Mom didn't like it. She didn't think it was romantic at all.

"I had to say yes," Mom said. "Your father wouldn't take no for an answer." Besides, she explained, she had to get away from her mother, who wouldn't let her make even the smallest decision on her own. "I had no idea your father would be even worse."

Dad left the air force after he got married because he wanted to make a fortune for his family, and you couldn't do that in the military. In a few months, Mom was pregnant. When Lori came out, she was mute and bald as an egg for the first three years of her life. Then suddenly, she sprouted curly hair the color of a new penny and started speaking non-stop. But it sounded like gibberish, and everyone thought she was addled except for Mom, who understood her perfectly and said she had an excellent vocabulary.

A year after Lori was born, Mom and Dad had a second daughter, Mary Charlene, who had coal-black hair and chocolate-brown eyes, just like Dad. But Mary Charlene died one night when she was nine months old. Crib death, Mom always said. Two years later, I was born. "You were to replace Mary Charlene," Mom said. She told me that she had ordered up a second redheaded girl so Lori wouldn't feel like she was weird. "You were such a skinny baby," Mom used to tell me. "The longest, boniest thing the nurses had ever seen."

Brian arrived when I was one. He was a blue baby, Mom said. When he was born, he couldn't breathe and came into this world having a seizure. Whenever Mom told the story, she would hold her arms rigid and clench her teeth and go bug-eyed to show how Brian looked. Mom said when she saw him like that, she thought, Uh-oh, looks like this one's a goner, too. But Brian lived. For the first year of his life, he kept having those seizures, then one day they just stopped. He turned into a tough little guy who never whined or cried, even the time I accidentally pushed him off the top bunk and he broke his nose.

Mom always said people worried too much about their children. Suffering when you're young is good for you, she said. It immunized your body and your soul, and that was why she ignored us kids when we cried. Fussing over children who cry only encourages them, she told us. That's positive reinforcement for negative behavior.

Mom never seemed upset about Mary Charlene's death. "God knows what He's doing," she said. "He gave me some perfect children, but He also gave me one that wasn't so perfect, so He said, 'Oops, I better take this one back.'" Dad, however, wouldn't talk about Mary Charlene. If her name came up, his face grew stony and he'd leave the room. He was the one who found her body in the crib, and Mom couldn't believe how much it shook him up. "When he found her, he stood there like he was in shock or something, cradling her stiff little body in his arms, and then he screamed like a wounded animal," she told us. "I never heard such a horrible sound."

Mom said Dad was never the same after Mary Charlene died. He started having dark moods, staying out late and coming home drunk, and losing jobs. One day soon after Brian was born, we were short on cash, so Dad pawned Mom's big diamond wedding ring, which her mother had paid for, and that upset Mom. After that, whenever Mom and Dad got in a fight, Mom brought up the ring, and Dad told her to quit her damn bellyaching. He'd say he was going to get her a ring even fancier than the one he pawned. That was why we had to find gold. To get Mom a new wedding ring. That and so we could build the Glass Castle.

"Do you like always moving around?" Lori asked me.

"Of course I do!" I said. "Don't you?"

"Sure," she said.

It was late afternoon, and we were parked outside of a bar in the Nevada desert. It was called the Bar None Bar. I was four and Lori was seven. We were on our way to Las Vegas. Dad had decided it would be easier, as he put it, to accumulate the capital necessary to finance the Prospector if he hit the casinos for a while. We'd been driving for hours when he saw the Bar None Bar, pulled over the Green Caboose—the Blue Goose had died, and we now had another car, a station wagon Dad had named the Green Caboose—and announced that he was going inside for a quick nip. Mom put on some red lipstick and joined him, even though she didn't drink anything stronger than tea. They had been inside for hours. The sun hung high in the sky, and there was not the slightest hint of a breeze. Nothing moved except some buzzards on the side of the road, pecking over an unrecognizable carcass. Brian was reading a dog-eared comic book.

"How many places have we lived?" I asked Lori.

"That depends on what you mean by 'lived,'" she said. "If you spend one night in some town, did you live there? What about two nights? Or a whole week?"

I thought. "If you unpack all your things," I said.

We counted eleven places we had lived, then we lost track. We couldn't remember the names of some of the towns or what the houses we had lived in looked like. Mostly, I remembered the inside of cars.

"What do you think would happen if we weren't always moving around?" I asked.

"We'd get caught," Lori said.

When Mom and Dad came out of the Bar None Bar, they brought us each a long piece of beef jerky and a candy bar. I ate the jerky first, and by the time I unwrapped my Mounds bar, it had melted into a brown, gooey mess, so I decided to save it until night, when the desert cold would harden it up again.

By then we had passed through the small town beyond the Bar None Bar. Dad was driving and smoking with one hand and holding a brown bottle of beer with the other. Lori was in the front seat between him and Mom, and Brian, who was in back with me, was trying to trade me half of his 3 Musketeers for half of my Mounds. Just then we took a sharp turn over some railroad tracks, the door flew open, and I tumbled out of the car.

I rolled several yards along the embankment, and when I came to a stop, I was too shocked to cry, with my breath knocked out and grit and pebbles in my eyes and mouth. I lifted my head in time to watch the Green Caboose get smaller and smaller and then disappear around a bend.

Blood was running down my forehead and flowing out of my nose. My knees and elbows were scraped raw and covered with sand. I was still holding the Mounds bar, but I had smashed it during the fall, tearing the wrapper and squeezing out the white coconut filling, which was also covered with grit.

Once I got my breath back, I crawled along the railroad embankment to the road and sat down to wait for Mom and Dad to come back. My whole body felt sore. The sun was small and white and broiling-hot. A wind had come up, and it was roiling the dust along the roadside. I waited for what seemed like a long time before I decided it was possible Mom and Dad might not come back for me. They might not notice I was missing. They might decide that it wasn't worth the drive back to retrieve me; that, like Quixote the cat, I was a bother and a burden they could do without.

The little town behind me was quiet, and there were no other cars on the road. I started crying, but that only made me feel more sore. I got up and began to walk back toward the houses, and then I decided that if Mom and Dad did come for me, they wouldn't be able to find me, so I returned to the railroad tracks and sat down again.

I was scraping the dried blood off my legs when I looked up and saw the Green Caboose come back around the bend. It hurtled up the road toward me, getting bigger and bigger, until it screeched to a halt right in front of me. Dad got out of the car, knelt down, and tried to give me a hug.

I pulled away from him. "I thought you were going to leave me behind," I said.

"Aww, I'd never do that," he said. "Your brother was trying to tell us that you'd fallen out, but he was blubbering so damned hard we couldn't understand a word he was saying."

Dad started pulling the pebbles out of my face. Some were buried deep in my skin, so he reached into the glove compartment for a pair of needle-nosed pliers. When he'd plucked all the pebbles from my cheeks and forehead, he took out his handkerchief and tried to stop my nose from bleeding. It was dripping like a broken faucet. "Damn, honey," he said. "You busted your snot locker pretty good."

I started laughing really hard. "Snot locker" was the funniest name I'd ever heard for a nose. After Dad cleaned me up and I got back in the car, I told Brian and Lori and Mom about the word, and they all started laughing as hard as me. Snot locker. It was hilarious.

WE LIVED IN LAS VEGAS for about a month, in a motel room with dark red walls and two narrow beds. We three kids slept in one, Mom and Dad in the other. During the day, we went to the casinos, where Dad said he had a sure-fire system for beating the house. Brian and I played hide-and-seek among the clicking slot machines, checking the trays for overlooked quarters, while Dad was winning money at the blackjack table. I'd stare at the long-legged showgirls when they sashayed across the casino floor, with huge feathers on their heads and behinds, sequins sparkling on their bodies, and glitter around their eyes. When I tried to imitate their walk, Brian said I looked like an ostrich.

At the end of the day, Dad came to get us, his pockets full of money. He bought us cowboy hats and fringed vests, and we ate chicken-fried steaks in restaurants with ice-cold air-conditioning and a miniature jukebox at each table. One night when Dad had made an especially big score, he said it was time to start living like the high rollers we had become. He took us to a restaurant with swinging doors like a saloon. Inside, the walls were decorated with real prospecting tools. A man with garters on his arms played a piano, and a woman with gloves that came up past her elbows kept hurrying over to light Dad's cigarettes.

Dad told us we were having something special for dessert—a flaming ice-cream cake. The waiter wheeled out a tray with the cake on it, and the woman with the gloves lit it with a taper. Everyone stopped eating to watch. The flames had a slow, watery movement, rolling up into the air like ribbons. Everyone started clapping, and Dad jumped up and raised the waiter's hand above his head as if he'd won first prize.

A few days later, Mom and Dad went off to the blackjack table and then almost immediately came looking for us. Dad said one of the dealers had figured out that he had a system and had put the word out on him. He told us it was time to do the skedaddle.

*　*　*

We had to get far away from Las Vegas, Dad said, because the Mafia, which owned the casinos, was after him. We headed west, through desert and then mountains. Mom said we should all live near the Pacific Ocean at least once in our lives, so we kept going all the way to San Francisco.

Mom didn't want us staying in one of those tourist-trap hotels near Fisherman's Wharf, which she said were inauthentic and cut off from the real life of the city, so we found one that had a lot more character, in a place called the Tenderloin District. Sailors and women with lots of makeup stayed there, too. Dad called it a flophouse, but Mom said it was an SRO, and when I asked what that stood for, she told me the hotel was for special residents only.

While Mom and Dad went out looking for investment money for the Prospector, we kids played in the hotel. One day I found a half-full box of matches. I was thrilled, because I much preferred the wooden matches that came in boxes over the flimsy ones in the cardboard books. I took them upstairs and locked myself in the bathroom. I pulled off some toilet paper, lit it, and when it started burning, I threw it down the toilet. I was torturing the fire, giving it life, and snuffing it out. Then I got a better idea. I made a pile of toilet paper in the toilet, lit it, and when it started burning, the flame shooting silently up out of the bowl, I flushed it down the toilet.

One night a few days later, I suddenly woke up. The air was hot and stifling. I smelled smoke and then saw flames leaping at the open window. At first I couldn't tell if the fire was inside or outside, but then I saw that one of the curtains, only a few feet from the bed, was ablaze.

Mom and Dad were not in the room, and Lori and Brian were still asleep. I tried to scream to warn them, but nothing came out of my throat. I wanted to reach over and shake them awake, but I couldn't move. The fire was growing bigger, stronger, and angrier.

Just then the door burst open. Someone was calling our names. It was Dad. Lori and Brian woke up and ran to him, coughing from the smoke. I still couldn't move. I watched the fire, expecting that at any moment my blanket would burst into flames. Dad wrapped the blanket around me and picked me up, then ran down the stairs, leading Lori and Brian with one arm and holding me in the other.

Dad took us kids across the street to a bar, then went back to help fight the fire. A waitress with red fingernails and blue-black hair asked if we wanted a Coca-Cola or, heck, even a beer, because we'd been through a lot that night. Brian and Lori said yes, please, to Cokes. I asked if I might please have a Shirley Temple, which was what Dad bought me whenever he took me to a bar. For some reason, the waitress laughed.

The people at the bar kept making jokes about women running naked out of the burning hotel. All I had on was my underwear, so I kept the blanket wrapped tightly around me. After I drank my Shirley Temple, I tried to go back across the street to watch the fire, but the waitress kept me at the bar, so I climbed up on a stool to watch through the window. The fire trucks had arrived. There were flashing lights and men in black rubber coats holding canvas hoses with big jets of water coming out of them.

I wondered if the fire had been out to get me. I wondered if all fire was related, like Dad said all humans were related, if the fire that had burned me that day while I cooked hot dogs was somehow connected to the fire I had flushed down the toilet and the fire burning at the hotel. I didn't have the answers to those questions, but what I did know was that I lived in a world that at any moment could erupt into fire. It was the sort of knowledge that kept you on your toes.

After the hotel burned down, we lived for a few days on the beach. When we put down the backseat of the Green Caboose, there was room for everyone to sleep, though sometimes someone's feet would be sticking in my face. One night a policeman tapped on our window and said we had to leave; it was illegal to sleep on the beach. He was nice and kept calling us "folks" and even drew us a map to a place where we could sleep without getting arrested.

But after he left, Dad called him the goddamn gestapo and said that people like that got their jollies pushing people like us around. Dad was fed up with civilization. He and Mom decided we should move back to the desert and resume our hunt for gold without our starter money. "These cities will kill you," he said.

AFTER WE PULLED UP stakes in San Francisco, we headed for the Mojave Desert. Near the Eagle Mountains, Mom made Dad stop the car. She'd seen a tree on the side of the road that had caught her fancy.

It wasn't just any tree. It was an ancient Joshua tree. It stood in a crease of land where the desert ended and the mountain began, forming a wind tunnel. From the time the Joshua tree was a tiny sapling, it had been so beaten down by the whipping wind that, rather than trying to grow skyward, it had grown in the direction that the wind pushed it. It existed now in a permanent state of windblownness, leaning over so far that it seemed ready to topple, although, in fact, its roots held it firmly in place.

I thought the Joshua tree was ugly. It looked scraggly and freakish, permanently stuck in its twisted, tortured position, and it made me think of how some adults tell you not to make weird faces because your features could freeze. Mom, however, thought it was one of the most beautiful trees she had ever seen. She told us she had to paint it. While she was setting out her easel, Dad drove up the road to see what was ahead. He found a scattering of parched little houses, trailers settling into the sand, and shacks with rusty tin roofs. It was called Midland. One of the little houses had a for-rent sign. "What the hell," Dad said, "this place is as good as any other."

The house we rented had been built by a mining company. It was white, with two rooms and a swaybacked roof. There were no trees, and the desert sand ran right up to the back door. At night you could hear coyotes howling.

When we first got to Midland, those coyotes kept me awake, and as I lay in bed, I'd hear other sounds—Gila monsters rustling in the underbrush, moths knocking against the screens, and the creosote crackling in the wind. One night when the lights were out and I could see a sliver of moon through the window, I heard a slithering noise on the floor.

"I think there's something under our bed," I said to Lori.

"It's merely a figment of your overly active imagination," Lori said. She talked like a grown-up when she was annoyed.

I tried to be brave, but I had heard something. In the moonlight, I thought I saw it move.

"Something's there," I whispered.

"Go to sleep," Lori said.

Holding my pillow over my head for protection, I ran into the living room, where Dad was reading. "What's up, Mountain Goat?" he asked. He called me that because I never fell down when we were climbing mountains—sure-footed as a mountain goat, he'd always say.

"Nothing, probably," I said. "I just think maybe I saw something in the bedroom." Dad raised his eyebrows. "But it was probably just a figment of my overly active imagination."

"Did you get a good look at it?" he asked.

"Not really."

"You must have seen it. Was it a big old hairy sonofabitch with the damnedest-looking teeth and claws?"

"That's it!"

"And did it have pointed ears and evil eyes with fire in 'em, and did it stare at you all wicked-like?" he asked.

"Yes! Yes! You've seen it, too?"

"Better believe I have. It's that old ornery bastard Demon."

Dad said he had been chasing Demon for years. By now, Dad said, that old Demon had figured out that it had better not mess with Rex Walls. But if that sneaky son of a gun thought it was going to terrorize Rex Walls's little girl, it had by God got another think coming. "Go fetch my hunting knife," Dad said.

I got Dad his knife with the carved bone handle and the blade of blue German steel, and he gave me a pipe wrench, and we went looking for Demon. We looked under my bed, where I had seen it, but it was gone. We looked all around the house—under the table, in the dark corners of the closets, in the toolbox, even outside in the trash cans.

"C'mere, you sorry-ass old Demon!" Dad called out in the desert night. "Come out and show your butt-ugly face, you yellow-bellied monster!"

"Yeah, c'mon, you old mean Demon!" I said, waving the pipe wrench in the air. "We're not scared of you!"

There was only the sound of the coyotes in the distance. "This is just like that chickenshit Demon," Dad said. He sat down on the front step and lit up a cigarette, then told me a story about the time Demon was terrorizing an entire town, and Dad fought it off in hand-to-hand combat, biting its ears and sticking his fingers in its eyes. Old Demon was terrified because that was the first time it had met anyone who wasn't afraid of it. "Damned old Demon didn't know what to think," Dad said, shaking his head with a chuckle. That was the thing to remember about all monsters, Dad said: They love to frighten people, but the minute you stare them down, they turn tail and run. "All you have to do, Mountain Goat, is show old Demon that you're not afraid."

Not much grew around Midland other than the Joshua tree, cacti, and the scrubby little creosote bushes that Dad said were some of the oldest plants on the planet. The great granddaddy creosote bushes were thousands of years old. When it rained, they let off a disgusting musty smell so animals wouldn't eat them. Only four inches of rain fell a year around Midland—about the same as in the northern Sahara—and water for humans came in on the train once a day in special containers. The only animals that could survive around Midland were lipless, scaly creatures such as Gila monsters and scorpions, and people like us.

A month after we moved to Midland, Juju got bitten by a rattlesnake and died. We buried him near the Joshua tree. It was practically the only time I ever saw Brian cry. But we had plenty of cats to keep us company. Too many, in fact. We had rescued lots of cats since we tossed Quixote out the window, and most of them had gone and had kittens, and it got to the point where we had to get rid of some of them. We didn't have many neighbors to give them to, so Dad put them in a burlap sack and drove to a pond made by the mining company to cool equipment. I watched him load the back of the car with bobbing, mewing bags.

"It doesn't seem right," I told Mom. "We rescued them. Now we're going to kill them."

"We gave them a little extra time on the planet," Mom said. "They should be grateful for that."

* * *

Dad finally got a job in the gypsum mine, digging out the white rocks that were ground into the powder used in drywall and plaster of paris. When he came home, he'd be covered with white gypsum powder, and sometimes we'd play ghost and he'd chase us. He also brought back sacks of gypsum, and Mom mixed it with water to make Venus de Milo sculptures from a rubber cast she ordered through the mail. It grieved Mom that the mine was destroying so much white rock—she said it was real marble and deserved a better fate and that, by making her sculptures, she was at least immortalizing some of it.

Mom was pregnant. Everyone hoped it would be a boy so Brian would have someone to play with other than me. When it got time for Mom to give birth, Dad's plan was for us to move to Blythe, twenty miles south, which was such a big town it had two movie theaters and two state prisons.

In the meantime, Mom devoted herself to her art. She spent all day working on oil paintings, watercolors, charcoal drawings, pen-and-ink sketches, clay and wire sculptures, silk screens, and wood blocks. She didn't have any particular style; some of her paintings were what she called primitive, some were impressionistic and abstract, some were realistic. "I don't want to be pigeonholed," she liked to say. Mom was also a writer and was always typing away on novels, short stories, plays, poetry, fables, and children's books, which she illustrated herself. Mom's writing was very creative. So was her spelling. She needed a proofreader, and when Lori was just seven years old, she would go over Mom's manuscripts, checking for errors.

While we were in Midland, Mom painted dozens of variations and studies of the Joshua tree. We'd go with her and she'd give us art lessons. One time I saw a tiny Joshua tree sapling growing not too far from the old tree. I wanted to dig it up and replant it near our house. I told Mom that I would protect it from the wind and water it every day so that it could grow nice and tall and straight.

Mom frowned at me. "You'd be destroying what makes it special," she said. "It's the Joshua tree's struggle that gives it its beauty."

I NEVER BELIEVED IN Santa Claus.

None of us kids did. Mom and Dad refused to let us. They couldn't afford expensive presents, and they didn't want us to think we weren't as good as other kids who, on Christmas morning, found all sorts of fancy toys under the tree that were supposedly left by Santa Claus. So they told us all about how other kids were deceived by their parents, how the toys the grown-ups claimed were made by little elves wearing bell caps in their workshop at the North Pole actually had labels on them saying MADE IN JAPAN.

"Try not to look down on those other children," Mom said. "It's not their fault that they've been brainwashed into believing silly myths."

We celebrated Christmas, but usually about a week after December 25, when you could find perfectly good bows and wrapping paper that people had thrown away and Christmas trees discarded on the roadside that still had most of their needles and even some silver tinsel hanging on them. Mom and Dad would give us a bag of marbles or a doll or a slingshot that had been marked way down in an after-Christmas sale.

Dad lost his job at the gypsum mine after getting in an argument with the foreman, and when Christmas came that year, we had no money at all. On Christmas Eve, Dad took each of us kids out into the desert night one by one. I had a blanket wrapped around me, and when it was my turn, I offered to share it with Dad, but he said no thanks. The cold never bothered him. I was five that year and I sat next to Dad and we looked up at the sky. Dad loved to talk about the stars. He explained to us how they rotated through the night sky as the earth turned. He taught us to identify the constellations and how to navigate by the North Star. Those shining stars, he liked to point out, were one of the special treats for people like us who lived out in the wilderness. Rich city folks, he'd say, lived in fancy apartments, but their air was so polluted they couldn't even see the stars. We'd have to be out of our minds to want to trade places with any of them.

"Pick out your favorite star," Dad said that night. He told me I could have it for keeps. He said it was my Christmas present.

"You can't give me a star!" I said. "No one owns the stars."

"That's right," Dad said. "No one else owns them. You just have to claim it before anyone else does, like that dago fellow Columbus claimed America for Queen Isabella. Claiming a star as your own has every bit as much logic to it."

I thought about it and realized Dad was right. He was always figuring out things like that.

I could have any star I wanted, Dad said, except Betelgeuse and Rigel, because Lori and Brian had already laid claim to them.

I looked up to the stars and tried to figure out which was the best one. You could see hundreds, maybe thousands or even millions, twinkling in the clear desert sky. The longer you looked and the more your eyes adjusted to the dark, the more stars you'd see, layer after layer of them gradually becoming visible. There was one in particular, in the west above the mountains but low in the sky, that shone more brightly than all the rest.

"I want that one," I said.

Dad grinned. "That's Venus," he said. Venus was only a planet, he went on, and pretty dinky compared to real stars. She looked bigger and brighter because she was much closer than the stars. Poor old Venus didn't even make her own light, Dad said. She shone only from reflected light. He explained to me that planets glowed because reflected light was constant, and stars twinkled because their light pulsed.

"I like it anyway," I said. I had admired Venus even before that Christmas. You could see it in the early evening, glowing on the western horizon, and if you got up early, you could still see it in the morning, after all the stars had disappeared.

"What the hell," Dad said. "It's Christmas. You can have a planet if you want."

And he gave me Venus.

That evening over Christmas dinner, we all discussed outer space. Dad explained light-years and black holes and quasars and told us about the special qualities of Betelgeuse, Rigel, and Venus.

Betelgeuse was a red star in the shoulder of the constellation Orion. It was one of the largest stars you could see in the sky, hundreds of times bigger than the sun. It had burned brightly for millions of years and would soon become a supernova and burn out. I got upset that Lori had chosen a clunker of a star, but Dad explained that "soon" meant hundreds of thousands of years when you were talking about stars.

Rigel was a blue star, smaller than Betelgeuse, Dad said, but even brighter. It was also in Orion—it was his left foot, which seemed appropriate, because Brian was an extra-fast runner.

Venus didn't have any moons or satellites or even a magnetic field, but it did have an atmosphere sort of similar to Earth's, except it was superhot—about five hundred degrees or more. "So," Dad said, "when the sun starts to burn out and Earth turns cold, everyone here might want to move to Venus to get warm. And they'll have to get permission from your descendants first."

We laughed about all the kids who believed in the Santa myth and got nothing for Christmas but a bunch of cheap plastic toys. "Years from now, when all the junk they got is broken and long forgotten," Dad said, "you'll still have your stars."

At twilight, once the sun had slid behind the Palen Mountains, the bats came out and swirled through the sky above the shacks of Midland. The old lady who lived next door warned us away from bats. She called them flying rats and said one got caught in her hair once and went crazy clawing at her scalp. But I loved those ugly little bats, the way they darted past, their wings in a furious blur. Dad explained how they had sonar detectors kind of like the ones in nuclear submarines. Brian and I would throw pebbles, hoping the bats would think they were bugs and eat them, and the weight of the pebbles would pull them down and we could keep them as pets, tying a long string to their claw so they could still fly around. I wanted to train one to hang upside down from my finger. But those darn bats were too clever to fall for our trick.

The bats were out, swooping and screeching, when we left Midland for Blythe. Earlier that day, Mom had told us that the baby had decided it was big enough to come out soon and join the family. Once we were on the road, Dad and Mom got in a big fight over how many months she'd been pregnant. Mom said she was ten months pregnant. Dad, who had fixed someone's transmission earlier that day and used the money he'd made to buy a bottle of tequila, said she probably lost track somewhere.

"I always carry children longer than most women," Mom said. "Lori was in my womb for fourteen months."

"Bullshit!" Dad said. "Unless Lori's part elephant."

"Don't you make fun of me or my children!" Mom yelled. "Some babies are premature. Mine were all postmature. That's why they're so smart. Their brains had longer to develop."

Dad said something about freaks of nature, and Mom called Dad a Mr. Know-It-All Smarty-Pants who refused to believe that she was special. Dad said something about Jesus H. Christ on a goddamn crutch not taking that much time to gestate. Mom got upset at Dad's blasphemy, reached her foot over to the driver's side, and stomped on the brake. It was the middle of the night, and Mom bolted out of the car and ran into the darkness.

"You crazy bitch!" Dad hollered. "Get your goddamn ass back in this car!"

"You make me, Mr. Tough Guy!" she screamed as she ran away.

Dad jerked the steering wheel to one side and drove off the road into the desert after her. Lori, Brian, and I braced one another with our arms, like we always did when Dad went on some wild chase that we knew would get bumpy.

Dad stuck his head out the window as he drove, hollering at Mom, calling her a "stupid whore" and a "stinking cunt" and ordering her to get back into the car. Mom refused. She was ahead of us, bobbing in and out of the desert brush. Since she never used curse words, she was calling Dad names like "blankety-blank" and "worthless drunk so-and-so." Dad stopped the car, then jammed down the accelerator and popped the clutch. We shot forward toward Mom, who screamed and jumped out of the way. Dad turned around and went for her again.

It was a moonless night, so we couldn't see Mom except when she ran into the beam of the headlights. She kept looking over her shoulder, her eyes wide like a hunted animal's. We kids cried and begged Dad to stop, but he ignored us. I was even more worried about the baby inside Mom's swollen belly than I was about her. The car bounced on holes and rocks, brush scratching against its sides and dust coming through the open windows. Finally, Dad cornered Mom against some rocks. I was afraid he might smush her with the car, but instead he got out and dragged her back, legs flailing, and threw her into the car. We banged back through the desert and onto the road. Everyone was quiet except Mom, who was sobbing that she really did carry Lori for fourteen months.

Mom and Dad made up the next day, and by late afternoon Mom was cutting Dad's hair in the living room of the apartment we'd rented in Blythe. He'd taken off his shirt and was sitting backward on a chair with his head bowed and his hair combed forward. Mom was snipping away while Dad pointed out the parts that were still too long. When they were finished, Dad combed his hair back and announced that Mom had done a helluva fine shearing job.

Our apartment was in a one-story cinder-block building on the out-skirts of town. It had a big blue-and-white plastic sign in the shape of an oval, and a boomerang that said: THE LBJ APARTMENTS. I thought it stood for Lori, Brian, and Jeannette, but Mom said LBJ were the initials of the president, who, she added, was a crook and a warmonger. A few truck drivers and cowboys had rooms at the LBJ Apartments, but most of the other people who lived there were migrant workers and their families, and we heard them talking through the thin Sheetrock walls. Mom said it was one of the bonuses of living at the LBJ Apartments, because we'd be able to pick up a little Spanish without even studying.

Blythe was in California, but the Arizona border was within spitting distance. People who lived there liked to say the town was 150 miles west of Phoenix, 250 miles east of Los Angeles, and smack dab in the middle of nowhere. But they always said it like they were bragging.

Mom and Dad weren't exactly crazy about Blythe. Too civilized, they said, and downright unnatural, too, since no town the size of Blythe had any business existing out in the Mojave Desert. It was near the Colorado River, founded back in the nineteenth century by some guy who figured he could get rich turning the desert into farmland. He dug a bunch of irrigation ditches that drained water out of the Colorado River to grow lettuce and grapes and broccoli right there in the middle of all the cactus and sagebrush. Dad got disgusted every time we drove past one of those farm fields with their irrigation ditches wide as moats. "It's a goddamn perversion of nature," he'd say. "If you want to live in the farmland, haul your sorry hide off to Pennsylvania. If you want to live in the desert, eat prickly pears, not iceberg pansy-assed lettuce."

"That's right," Mom would say. "Prickly pears have more vitamins anyway."

Living in a big city like Blythe meant I had to wear shoes. It also meant I had to go to school.

School wasn't so bad. I was in the first grade, and my teacher, Miss Cook, always chose me to read aloud when the principal came into the classroom. The other students didn't like me very much because I was so tall and pale and skinny and always raised my hand too fast and waved it frantically in the air whenever Miss Cook asked a question. A few days after I started school, four Mexican girls followed me home and jumped me in an alleyway near the LBJ Apartments. They beat me up pretty bad, pulling my hair and tearing my clothes and calling me a teacher's pet and a matchstick.

I came home that night with scraped knees and elbows and a busted lip. "Looks to me like you got in a fight," Dad said. He was sitting at the table, taking apart an old alarm clock with Brian.

"Just a little dustup," I said. That was the word Dad always used after he'd been in a fight.

"How many were there?"

"Six," I lied.

"Is that split lip okay?" he asked.

"This lil' ol' scratch?" I asked. "You should have seen what I did to them."

"That's my girl!" Dad said and went back to the clock, but Brian kept looking over at me.

The next day when I got to the alley, the Mexican girls were waiting for me. Before they could attack, Brian jumped out from behind a clump of sagebrush, waving a yucca branch. Brian was shorter than me and just as skinny, with freckles across his nose and sandy red hair that fell into his eyes. He wore my hand-me-down pants, which I had inherited from Lori and then passed on to him, and they were always sliding off his bony behind.

"Just back off now, and everyone can walk away with all their limbs still attached," Brian said. It was another one of Dad's lines.

The Mexican girls stared at him before bursting into laughter. Then they surrounded him. Brian did fairly well fending them off until the yucca branch broke. Then he disappeared beneath a flurry of swinging fists and kicking feet. I grabbed the biggest rock I could find and hit one of the girls on the head with it. From the jolt in my arm, I thought I'd cracked her skull. She sank to her knees. One of her friends pushed me to the ground and kicked me in the face; then they all ran off, the girl I had hit holding her head as she staggered along.

Brian and I sat up. His face was covered with sand. All I could see were his blue eyes peering out and a couple of spots of blood seeping through. I wanted to hug him, but that would have been too weird. Brian stood up and gestured for me to follow him. We climbed through a hole in the chain-link fence he had discovered that morning and ran into the iceberg-lettuce farm next to the apartment building. I followed him through the rows of big green leaves, and we eventually settled down to feast, burying our faces in the huge wet heads of lettuce and eating until our stomachs ached.

"I guess we scared them off pretty good," I said to Brian.

"I guess," he said.

He never liked to brag, but I could tell he was proud that he had taken on four bigger, tougher kids, even if they were girls.

"Lettuce war!" Brian shouted. He tossed a half-eaten head at me like a grenade. We ran along the rows, pulling up heads and throwing them at each other. A crop duster flew overhead. We waved as it made a pass above the field. A cloud sprayed out from behind the plane, and a fine white powder came sprinkling down on our heads.

Two months after we moved to Blythe, when Mom said she was twelve months pregnant, she at last gave birth. After she'd been in the hospital for two days, we all drove out to pick her up. Dad left us kids waiting in the car with the engine idling while he went in for Mom. They came running out with Dad's arm around Mom's shoulders. Mom was cradling a bundle in her arms and giggling sort of guiltily, like she'd stolen a candy bar from a dime store. I figured they had checked out Rex Walls–style.

"What is it?" Lori asked as we sped away.

"Girl!" Mom said.

Mom handed me the baby. I was going to turn six in a few months, and Mom said I was mature enough to hold her the entire way home. The baby was pink and wrinkly but absolutely beautiful, with big blue eyes, soft wisps of blond hair, and the tiniest fingernails I had ever seen. She moved in confused, jerky motions, as if she couldn't understand why Mom's belly wasn't still around her. I promised her I'd always take care of her.

The baby went without a name for weeks. Mom said she wanted to study it first, the way she would the subject of a painting. We had a lot of arguments over what the name should be. I wanted to call her Rosita, after the prettiest girl in my class, but Mom said that name was too Mexican.

"I thought we weren't supposed to be prejudiced," I said.

"It's not being prejudiced," Mom said. "It's a matter of accuracy in labeling."

She told us that both our grandmothers were angry because neither Lori nor I had been named after them, so she decided to call the baby Lilly Ruth Maureen. Lilly was Mom's mother's name, and Erma Ruth was Dad's mother's name. But we'd call the baby Maureen, a name Mom liked because it was a diminutive of Mary, so she'd also be naming the baby after herself but pretty much no one would know it. That, Dad told us, would make everyone happy except his mom, who hated the name Ruth and wanted the baby called Erma, and Mom's mom, who would hate sharing her namesake with Dad's mom.

A FEW MONTHS AFTER Maureen was born, a squad car tried to pull us over because the brake lights on the Green Caboose weren't working. Dad took off. He said that if the cops stopped us, they'd find out that we had no registration or insurance and that the license plate had been taken off another car, and they'd arrest us all. After barreling down the highway, he made a screeching U-turn, with us kids feeling like the car was going to tumble over on its side, but the squad car made one, too. Dad peeled through Blythe at a hundred miles an hour, ran a red light, cut the wrong way up a one-way street, the other cars honking and pulling over. He made a few more turns, then headed down an alley and found an empty garage to hide in.

We heard the sound of the siren a couple of blocks away and then it faded. Dad said that since the gestapo would have their eyes out for the Green Caboose, we'd have to leave it in the garage and walk home.

The next day he announced that Blythe had become a little too hot and we were hitting the road again. This time he knew where we were going. Dad had been doing some research and settled on a town in northern Nevada called Battle Mountain. There was gold in Battle Mountain, Dad said, and he intended to go after it with the Prospector. Finally, we were going to strike it rich.

Mom and Dad rented a great big U-Haul truck. Mom explained that since only she and Dad could fit in the front of the U-Haul, Lori, Brian, Maureen, and I were in for a treat: We got to ride in the back. It would be fun, she said, a real adventure, but there wouldn't be any light, so we would have to use all our resources to entertain one another. Plus we were not allowed to talk. Since it was illegal to ride in the back, anyone who heard us might call the cops. Mom told us the trip would be about fourteen hours if we took the highway, but we should tack on another couple of hours because we might make some scenic detours.

We packed up what furniture we had. There wasn't much, mostly parts for the Prospector and a couple of chairs and Mom's oil paintings and art supplies. When we were ready to leave, Mom wrapped Maureen in a lavender blanket and passed her to me, and we kids all climbed into the back of the U-Haul. Dad closed the doors. It was pitch black and the air smelled stale and dusty. We were sitting on the ribbed wooden floor, on frayed, stained blankets used to wrap furniture, feeling for one another with our hands.

"Here goes the adventure!" I whispered.

"Shhhh!" Lori said.

The U-Haul started up and lurched forward. Maureen let loose with a loud, high-pitched wail. I shushed her and rocked her and patted her, but she kept crying. So I gave her to Lori, who whispered singsong into her ear and told jokes. That didn't work, either, so we begged Maureen to please stop crying. Then we just put our hands over our ears.

After a while, it got cold and uncomfortable in the back of the dark U-Haul. The engine made the floor vibrate, and we'd all go tumbling whenever we hit a bump. Several hours passed. By then we were all dying to pee and wondering if Dad was going to pull over for a rest stop. Suddenly, with a bang, we hit a huge pothole and the back doors on the U-Haul flew open. The wind shrieked through the compartment. We were afraid we were going to get sucked out, and we all shrank back against the Prospector. The moon was out. We could see the glow from the U-Haul's taillights and the road we'd come down, stretching back through the silvery desert. The unlocked doors swung back and forth with loud clangs.

Since the furniture was stored between us and the cabin, we couldn't knock on the wall to get Mom's and Dad's attention. We banged on the sides of the U-Haul and hollered as loud as we could, but the engine was too noisy and they didn't hear us.

Brian crawled to the back of the van. When one of the doors swung in, he grabbed at it, but it flew open again, jerking him forward. I thought the door was going to drag Brian out, but he jumped back just in time and scrambled along the wooden floor toward Lori and me.

Brian and Lori held tight to the Prospector, which Dad had tied securely with ropes. I was holding Maureen, who for some strange reason had stopped crying. I wedged myself into a corner. It seemed like we'd have to ride it out.

Then a pair of headlights appeared way in the distance behind us. We watched as the car slowly caught up with the U-Haul. After a few minutes, it pulled up right behind us, and its headlights caught us there in the back of the cab. The car started honking and flashing its brights. Then it pulled up and passed us. The driver must have signaled Mom and Dad, because the U-Haul slowed to a stop and Dad came running back with a flashlight.

"What the hell is going on?" he asked. He was furious. We tried to explain that it wasn't our fault the doors blew open, but he was still angry. I knew that he was scared, too. Maybe even more scared than angry.

"Was that a cop?" Brian asked.

"No," Dad said. "And you're sure as hell lucky it wasn't, or he'd be hauling your asses off to jail."

After we peed, we climbed back into the truck and watched as Dad closed the doors. The darkness enveloped us again. We could hear Dad locking the doors and double-checking them. The engine restarted, and we continued on our way.

BATTLE MOUNTAIN HAD started out as a mining post, settled a hundred years earlier by people hoping to strike it rich, but if anyone ever had struck it rich in Battle Mountain, they must have moved somewhere else to spend their fortune. Nothing about the town was grand except the big empty sky and, off in the distance, the stony purple Tuscarora Mountains running down to the table-flat desert.

The main street was wide—with sun-bleached cars and pickups parked at an angle to the curb—but only a few blocks long, flanked on both sides with low, flat-roofed buildings made of adobe or brick. A single streetlight flashed red day and night. Along Main Street was a grocery store, a drugstore, a Ford dealership, a Greyhound bus station, and two big casinos, the Owl Club and the Nevada Hotel. The buildings, which seemed puny under the huge sky, had neon signs that didn't look like they were on during the day because the sun was so bright.

We moved into a wooden building on the edge of town that had once been a railroad depot. It was two stories tall and painted an industrial green, and was so close to the railroad tracks that you could wave to the engineer from the front window. Our new home was one of the oldest buildings in town, Mom proudly told us, with a real frontier quality to it.

Mom and Dad's bedroom was on the second floor, where the station manager once had his office. We kids slept downstairs in what had been the waiting room. The old restrooms were still there, but the toilet had been ripped out of one and a bathtub put in its place. The ticket booth had been converted into a kitchen. Some of the original benches were still bolted to the unpainted wood walls, and you could see the dark, worn spots where prospectors and miners and their wives and children had sat waiting for the train, their behinds polishing the wood.

Since we didn't have money for furniture, we improvised. A bunch of huge wooden spools, the kind that hold industrial cable, had been dumped on the side of the tracks not far from our house, so we rolled them home and turned them into tables. "What kind of fools would go waste money on store-bought tables when they can have these for free?" Dad said as he pounded the tops of the spools to show us how sturdy they were.

For chairs, we used some smaller spools and a few crates. Instead of beds, we kids each slept in a big cardboard box, like the ones refrigerators get delivered in. A little while after we'd moved into the depot, we heard Mom and Dad talking about buying us kids real beds, and we said they shouldn't do it. We liked our boxes. They made going to bed seem like an adventure.

Shortly after we moved into the depot, Mom decided that what we really needed was a piano. Dad found a cheap upright when a saloon in the next town over went out of business, and he borrowed a neighbor's pickup to bring it home. We slid it off the pickup down a ramp, but it was too heavy to carry. To get it into the depot, Dad devised a system of ropes and pulleys that he attached to the piano in the front yard and ran through the house and out the back door, where they were tied to the pickup. The plan was for Mom to ease the truck forward, pulling the piano into the house while Dad and we kids guided it up a ramp of planks and through the front door.

"Ready!" Dad hollered when we were all in our positions.

"Okeydoke!" Mom shouted. But instead of easing forward, Mom, who had never quite gotten the hang of driving, hit the gas pedal hard, and the truck shot ahead. The piano jerked out of our hands, sending us lurching forward, and bounced into the house, splintering the door frame. Dad screamed at Mom to slow down, but she kept going and dragged the screeching, chord-banging piano across the depot floor and right through the rear door, splintering its frame, too, then out into the backyard, where it came to rest next to a thorny bush.

Dad came running through the house. "What the Sam Hill were you doing?" he yelled at Mom. "I told you to go slow!"

"I was only doing twenty-five!" Mom said. "You get mad at me when I go that slow on the highway." She looked behind her and saw the piano sitting in the backyard. "Oopsie-daisy," she said.

Mom wanted to turn around and drag it back into the house from the other direction, but Dad said that was impossible because the railroad tracks were too close to the front door to get the pickup in position. So the piano stayed where it was. On the days Mom felt inspired, she took her sheet music and one of our spool chairs outside and pounded away at her music back there. "Most pianists never get the chance to play in the great out-of-doors," she said. "And now the whole neighborhood can enjoy the music, too."

DAD GOT A JOB AS an electrician in a barite mine. He left early and came home early, and in the afternoons we all played games. Dad taught us cards. He tried to show us how to be steely-eyed poker players, but I wasn't very good. Dad said you could read my face like a traffic light. Even though I wasn't much of a bluffer, I'd sometimes win a hand because I was always getting excited by even mediocre cards, like a pair of fives, which made Brian and Lori think I'd been dealt aces. Dad also invented games for us to play, like the Ergo Game, in which he'd make two statements of fact and we had to answer a question based on those statements, or else say "Insufficient information to draw a conclusion" and explain why.

When Dad wasn't there, we invented our own games. We didn't have many toys, but you didn't need toys in a place like Battle Mountain. We'd get a piece of cardboard and go tobogganing down the depot's narrow staircase. We'd jump off the roof of the depot, using an army-surplus blanket as our parachute and letting our legs buckle under us when we hit the ground, like Dad had taught us real parachutists do. We'd put a piece of scrap metal—or a penny, if we were feeling extravagant—on the railroad tracks right before the train came. After the train had roared by, the massive wheels churning, we'd run to get our newly flattened, hot and shiny piece of metal.

The thing we liked to do most was go exploring in the desert. We'd get up at dawn, my favorite time, when the shadows were long and purple and you still had the whole day ahead of you. Sometimes Dad went with us, and we'd march through the sagebrush military-style, with Dad calling out orders in a singsong chant—*hup, two, three, four*—and then we'd stop and do push-ups or Dad would hold out his arm so we could do pull-ups on it. Mostly, Brian and I went exploring by ourselves. That desert was filled with all sorts of amazing treasures.

We had moved to Battle Mountain because of the gold in the area, but the desert also had tons of other mineral deposits. There was silver and copper and uranium and barite, which Dad said oil-drilling rigs used. Mom and Dad could tell what kind of minerals and ore were in the ground from the color of the rock and soil, and they taught us what to look for. Iron was in the red rocks, copper in the green. There was so much turquoise—nuggets and even big chunks of it lying on the desert floor—that Brian and I could fill our pockets with it until the weight practically pulled our pants down. You could also find arrowheads and fossils and old bottles that had turned deep purple from lying under the broiling sun for years. You could find the sun-parched skulls of coyotes and empty tortoise shells and the rattles and shed skins of rattlesnakes. And you could find great big bullfrogs that had stayed in the sun too long and were completely dried up and as light as a piece of paper.

On Sunday night, if Dad had money, we'd all go to the Owl Club for dinner. The Owl Club was "World Famous," according to the sign, where a hoot owl wearing a chef's hat pointed the way to the entrance. Off to one side was a room with rows of slot machines that were constantly clinking and ticking and flashing lights. Mom said the slot players were hypnotized. Dad said they were damn fools. "Never play the slots," Dad told us. "They're for suckers who rely on luck." Dad knew all about statistics, and he explained how the casinos stacked the odds against the slot players. When Dad gambled, he preferred poker and pool—games of skill, not chance. "Whoever coined the phrase 'a man's got to play the hand that was dealt him' was most certainly one piss-poor bluffer," Dad said.

The Owl Club had a bar where groups of men with sunburned necks huddled together over beers and cigarettes. They all knew Dad, and whenever he walked in, they insulted him in a loud funny way that was meant to be friendly. "This joint must be going to hell in a handbasket if they're letting in sorry-ass characters like you!" they'd shout.

"Hell, my presence here has a positively elevating effect compared to you mangy coyotes," Dad would yell back. They'd all throw their heads back and laugh and slap one another between the shoulder blades.

We always sat at one of the red booths. "Such good manners," the waitress would exclaim, because Mom and Dad made us say "sir" and "ma'am" and "yes, please" and "thank you."

"They're damned smart, too!" Dad would declare. "Finest damn kids ever walked the planet." And we'd smile and order hamburgers or chili dogs and milk shakes and big plates of onion rings that glistened with hot grease. The waitress brought the food to the table and poured the milk shakes from a sweating metal container into our glasses. There was always some left over, so she kept the container on the table for us to finish. "Looks like you hit the jackpot and got something extra," she'd say with a wink. We always left the Owl Club so stuffed we could hardly walk. "Let's waddle home, kids," Dad would say.

The barite mine where Dad worked had a commissary, and the mine owner deducted our bill and the rent for the depot out of Dad's paycheck every month. At the beginning of each week, we went to the commissary and brought home bags and bags of food. Mom said only people brainwashed by advertising bought prepared foods such as SpaghettiOs and TV dinners. She bought the basics: sacks of flour or cornmeal, powdered milk, onions, potatoes, twenty-pound bags of rice or pinto beans, salt, sugar, yeast for making bread, cans of jack mackerel, a canned ham or a fat slab of bologna, and for dessert, cans of sliced peaches.

Mom didn't like cooking much—"Why spend the afternoon making a meal that will be gone in an hour," she'd ask us, "when in the same amount of time, I can do a painting that will last forever?"—so once a week or so, she'd fix a big cast-iron vat of something like fish and rice or, usually, beans. We'd all sort through the beans together, picking out the rocks, then Mom would soak them overnight, boil them the next day with an old ham bone to give them flavor, and for that entire week, we'd have beans for breakfast, lunch, and dinner. If the beans started going bad, we'd just put extra spice in them, like the Mexicans at the LBJ Apartments always did.

We bought so much food that we never had much money come payday. One payday Dad owed the mine company eleven cents. He thought it was funny and told them to put it on his tab. Dad almost never went out drinking at night like he used to. He stayed home with us. After dinner, the whole family stretched out on the benches and the floor of the depot and read, with the dictionary in the middle of the room so we kids could look up words we didn't know. Sometimes I discussed the definitions with Dad, and if we didn't agree with what the dictionary writers said, we sat down and wrote a letter to the publishers. They'd write back defending their position, which would prompt an even longer letter from Dad, and if they replied again, so would he, until we stopped hearing from the dictionary people.

Mom read everything: Charles Dickens, William Faulkner, Henry Miller, Pearl Buck. She even read James Michener—apologetically—saying she knew it wasn't great literature, but she couldn't help herself. Dad preferred science and math books, biographies and history. We kids read whatever Mom brought home from her weekly trips to the library.

Brian read thick adventure books, ones written by guys like Zane Grey. Lori especially loved Freddy the Pig and all the Oz books. I liked the Laura Ingalls Wilder stories and the We Were There series about kids who lived at great historical moments, but my very favorite was *Black Beauty*. Occasionally, on those nights when we were all reading together, a train would thunder by, shaking the house and rattling the windows. The noise was thunderous, but after we'd been there a while, we didn't even hear it.

MOM AND DAD enrolled us in the Mary S. Black Elementary School, a long, low building with an asphalt playground that turned gooey in the hot sun. My second-grade class was filled with the children of miners and gamblers, scabby-kneed and dusty from playing in the desert, with uneven home-scissored bangs. Our teacher, Miss Page, was a small, pinched woman, given to sudden rages and savage thrashings with her ruler.

Mom and Dad had already taught me nearly everything Miss Page was teaching the class. Since I wanted the other kids to like me, I didn't raise my hand all the time the way I had in Blythe. Dad accused me of coasting. Sometimes he made me do my arithmetic homework in binary numbers because he said I needed to be challenged. Before class, I'd have to recopy it into Arabic numbers, but one day I didn't have time, so I turned in the assignment in its binary version.

"What's this?" Miss Page asked. She pressed her lips together as she studied the circles and lines that covered my paper, then looked up at me suspiciously. "Is this a joke?"

I tried to explain to her about binary numbers, and how they were the system that computers used and how Dad said they were far superior to other numeric systems. Miss Page stared at me.

"It wasn't the assignment," she said impatiently. She made me stay late and redo the homework. I didn't tell Dad, because I knew he'd come to school to debate Miss Page about the virtues of various numeric systems.

Lots of other kids lived in our neighborhood, which was known as the Tracks, and after school we all played together. We played red-light-green-light, tag, football, Red Rover, or nameless games that involved running hard, keeping up with the pack, and not crying if you fell down. All the families who lived around the Tracks were tight on cash. Some were tighter than others, but all of us kids were scrawny and sunburned and wore faded shorts and raggedy shirts and sneakers with holes or no shoes at all.

What was most important to us was who ran the fastest and whose daddy wasn't a wimp. My dad was not only not a wimp, he came out to play with the gang, running alongside us, tossing us up in the air, and wrestling against the entire pack without getting hurt. Kids from the Tracks came knocking at the door, and when I answered, they asked, "Can your dad come out and play?"

Lori, Brian, and I, and even Maureen, could go pretty much anywhere and do just about anything we wanted. Mom believed that children shouldn't be burdened with a lot of rules and restrictions. Dad whipped us with his belt, but never out of anger, and only if we back-talked or disobeyed a direct order, which was rare. The only rule was that we had to come home when the streetlights went on. "And use your common sense," Mom said. She felt it was good for kids to do what they wanted because they learned a lot from their mistakes. Mom was not one of those fussy mothers who got upset when you came home dirty or played in the mud or fell and cut yourself. She said people should get things like that out of their systems when they were young. Once an old nail ripped my thigh while I was climbing over a fence at my friend Carla's house. Carla's mother thought I should go to the hospital for stitches and a tetanus shot. "Nothing but a minor flesh wound," Mom declared after studying the deep gash. "People these days run to the hospital every time they skin their knees," she added. "We're becoming a nation of sissies." With that, she sent me back out to play.

Some of the rocks I found while I was exploring out in the desert were so beautiful that I could not bear the idea of leaving them there. So I started a collection. Brian helped me with it, and together we found garnets and granite and obsidian and Mexican crazy lace, and more and more turquoise. Dad made necklaces for Mom out of all that turquoise. We discovered large sheets of mica that you could pound into powder and then rub all over your body so you'd shimmer under the Nevada sun as if you were coated with diamonds. Lots of times Brian and I thought we'd found gold, and we'd stagger home with an entire bucketful of sparkling nuggets, but it was always iron pyrite—fool's gold. Some of it

Dad said we should keep because it was especially good-quality for fool's gold.

My favorite rocks to find were geodes, which Mom said came from the volcanoes that had erupted to form the Tuscarora Mountains millions of years ago, during the Miocene period. From the outside, geodes looked like boring round rocks, but when you broke them open with a chisel and hammer, the insides were hollow, like a cave, and the walls were covered with glittering white quartz crystals or sparkling purple amethysts.

I kept my rock collection behind the house, next to Mom's piano, which was getting a little weathered. Lori and Brian and I would use the rocks to decorate the graves of our pets that had died or of the dead animals we found and decided should get a proper burial. I also held rock sales. I didn't have that many customers, because I charged hundreds of dollars for a piece of flint. In fact, the only person who ever bought one of my rocks was Dad. He came out behind the house one day with a pocketful of change and was startled when he saw the price tags I'd taped to each rock.

"Honey, your inventory might move a little faster if you dropped your prices," he said.

I explained that all my rocks were incredibly valuable and I'd rather keep them than sell them for less than they were worth.

Dad gave me his crooked smile. "Sounds like you've thought this through pretty well," he said. He told me he had his heart set on buying a particular piece of rose quartz but didn't have the six hundred dollars I was charging, so I cut the price to five hundred and let him have it on credit.

Brian and I loved to go to the dump. We looked for treasures among the discarded stoves and refrigerators, the broken furniture and stacks of bald tires. We chased after the desert rats that lived in the wrecked cars, or caught tadpoles and frogs in the scum-topped pond. Buzzards circled overhead, and the air was filled with dragonflies the size of small birds. There were no trees to speak of in Battle Mountain, but one corner of the dump had huge piles of railroad ties and rotting lumber that were great for climbing and carving your initials on. We called it the Woods.

Toxic and hazardous wastes were stored in another corner of the dump, where you could find old batteries, oil drums, paint cans, and bottles with skulls and crossbones. Brian and I decided some of this stuff would make for a neat scientific experiment, so we filled up a couple of boxes with different bottles and jars and took them to an abandoned shed we named our laboratory. At first we mixed things together, hoping they would explode, but nothing happened, so I decided we should conduct an experiment to see if any of the stuff was flammable.

The next day after school we came back to the laboratory with a box of Dad's matches. We unscrewed the lids of some of the jars, and I dropped in matches, but still nothing happened. So we mixed up a batch of what Brian called nuclear fuel, pouring different liquids into a can. When I tossed in the match, a cone of flame shot up with a whoosh like a jet afterburner.

Brian and I were knocked to our feet. When we stood up, one of the walls was on fire. I yelled to Brian that we had to get out of there, but he was throwing sand at the fire, saying that we had to put it out or we'd get in trouble. The flames were spreading toward the door, eating up that dry old wood in no time. I kicked out a board in the back wall and squeezed through. When Brian didn't follow, I ran up the street calling for help. I saw Dad walking home from work. We ran back to the shack. Dad kicked in more of the wall and pulled Brian out coughing.

I thought Dad would be furious, but he wasn't. He was sort of quiet. We stood on the street watching the flames devour the shack. Dad had an arm around each of us. He said it was an incredible coincidence that he happened to be walking by. Then he pointed to the top of the fire, where the snapping yellow flames dissolved into an invisible shimmery heat that made the desert beyond seem to waver, like a mirage. Dad told us that zone was known in physics as the boundary between turbulence and order. "It's a place where no rules apply, or at least they haven't figured 'em out yet," he said. "You-all got a little too close to it today."

NONE OF US KIDS got allowances. When we wanted money, we walked along the roadside picking up beer cans and bottles that we redeemed for two cents each. Brian and I also collected scrap metal that we sold to the junk dealer for a penny a pound—three cents a pound for copper. After we redeemed the bottles or sold the scrap metal, we walked into town, to the drugstore next door to the Owl Club. There were so many rows and rows of delicious candies to choose from that we'd spend an hour trying to decide how to spend the ten cents we'd each made. We'd pick a piece of candy and then, as we got ready to pay for it, change our minds and pick another piece, until the man who owned the store got mad and told us to stop fingering all his candy and make a purchase and get out.

Brian's favorite was the giant SweeTart candies, which he licked until his tongue was so raw it bled. I loved chocolate, but it was gone too quickly, so I usually got a Sugar Daddy, which lasted practically half the day and always had a funny poem printed in pink letters on the stick, like: *To keep your feet / From falling asleep / Wear loud socks / They can't be beat.*

On our way back from the candy store, Brian and I liked to spy on the Green Lantern—a big dark green house with a sagging porch right near the highway. Mom said it was a cathouse, but I never saw any cats there, only women wearing bathing suits or short dresses who sat or lay out on the porch, waving at the cars that drove by. There were Christmas lights over the door all year round, and Mom said that was how you could tell it was a cathouse. Cars would stop in front, and men would get out and duck inside. I couldn't figure out what went on at the Green Lantern, and Mom refused to discuss it. She would say only that bad things happened there, which made the Green Lantern a place of irresistible mystery to us.

Brian and I would hide behind the sagebrush across the highway, trying to peer inside the front door when someone went in or out, but we could never see what was going on. A couple of times we sneaked up close and tried to look in the windows, but they were painted black. Once a woman on the porch saw us in the brush and waved to us, and we ran away shrieking.

One day when Brian and I were hiding in the sagebrush, spying, I double-dared him to go talk to the woman lying out on the porch. Brian was almost six by then, a year younger than me, and wasn't afraid of anything. He hitched up his pants, handed me his half-eaten SweeTart for safekeeping, walked across the street, and went right up to the woman. She had long black hair, her eyes were outlined with black mascara thick as tar, and she wore a short blue dress printed with black flowers. She had been lying on her side on the porch floor, her head propped up on one arm, but when Brian walked up to her, she rolled over on her stomach and rested her chin on her hand.

From my hiding place, I could see that Brian was talking with her, but I couldn't hear what they were saying. Then she reached out a hand to Brian. I held my breath to see what this woman who did bad things inside the Green Lantern was going to do to him. She put her hand on his head and ruffled his hair. Grown-up women always did that to Brian, because his hair was red and he had freckles. It annoyed him; he usually swatted their hands away. But not this time. Instead, he stayed and talked with the woman for a while. When he came back across the highway, he didn't look scared at all.

"What happened?" I asked.

"Nothing much," Brian said.

"What did you talk about?"

"I asked her what goes on inside the Green Lantern," he said.

"Really?" I was impressed. "What did she say?"

"Nothing much," he said. "She told me that men came in and the women there were nice to them."

"Oh," I said. "Anything else?"

"Naw," Brian said. He started kicking at the dirt like he didn't want to talk about it anymore. "She was kinda nice," he said.

After that, Brian waved to the women on the porch of the Green Lantern, and they smiled real big and waved back, but I was still a little afraid of them.

OUR HOUSE IN BATTLE MOUNTAIN was filled with animals. They came and went, stray dogs and cats, their puppies and kittens, nonpoisonous snakes, and lizards and tortoises we caught in the desert. A coyote that seemed pretty tame lived with us for a while, and once Dad brought home a wounded buzzard that we named Buster. He was the ugliest pet we ever owned. Whenever we fed Buster scraps of meat, he turned his head sideways and stared at us out of one angry-looking yellow eye. Then he'd scream and frantically flap his good wing. I was secretly glad when his hurt wing healed and he flew away. Every time we saw buzzards circling overhead, Dad would say that he recognized Buster among them and that he was coming back to thank us. But I knew Buster would never even consider returning. That buzzard didn't have an ounce of gratitude in him.

We couldn't afford pet food, so the animals had to eat our leftovers, and there usually wasn't much. "If they don't like it, they can leave," said Mom. "Just because they live here doesn't mean I'm going to wait on them hand and foot." Mom told us that we were actually doing the animals a favor by not allowing them to become dependent on us. That way, if we ever had to leave, they'd be able to get by on their own. Mom liked to encourage self-sufficiency in all living creatures.

Mom also believed in letting nature take its course. She refused to kill the flies that always filled the house; she said they were nature's food for the birds and lizards. And the birds and lizards were food for the cats. "Kill the flies and you starve the cats," she said. Letting the flies live, in her view, was the same as buying cat food, only cheaper.

One day I was visiting my friend Carla when I noticed that her house didn't have any flies. I asked her mother why.

She pointed toward a shiny gold contraption dangling from the ceiling, which she proudly identified as a Shell No-Pest Strip. She said it could be bought at the filling station and that her family had one in every room. The No-Pest Strips, she explained, released a poison that killed all the flies.

"What do your lizards eat?" I asked.

"We don't have any lizards, either," she said.

I went home and told Mom we needed to get a No-Pest Strip like Carla's family, but she refused. "If it kills the flies," she said, "it can't be very good for us."

Dad bought a souped-up old Ford Fairlane that winter, and one weekend when the weather got cold, he announced that we were going swimming at the Hot Pot. The Hot Pot was a natural sulfur spring in the desert north of town, surrounded by craggy rocks and quicksand. The water was warm to the touch and smelled like rotten eggs. It was so full of minerals that rough, chalky encrustations had built up along the edges, like a coral reef. Dad was always saying we should buy the Hot Pot and develop it as a spa.

The deeper you went into the water, the hotter it got. It was very deep in the middle. Some people around Battle Mountain said the Hot Pot had no bottom at all, that it went clean through to the center of the earth. A couple of drunks and wild teenagers had drowned there, and people at the Owl Club said when their bodies floated back to the surface, they'd been literally boiled.

Both Brian and Lori knew how to swim, but I had never learned. Large bodies of water scared me. They seemed unnatural—oddities in the desert towns where we'd lived. We had once stayed at a motel with a swimming pool, and I worked up enough nerve to make my way around the entire length of the pool, clinging to the side. But the Hot Pot didn't have any neat edges like that swimming pool. There was nothing to cling to.

I waded in up to my shoulders. The water around my chest was warm, and the rocks I was standing on felt so hot I wanted to keep moving. I looked back at Dad, who watched me, unsmiling. I tried to push out into deeper water, but something held me back. Dad dived in and splashed his way toward me. "You're going to learn to swim today," he said.

He put an arm around me, and we started across the water. Dad was dragging me. I felt terrified and clutched his neck so tightly that his skin turned white. "There, that wasn't so bad, was it?" Dad asked when we got to the other side.

We started back, and this time, when we got to the middle, Dad pried my fingers from around his neck and pushed me away. My arms flailed around, and I sank into the hot, smelly water. I instinctively breathed in. Water surged into my nose and mouth and down my throat. My lungs burned. My eyes were open, the sulfur stinging them, but the water was dark and my hair was wrapped around my face and I couldn't see anything. A pair of hands grabbed me around the waist. Dad pulled me into the shallow water. I was spitting and coughing and breathing in uneven choking gasps.

"That's okay," Dad said. "Catch your breath."

When I recovered, Dad picked me up and heaved me back into the middle of the Hot Pot. "Sink or swim!" he called out. For the second time, I sank. The water once more filled my nose and lungs. I kicked and flailed and thrashed my way to the surface, gasping for air, and reached out to Dad. But he pulled back, and I didn't feel his hands around me until I'd sunk one more time.

He did it again and again, until the realization that he was rescuing me only to throw me back into the water took hold, and so, rather than reaching for Dad's hands, I tried to get away from them. I kicked at him and pushed away through the water with my arms, and finally, I was able to propel myself beyond his grasp.

"You're doing it, baby!" Dad shouted. "You're swimming!"

I staggered out of the water and sat on the calcified rocks, my chest heaving. Dad came out of the water, too, and tried to hug me, but I wouldn't have anything to do with him, or with Mom, who'd been floating on her back as if nothing were happening, or with Brian and Lori, who gathered around and were congratulating me. Dad kept telling me that he loved me, that he never would have let me drown, but you can't cling to the side your whole life, that one lesson every parent needs to teach a child is "If you don't want to sink, you better figure out how to swim." What other reason, he asked, would possibly make him do this?

Once I got my breath back, I figured he must be right. There was no other way to explain it.

"BAD NEWS," LORI SAID one day when I got home from exploring. "Dad lost his job."

Dad had kept this job for nearly six months—longer than any other. I figured we were through with Battle Mountain and that within a few days, we'd be on the move again.

"I wonder where we'll live next," I said.

Lori shook her head. "We're staying here," she said. Dad insisted he hadn't exactly lost his job. He had arranged to have himself fired because he wanted to spend more time looking for gold. He had all sorts of plans to make money, she added, inventions he was working on, odd jobs he had lined up. But for the time being, things might get a little tight around the house. "We all have to help out," Lori said.

I thought of what I could do to contribute, besides collecting bottles and scrap metal. "I'll cut the prices on my rocks," I said.

Lori paused and looked down. "I don't think that will be enough," she said.

"I guess we can eat less," I said.

"We have before," Lori said.

We did eat less. Once we lost our credit at the commissary, we quickly ran out of food. Sometimes one of Dad's odd jobs would come through, or he'd win some money gambling, and we'd eat for a few days. Then the money would be gone and the refrigerator would be empty again.

Before, whenever we were out of food, Dad was always there, full of ideas and ingenuity. He'd find a can of tomatoes on the back of a shelf that everyone else had missed, or he'd go off for an hour and come back with an armful of vegetables—never telling us where he got them—and whip up a stew. But now he began disappearing a lot.

"Where Dad?" Maureen asked all the time. She was a year and a half old, and these were almost her first words.

"He's out finding us food and looking for work," I'd say. But I wondered if he didn't really want to be around us unless he could provide for us. I tried to never complain.

If we asked Mom about food—in a casual way, because we didn't want to cause any trouble—she'd simply shrug and say she couldn't make something out of nothing. We kids usually kept our hunger to ourselves, but we were always thinking of food and how to get our hands on it. During recess at school, I'd slip back into the classroom and find something in some other kid's lunch bag that wouldn't be missed—a package of crackers, an apple—and I'd gulp it down so quickly I would barely be able to taste it. If I was playing in a friend's yard, I'd ask if I could use the bathroom, and if no one was in the kitchen, I'd grab something out of the refrigerator or cupboard and take it into the bathroom and eat it there, always making a point of flushing the toilet before leaving.

Brian was scavenging, too. One day I discovered him upchucking behind our house. I wanted to know how he could be spewing like that when we hadn't eaten in days. He told me he had broken into a neighbor's house and stolen a gallon jar of pickles. The neighbor had caught him, but instead of reporting him to the cops, he made Brian eat the entire jarful as punishment. I had to swear I wouldn't tell Dad.

A couple of months after Dad lost his job, he came home with a bag of groceries: a can of corn, a half gallon of milk, a loaf of bread, two tins of deviled ham, a sack of sugar, and a stick of margarine. The can of corn disappeared within minutes. Somebody in the family had stolen it, and no one except the thief knew who. But Dad was too busy making deviled-ham sandwiches to launch an investigation. We ate our fill that night, washing down the sandwiches with big glasses of milk. When I got back from school the next day, I found Lori in the kitchen eating something out of a cup with a spoon. I looked in the refrigerator. There was nothing inside but a half-gone stick of margarine.

"Lori, what are you eating?"

"Margarine," she said.

I wrinkled my nose. "Really?"

"Yeah," she said. "Mix it with sugar. Tastes just like frosting."

I made some. It didn't taste like frosting. It was sort of crunchy, because the sugar didn't dissolve, and it was greasy and left a filmy coat in my mouth. But I ate it all anyway.

When Mom got home that evening, she looked in the refrigerator. "What happened to the stick of margarine?" she asked.

"We ate it," I said.

Mom got angry. She was saving it, she said, to butter the bread. We already ate all the bread, I said. Mom said she was thinking of baking some bread if a neighbor would loan us some flour. I pointed out that the gas company had turned off our gas.

"Well," Mom said. "We should have saved the margarine just in case the gas gets turned back on. Miracles happen, you know." It was because of my and Lori's selfishness, she said, that if we had any bread, we'd have to eat it without butter.

Mom wasn't making any sense to me. I wondered if she had been looking forward to eating the margarine herself. And that made me wonder if she was the one who'd stolen the can of corn the night before, which got me a little mad. "It was the only thing to eat in the whole house," I said. Raising my voice, I added, "I was *hungry*."

Mom gave me a startled look. I'd broken one of our unspoken rules: We were always supposed to pretend our life was one long and incredibly fun adventure. She raised her hand, and I thought she was going to hit me, but then she sat down at the spool table and rested her head on her arms. Her shoulders started shaking. I went over and touched her arm. "Mom?" I said.

She shook off my hand, and when she raised her head, her face was swollen and red. "It's not my fault if you're hungry!" she shouted. "Don't blame me. Do you think I like living like this? Do you?"

That night when Dad came home, he and Mom got into a big fight. Mom was screaming that she was tired of getting all the blame for everything that went wrong. "How did this become my problem?" she shouted. "Why aren't you helping? You spend your whole day at the Owl Club. You act like it's not your responsibility."

Dad explained that he was out trying to earn money. He had all sorts of prospects that he was on the brink of realizing. Problem was, he needed cash to make them happen. There was a lot of gold in Battle Mountain, but it was trapped in the ore. It was not like there were gold nuggets lying around for the Prospector to sort through. He was perfecting a technique by which the gold could be leached out of the rock by processing it with a cyanide solution. But that took money. Dad told

Mom she needed to ask her mother for the money to fund the cyanide-leaching process he was developing.

"You want me to beg from my mother again?" Mom asked.

"Goddammit, Rose Mary! It's not like we're asking for a handout," he yelled. "She'd be making an *investment*."

Grandma was always lending us money, Mom said, and she was sick of it. Mom told Dad that Grandma had said if we couldn't take care of ourselves, we could go live in Phoenix, in her house.

"Maybe we should," Mom said.

That got Dad really angry. "Are you saying I can't take care of my own family?"

"Ask them," Mom snapped.

We kids were sitting on the old passenger benches. Dad turned to me. I studied the scuff marks on the floor.

Their argument continued the next morning. We kids were downstairs lying in our boxes, listening to them fighting upstairs. Mom was carrying on about how things had gotten so desperate around the house that we didn't have anything to eat except margarine, and now that was gone, too. She was sick, she said, of Dad's ridiculous dreams and his stupid plans and his empty promises.

I turned to Lori, who was reading a book. "Tell them that we like eating margarine," I said. "Then maybe they'll stop fighting."

Lori shook her head. "That'll make Mom think we're taking Dad's side," she said. "It would only make it worse. Let them work it out."

I knew Lori was right. The only thing to do when Mom and Dad fought was to pretend it wasn't happening or act like it didn't matter. Pretty soon they'd be friends again, kissing and dancing in each other's arms. But this particular argument just would not stop. After going on about the margarine, they started fighting about whether or not some painting Mom had done was ugly. Then they argued about whose fault it was that we lived like we did. Mom told Dad he should get another job. Dad said that if Mom wanted someone in the family to be punching a time clock, then she could get a job. She had a teaching degree, he pointed out. She could work instead of sitting around on her butt all day painting pictures no one ever wanted to buy.

"Van Gogh didn't sell any paintings, either," Mom said. "I'm an artist!"

"Fine," Dad said. "Then quit your damned bellyaching. Or go peddle your ass at the Green Lantern."

Mom and Dad's shouting was so loud that you could hear it throughout the neighborhood. Lori, Brian, and I looked at one another. Brian nodded at the front door, and we all went outside and started making sand castles for scorpions. We figured that if we were all in the yard acting like the fighting was no big deal, maybe the neighbors would feel the same way.

But as the screaming continued, neighbors started gathering on the street. Some were simply curious. Moms and dads got into arguments all the time in Battle Mountain, so it didn't seem that big a deal, but this fight was raucous even by local standards, and some people thought they should step in and break it up. "Aw, let 'em work out their differences," one of the men said. "No one's got a right to interfere." So they leaned back against car fenders and fence posts, or sat on pickup tailgates, as if they were at a rodeo.

Suddenly, one of Mom's oil paintings came flying through an upstairs window. Next came her easel. The crowd below scurried back to avoid getting hit. Then Mom's feet appeared in the window, followed by the rest of her body. She was dangling from the second floor, her legs swinging wildly. Dad was holding her by the arms while she tried to hit him in the face.

"Help!" Mom screamed. "He's trying to kill me!"

"Goddammit, Rose Mary, get back in here!" Dad said.

"Don't hurt her!" Lori yelled.

Mom was swinging back and forth. Her yellow cotton dress had gotten bunched up around her waist, and the crowd could see her white underwear. They were sort of old and baggy, and I was afraid they might fall off altogether. Some of the grown-ups called out, worried that Mom might fall, but one group of kids thought Mom looked like a chimpanzee swinging from a tree, and they began making monkey noises and scratching their armpits and laughing. Brian's face turned dark and his fists clenched up. I felt like punching them, too, but I pulled Brian back.

Mom was thrashing around so hard that her shoes fell off. It looked like she might slip from Dad's grasp or pull him out the window. Lori turned to Brian and me. "Come on." We ran inside and up the stairs and held on to Dad's legs so that Mom's weight wouldn't drag him through the window as well. Finally, he pulled Mom back inside. She collapsed onto the floor.

"He tried to kill me," Mom sobbed. "Your father wants to watch me die."

"I didn't push her," Dad protested. "I swear to God I didn't. She jumped." He was standing over Mom, holding out his hands, palms up, pleading his innocence.

Lori stroked Mom's hair and dried her tears. Brian leaned against the wall and shook his head.

"Everything's okay now," I said over and over again.

THE NEXT MORNING, instead of sleeping late the way she usually did, Mom got up with us kids and walked over to the Battle Mountain Intermediate School, which was across the street from the Mary S. Black Elementary School. She applied for a job and was hired right away, since she had a degree, and there were never enough teachers in Battle Mountain. The few teachers the town did have were not exactly the pick of the litter, as Dad liked to say, and despite the shortage, one would get fired from time to time. A couple of weeks earlier, Miss Page had gotten the ax when the principal caught her toting a loaded rifle down the school hall. Miss Page said all she wanted to do was motivate her students to do their homework.

Lori's teacher had stopped showing up around the same time Miss Page was fired, so Mom was assigned to teach Lori's class. Her students really liked her. She had the same philosophy about educating children that she had about rearing them. She thought rules and discipline held people back and felt that the best way to let children fulfill their potential was by providing freedom. She didn't care if her students were late or didn't do their homework. If they wanted to act out, that was fine with her, as long as they didn't hurt anyone else.

Mom was all the time hugging her students and letting them know how wonderful and special she thought they were. She'd tell the Mexican kids never to let anyone say they weren't as good as white kids. She'd tell the Navaho and Apache kids they should be proud of their noble Indian heritage. Students who were considered problem kids or mentally slow started doing well. Some followed Mom around like stray dogs.

Even though her students liked her, Mom hated teaching. She had to leave Maureen, who was not yet two, with a woman whose drug-dealer husband was serving time in the state prison. But what really bothered Mom was that her mother had been a teacher and had pushed Mom into getting a teaching degree so she would have a job to fall back on just in case her dreams of becoming an artist didn't pan out. Mom felt Grandma

Smith had lacked faith in her artistic talent, and by becoming a teacher now, she was acknowledging that her mother had been right all along. At night she sulked and muttered under her breath. In the morning she slept late and pretended to be sick. It was up to Lori, Brian, and me to get her out of bed and see to it that she was dressed and at school on time.

"I'm a grown woman now," Mom said almost every morning. "Why can't I do what I want to do?"

"Teaching is rewarding and fun," Lori said. "You'll grow to like it."

Part of the problem was that the other teachers and the principal, Miss Beatty, thought Mom was a terrible teacher. They'd stick their heads into her classroom and see the students playing tag and throwing erasers while Mom was up front, spinning like a top and letting pieces of chalk fly from her hands to demonstrate centrifugal force.

Miss Beatty, who wore her glasses on a chain around her neck and had her hair done at the beauty parlor over in Winnemucca every week, told Mom she needed to discipline her students. Miss Beatty also told Mom to submit weekly lesson plans, keep her classroom tidy, and grade the homework promptly. But Mom was always getting confused and filling in the wrong dates on the lesson plans or losing the homework.

Miss Beatty threatened to fire Mom, so Lori, Brian, and I started helping Mom with her schoolwork. I'd go to her classroom after school and clean her chalkboard, dust her erasers, and pick the paper up off the floor. At night Lori, Brian, and I went over her students' homework and tests. Mom let us grade papers that had multiple-choice, true-false, and fill-in-the-blank answers—just about anything except essay questions, which she thought she had to evaluate because they could be answered correctly in all sorts of different ways. I liked grading homework. I liked knowing that I could do what grown-ups did for a living. Lori also helped Mom with her lesson plans. She'd make sure Mom filled them in accurately, and she'd correct Mom's spelling and math.

"Mom, double Ls in Halloween," Lori said, erasing Mom's writing and penciling in the changes. "Double Es as well, and no silent E at the end."

Mom marveled at how brilliant Lori was. "Lori gets straight As," she once told me.

"So do I," I said.

"Yes, but you have to work for them."

Mom was right, Lori was brilliant. I think helping Mom like that was one of Lori's favorite things in the world. She wasn't very athletic and didn't like exploring as much as Brian and I did, but she loved anything having to do with pencil and paper. After Mom and Lori finished the lesson plans, they'd sit around the spool table, sketching each other and cutting out magazine photos of animals and landscapes and people with wrinkled faces and putting them in Mom's folder of potential painting subjects.

Lori understood Mom better than anyone. It didn't bother her that when Miss Beatty showed up to observe Mom's class, Mom started yelling at Lori to prove to Miss Beatty that she was capable of disciplining her students. One time Mom went so far as to order Lori up to the front of the class, where she gave her a whipping with a wooden paddle.

"Were you acting up?" I asked Lori when I heard about the whipping.

"No," Lori said.

"Then why would Mom paddle you?"

"She had to punish someone, and she didn't want to upset the other kids," Lori said.

ONCE MOM STARTED TEACHING, I thought maybe we'd be able to buy new clothes, eat cafeteria lunches, and even spring for nifty extras like the class pictures the school took every year. Mom and Dad had never been able to buy the class pictures for us, though a couple of times, Mom secretly snipped a snapshot out of the packet before returning it. Despite Mom's salary, we didn't buy the class pictures that year—or even steal them—but that was probably just as well. Mom had read somewhere that mayonnaise was good for your hair, and the morning the photographer was coming to school, she slathered a few spoonfuls on mine. She didn't realize you were supposed to wash out the mayonnaise, and in the picture that year I was peering out from under one stiff shingle of hair.

Still, things did improve. Even though Dad had been fired from the barite mine, we were able to continue living in the depot by paying rent to the mining company, since not a lot of other families were vying for the place. We now had food in the fridge, at least until it got toward the end of the month, when we usually ran out of money because neither Mom nor Dad ever mastered the art of budgeting.

But Mom's salary created a whole new set of problems. While Dad liked it that Mom was bringing home a paycheck, he saw himself as the head of the household, and he maintained that the money should be turned over to him. It was his responsibility, he'd say, to handle the family finances. And he needed money to fund his gold-leaching research.

"The only research you're doing is on the liver's capacity to absorb alcohol," Mom said. Still, she found it hard to straight-out defy Dad. For some reason, she didn't have it in her to say no to him. If she tried, he'd argue and wheedle and sulk and bully and plain wear her down. So she resorted to evasive tactics. She'd tell Dad she hadn't cashed her paycheck yet, or she'd pretend she'd left it at school and hide it until she could sneak off to the bank. Then she'd pretend she'd lost all the money.

Pretty soon Dad took to showing up at school on payday, waiting outside in the car, and taking us all straight to Winnemucca, where the bank was located, so Mom could cash her paycheck immediately. Dad insisted on escorting Mom into the bank. Mom had us kids come along so she could try to slip some of the cash to us first. Back in the car, Dad would go through Mom's purse and take the money out.

On one trip, Mom went into the bank alone because Dad couldn't find a place to park. When she came out, she was missing a sock. "Jeannette, I'm going to give you a *sock* that I want you to put in a safe place," Mom said once she got in the car. She winked hard at me as she reached inside her bra and pulled out her other sock, knotted in the middle and bulging at the toe. "Hide it where no one can get it, because you know how scarce *socks* can get in our house."

"Goddammit, Rose Mary," Dad snapped. "Do you think I'm a fucking idiot?"

"What?" Mom asked, throwing her arms up in the air. "Am I not allowed to give my daughter a sock?" She winked at me again, just in case I didn't get it.

Back in Battle Mountain, Dad insisted we go to the Owl Club to celebrate payday, and ordered steaks for all of us. They tasted so good we forgot we were eating a week's worth of groceries. "Hey, Mountain Goat," Dad said at the end of the dinner, while Mom was putting our table scraps in her purse. "Why don't you let me borrow that sock for a second?"

I looked around the table. No one met my eye except Dad, who was grinning like an alligator. I handed over the sock. Mom gave a dramatic sigh of defeat and let her head drop down on the table. To show who was in charge, Dad left the waitress a ten-dollar tip, but on the way out, Mom slipped it into her purse.

Soon we were out of money again. When Dad dropped Brian and me off at school, he noticed that we weren't carrying lunch bags.

"Where are your lunches?" Dad asked us.

We looked at each other and shrugged.

"There's no food in the house," Brian said.

When Dad heard that, he acted outraged, as though he'd learned for the first time that his children were going hungry.

"Dammit, that Rose Mary keeps spending money on art supplies!" he muttered, pretending to be talking to himself. Then he declared more loudly, "No child of mine has to go hungry!" After he dropped us off, he called after us, "Don't you kids worry about a thing."

At lunch Brian and I sat together in the cafeteria. I was pretending to help him with his homework so that no one would ask us why we weren't eating when Dad appeared in the doorway, carrying a big grocery bag. I saw him scanning the room, looking for us. "My young 'uns forgot to take their lunch to school today," he announced to the teacher on cafeteria duty as he walked toward us. He set the bag on the table in front of Brian and me and took out a loaf of bread, a whole package of bologna, a jar of mayonnaise, a half-gallon jug of orange juice, two apples, a jar of pickles, and two candy bars.

"Have I ever let you down?" he asked Brian and me and then turned and walked away.

In a voice so low that Dad didn't hear him, Brian said, "Yes."

"Dad has to start carrying his weight," Lori said as she stared into the empty refrigerator.

"He does!" I said. "He brings in money from odd jobs."

"He spends more than he earns on booze," Brian said. He was whittling, the shavings falling to the floor right outside the kitchen where we were standing. Brian had taken to carrying a pocketknife with him at all times, and he often whittled pieces of scrap wood when he was working something out in his head.

"It's not all for booze," I said. "Most of it's for research on cyanide leaching."

"Dad doesn't need to do research on leaching," Brian said. "He's an expert." He and Lori cracked up. I glared at them. I knew more about Dad's situation than they did because he talked to me more than anyone else in the family. We'd still go Demon Hunting in the desert together, for old time's sake, since by then I was seven and too grown up to believe in demons. Dad told me about all his plans and showed me his pages of graphs and calculations and geological charts, depicting the layers of sediment where the gold was buried.

He told me I was his favorite child, but he made me promise not to tell Lori or Brian or Maureen. It was our secret. "I swear, honey, there are times when I think you're the only one around who still has faith in me," he said. "I don't know what I'd do if you ever lost it." I told him that I would never lose faith in him. And I promised myself I never would.

A few months after Mom had started working as a teacher, Brian and I passed by the Green Lantern. The clouds above the setting sun were streaked scarlet and purple. The temperature was dropping quickly, from searing hot to chilly within a matter of minutes, like it always did in the desert at dusk. A woman with a fringed shawl draped over her shoulders was smoking a cigarette on the Green Lantern's front porch. She waved at Brian, but he didn't wave back.

"Yoo-hoo! Brian, it's me, sugar! Ginger!" she called.

Brian ignored her.

"Who's that?" I asked.

"Some friend of Dad's," he said. "She's dumb."

"Why is she dumb?"

"She doesn't even know all the words in a Sad Sack comic book," Brian said.

He told me that Dad had taken him out for his birthday awhile back. In the drugstore, Dad had let Brian pick out whatever present he wanted, so Brian chose a Sad Sack comic book. Then they went to the Nevada Hotel, which was near the Owl Club and had a sign outside saying BAR GRILL CLEAN MODERN. They had dinner with Ginger, who kept laughing and talking real loud and touching both Dad and Brian. Then all three climbed the stairs to one of the hotel rooms. It was a suite, with a small front room and a bedroom. Dad and Ginger went into the bedroom while Brian stayed in the front room and read his new comic book. Later, when Dad and Ginger came out, she sat down next to Brian. He didn't look up. He kept staring at the comic book, even though he'd already read it all the way through twice. Ginger declared that she loved Sad Sack. So Dad made Brian give Ginger the comic book, telling him it was the gentlemanly thing to do.

"It was mine!" Brian said. "And she kept asking me to read the bigger words. She's a grown-up, and she can't even read a comic book."

Brian had taken such a powerful dislike to Ginger that I realized she must have done something more than shanghai his comic book. I wondered if he had figured out something about Ginger and the other ladies at the Green Lantern. Maybe he knew why Mom said they were bad. Maybe that was why he was mad. "Did you learn what they do inside the Green Lantern?" I asked.

Brian stared off ahead. I tried to see what he was looking at, but there was nothing there except for the Tuscarora Mountains rising up to meet the darkening sky. Then he shook his head. "She makes a lot of money," he said, "and she should buy her own darn comic book."

SOME PEOPLE LIKED to make fun of Battle Mountain. A big newspaper out east once held a contest to find the ugliest, most forlorn, most godforsaken town in the whole country, and it declared Battle Mountain the winner. The people who lived there didn't hold it in much regard, either. They'd point to the big yellow-and-red sign way up on a pole at the Shell station—the one with the burned-out S—and say with a sort of perverse pride, "Yep, that's where we live: hell!"

But I was happy in Battle Mountain. We'd been there for nearly a year, and I considered it home—the first real home I could remember. Dad was on the verge of perfecting his cyanide gold process, Brian and I had the desert, Lori and Mom painted and read together, and Maureen, who had silky white-blond hair and a whole gang of imaginary friends, was happy running around with no diaper on. I thought our days of packing up and driving off in the middle of the night were over.

Just after my eighth birthday, Billy Deel and his dad moved into the Tracks. Billy was three years older than me, tall and skinny with a sandy crew cut and blue eyes. But he wasn't handsome. The thing about Billy was that he had a lopsided head. Bertha Whitefoot, a half-Indian woman who lived in a shack near the depot and kept about fifty dogs fenced in her yard, said it was because Billy's mom hadn't turned him over at all when he was a baby. He just lay there in the same position day in and day out, and the side of his head that was pressed against the mattress got a little flat. You didn't notice it all that much unless you looked at him straight on, and not a lot of people did, because Billy was always moving around like he was itchy. He kept his Marlboros rolled up in one of his T-shirt sleeves, and he lit his cigarettes with a Zippo lighter stamped with a picture of a naked lady bending over.

Billy lived with his dad in a house made of tar paper and corrugated tin, down the tracks from our house. He never mentioned his mom and made it clear that you weren't supposed to bring her up, so I never knew if she had run off or died. His dad worked in the barite mine and spent his evenings at the Owl Club, so Billy had a lot of unsupervised time on his hands.

Bertha Whitefoot took to calling Billy "the devil with a crew cut" and "the terror of the Tracks." She claimed he set fire to a couple of her dogs and skinned some neighborhood cats and strung their naked pink bodies up on a clothesline to make jerky. Billy said Bertha was a big fat liar. I didn't know whom to believe. After all, Billy was a certified JD—juvenile delinquent. He had told us that he spent time in a detention center in Reno for shoplifting and vandalizing cars. Shortly after he moved to the Tracks, Billy started following me around. He was always looking at me and telling the other kids he was my boyfriend.

"No, he's not!" I would yell, though I secretly liked it that he wanted to be.

A few months after he'd moved to town, Billy told me he wanted to show me something really funny.

"If it's a skinned cat, I don't want to see it," I said.

"Naw, it ain't nothing like that," he said. "It's really funny. You'll laugh and laugh. I promise. Unless you're scared."

"'Course I'm not scared," I said.

The funny thing Billy wanted to show me was in his house, which was dark inside and smelled like pee, and was even messier than our house, although in a different way. Our house was filled with stuff: papers, books, tools, lumber, paintings, art supplies, and statues of Venus de Milo painted all different colors. There was hardly anything in Billy's house. No furniture. Not even wooden spool tables. It had only one room with two mattresses on the floor next to a TV. There was nothing on the walls, not a single painting or drawing. A naked lightbulb hung from the ceiling, right next to three or four dangling spiral strips of flypaper so thick with flies that you couldn't see the sticky yellow surface underneath. Empty beer cans and whiskey bottles and a few half-eaten tins of Vienna sausages littered the floor. On one of the mattresses, Billy's father was snoring unevenly. His mouth hung open, and flies were gathered in the stubble of his beard. A wet stain had darkened his pants nearly to his knees. His zipper was undone, and his gross penis dangled to one side. I stared quietly, then asked, "What's the funny thing?"

"Don't you see?" said Billy, pointing at his dad. "He *pissed* himself!" Billy started laughing.

I felt my face turning hot. "You're not supposed to laugh at your own father," I said to him. "Ever."

"Aw, now, don't go get all high-and-mighty on me," Billy said. "Don't go and try and pretend you're better than me. 'Cause I know your daddy ain't nothing but a drunk like mine."

I hated Billy at that moment, I really did. I thought of telling him about binary numbers and the Glass Castle and Venus and all the things that made my dad special and completely different from his dad, but I knew Billy wouldn't understand. I started to run out of the house, but then I stopped and turned around.

"My daddy is nothing like your daddy!" I shouted. "When my daddy passes out, he *never* pisses himself!"

At dinner that night, I started telling everyone about Billy Deel's disgusting dad and the ugly dump they lived in.

Mom put down her fork. "Jeannette, I'm disappointed in you," she said. "You should show more compassion."

"Why?" I said. "He's bad. He's a JD."

"No child is born a delinquent," Mom said. They only became that way, she went on, if nobody loved them when they were kids. Unloved children grow up to become serial murderers or alcoholics. Mom looked pointedly at Dad and then back at me. She told me I should try to be nicer to Billy . "He doesn't have all the advantages you kids do," she said.

The next time I saw Billy, I told him I'd be his friend—but not his girlfriend—if he promised not to make fun of anyone's dad. Billy promised. But he kept trying to be my boyfriend. He told me that if I'd be his girlfriend, he would always protect me and make sure nothing bad ever happened to me and buy me expensive presents. If I wouldn't be his girlfriend, he said, I'd be sorry. I told him if he didn't want to be just friends, fine with me, I wasn't scared of him.

After about a week, I was hanging out with some other kids from the

Tracks, watching garbage burn in a big rusty trash can. They were all throwing in pieces of brush to keep the fire going, plus chunks of tire treads, and we cheered at the thick black rubber smoke that made our noses sting as it rolled past us into the air.

Billy came up to me and pulled my arm, motioning me away from the other kids. He dug into his pocket and pulled out a turquoise and silver ring. "It's for you," he said.

I took it and turned it over in my hand. Mom had a collection of turquoise and silver Indian jewelry that she kept at Grandma's house so Dad wouldn't pawn it. Most of it was antique and very valuable—some man from a museum in Phoenix kept trying to buy pieces from her—and when we visited Grandma, Mom would let me and Lori put on the heavy necklaces and bracelets and concha belts. Billy's ring looked like one of Mom's. I ran it across my teeth and tongue like Mom had taught me to. I could tell by the slightly bitter taste that it was real silver.

"Where'd you get this?" I asked.

"It used to be my mom's," Billy said.

It sure was a pretty ring. It had a simple thin band and an oval-shaped piece of dark turquoise held in place by snaking silver strands. I didn't have any jewelry and it had been a long time since anyone had given me a present, except for the planet Venus.

I tried on the ring. It was way too big for my finger, but I could wrap yarn around the band the way high school girls did when they wore their boyfriend's rings. I was afraid, however, that if I took the ring, Billy might start thinking that I had agreed to be his girlfriend. He'd tell all the other kids, and if I said it wasn't true, he'd point to the ring. On the other hand, I figured Mom would approve, since accepting it would make Billy feel good about himself. I decided to compromise.

"I'll keep it," I said. "But I'm not going to wear it."

Billy's smile spread all across his face.

"But don't think this means we're boyfriend and girlfriend," I said. "And don't think this means you can kiss me."

I didn't tell anyone about the ring, not even Brian. I kept it in my pants pocket during the day, and at night I hid it in the bottom of the cardboard box where I kept my clothes.

But Billy Deel had to go and shoot his mouth off about giving me the ring. He started telling the other kids things like how, as soon as I was old enough, me and him were going to get married. When I found out what he was saying, I knew accepting the ring had been a big mistake. I also knew I should return it. But I didn't. I meant to, and every morning I'd put it in my pocket with the intention of giving it back, but I couldn't bring myself to do it. That ring was too darn pretty.

A few weeks later, I was playing hide-and-seek along the tracks with some of the neighborhood kids. I found the perfect hiding place, a small tool shed behind a clump of sagebrush that no one had hid in before. But just as the kid who was It was finishing counting, the door opened and someone else tried to get in. It was Billy Deel. He hadn't even been playing with us.

"You can't hide with me," I hissed at him. "You're supposed to find your own place."

"It's too late," he said. "He's almost done counting."

Billy crawled inside. The shed was tiny, with barely enough room for one person to fit in crouched over. I wasn't about to say so, but being that close to Billy scared me. "It's too crowded!" I whispered. "You gotta leave."

"No," Billy said. "We can fit." He rearranged his legs so they were pressed up against mine. We were so close I could feel his breath on my face.

"It's too crowded," I said again. "And you're breathing on me."

He pretended not to hear me. "You know what they do in the Green Lantern, don't you?" he asked.

I could hear the muffled shouts of the other kids being chased by the boy who was It. I wished I hadn't chosen such a good hiding place. "Sure," I said.

"What?"

"The women are nice to the men."

"But what do they do?" He paused. "See, you don't know."

"I do," I said.

"Want me to tell you?"

"I want you to find your own hiding place."

"They start by kissing," he said. "Ever kissed anyone?"

In the narrow rays of light that shot through the gaps in the sides of the shed, I could see the rings of dirt around his skinny neck. "Of course I have. Lots of times."

"Who?"

"My dad."

"Your dad doesn't count. Someone not in your family. And with your eyes closed. It doesn't count unless your eyes are closed."

I told Billy that was about the dumbest thing I'd ever heard. If your eyes were closed, you couldn't see who you were kissing.

Billy said there was an awful lot about men and women I didn't know. He said some men stuck knives into women while they were kissing them, especially if the women were being mean and didn't want to be kissed. But he told me he'd never do that to me. He put his face up next to mine.

"Close your eyes," he said.

"No way," I said.

Billy smushed his face against mine, then grabbed my hair and made my head bend sideways and stuck his tongue in my mouth. It was slimy and disgusting, but when I tried to pull away, he pushed in toward me. The more I pulled, the more he pushed, until he was on top of me and I felt his fingers tugging at my shorts. His other hand was unbuttoning his own pants. To stop him, I put my hand down there, and when I touched it, I knew what it was, even though I had never touched one before.

I couldn't knee him in the groin like Dad had told me to if a guy jumped on me, because my knees were outside his legs, so I bit him hard on the ear. It must have hurt, because he yelled and hit me in the face. Blood started gushing out of my nose.

The other kids heard the ruckus and came running. One of them opened the shed door, and Billy and I scrambled out, pulling on our clothes.

"I kissed Jeannette!" Billy yelled.

"Did not!" I said. "He's a liar! We just got into a fight, that's all."

He *was* a liar, I told myself all the rest of the day. I hadn't really kissed him, or at least it didn't count. My eyes had been open the entire time.

The next day I took the ring to Billy Deel's house. I found him out back, sitting in an abandoned car. Its red paint had been bleached by the desert sun and had turned orange along the rusting trim. The tires had collapsed a long time ago, and the black rag roof was peeling. Billy was sitting in the driver's seat, making engine noises in his throat and pretending to work a phantom stick shift.

I stood nearby, waiting for him to acknowledge me. He didn't, so I spoke first. "I don't want to be your friend," I said. "And I don't want your ring anymore."

"I don't care," he said. "I don't want it, either." He kept looking straight ahead through the cracked windshield. I reached through the open window, dropped the ring in his lap, and turned and walked away. I heard the click and clunk of the car door opening and closing behind me. I kept walking. Then I felt a sharp sting on the back of my head as if a little rock had hit me. Billy had thrown the ring at me. I kept walking.

"Guess what?" Billy shouted. "I raped you!"

I turned around and saw him standing there by the car, looking hurt and angry but not as tall as usual. I searched my mind for a cutting comeback, but since I didn't know what "rape" meant, all I could think to say was "Big deal!"

At home I looked up the word in the dictionary. Then I looked up the words that explained it, and though I still couldn't figure it out completely, I knew it wasn't good. Usually, when I didn't understand a word, I'd ask Dad about it, and we'd read over the definition together and discuss it. I didn't want to do that now. I had a hunch it would cause problems.

The next day Lori, Brian, and I were sitting at one of the spool tables in the depot, playing five-card draw and keeping an eye on Maureen while Mom and Dad spent some downtime at the Owl Club. We heard Billy Deel outside, calling my name. Lori looked at me, and I shook my head. We went back to our card game, but Billy kept on, so Lori went out on the porch, which was the old platform where people used to board the train, and told Billy to go away. She came back in and said, "He's got a gun."

Lori picked up Maureen. One of the windows shattered, and then Billy appeared framed in it. He used the butt of his rifle to knock out the remaining pieces of glass, then pointed the barrel inside.

"It's just a BB gun," Brian said.

"I told you you'd be sorry," Billy said to me and pulled the trigger. It felt like a wasp had stung me in the ribs. Billy started firing at us all, working the pump action quickly back and forth before each shot. Brian pushed over the spool table and we all crouched behind it.

The BBs pinged off the tabletop. Maureen was howling. I turned to Lori, who was the oldest and in charge. She was biting her lower lip, thinking. She handed Maureen to me and took off running across the room. Billy got her once or twice—Brian stood up to try to draw the fire—but she made it upstairs to the second floor. Then she came down again. She had Dad's pistol, and she pointed it dead at Billy.

"That's just a toy," Billy said, but his voice was a little shaky.

"It's real, all right!" I shouted. "It's my dad's gun!"

"If it is," he said, "she ain't got the cojones to use it."

"Try me," Lori told him.

"Go on, then," Billy said. "Shoot me and see what happens."

Lori wasn't as good a shot as me, but she pointed the gun in Billy's general direction and pulled the trigger. I squeezed my eyes shut at the explosion, and when I opened them, Billy had disappeared.

We all ran outside, wondering if Billy's blood-soaked body would be lying on the ground, but he had ducked under the window. When he saw us, he hightailed it down the street along the tracks. He got about fifty yards away and started shooting at us again with his BB gun. I yanked the pistol out of Lori's hand, aimed low, and pulled the trigger. I was too carried away to hold the gun the way Dad had taught me, and the recoil nearly pulled my shoulder out of its socket. The dirt kicked up a few feet in front of Billy. He jumped what seemed about three feet up in the air and broke into a dead run down the tracks.

We all started laughing, but it seemed funny only for a second or two, and then we stood there looking at one another in silence. I realized my hand was shaking so bad I could hardly hold the gun.

A little while later, a squad car pulled up outside the depot, and Mom and Dad got out. Their faces were grave. An officer got out also and walked alongside them to the door. We kids were all sitting inside on the benches wearing polite, respectful expressions. The officer looked at each of us individually, as if counting us. I clasped my hands in my lap to show I was well behaved.

Dad squatted in front of us, one knee to the floor, his arms folded across the other knee, cowboy-style. "So what happened here?" he asked.

"It was self-defense," I piped up. Dad had always said that self-defense was a justifiable reason for shooting someone.

"I see," Dad said.

The policeman told us that some of the neighbors had reported seeing kids shooting guns at each other, and he wanted to know what had happened. We tried to explain that Billy had started it, that we'd been provoked and were defending ourselves and didn't even aim to kill, but the cop wasn't interested in the nuances of the situation. He told Dad that the whole family would need to come down to the courthouse the next morning and see the magistrate. Billy Deel and his dad would be there, too. The magistrate would get to the bottom of the matter and decide what measures needed to be taken.

"Are we going to be sent away?" Brian asked the officer.

"That's up to the magistrate," he said.

That night Mom and Dad spent a long time upstairs talking in low voices while we kids lay in our boxes. Finally, late in the evening, they came down, their faces still grave.

"We're going to Phoenix," Dad said.

"When?" I asked.

"Tonight."

Dad allowed each of us to bring only one thing. I ran outside with a paper bag to gather up my favorite rocks. When I returned, holding the heavy bag at the bottom so it wouldn't split, Dad and Brian were arguing over the plastic jack-o'-lantern filled with green plastic army soldiers that Brian wanted to bring.

"You're bringing toys?" Dad asked.

"You said I could take one thing, and this is my thing," Brian said.

"This is my one thing," I said, holding up the bag. Lori, who was bringing *The Wizard of Oz*, objected, saying that a rock collection wasn't one thing but several things. It would be like her bringing her entire book collection. I pointed out that Brian's army soldiers were a collection. "And anyway, it's not the entire rock collection. Just the best ones."

Dad, who usually liked debates on questions such as whether a bag of things is one thing, was not in the mood and told me the rocks were too heavy. "You can bring one," he said.

"There are plenty of rocks in Phoenix," Mom added.

I picked out a single geode, its insides coated with tiny white crystals, and held it in both hands. As we pulled out, I looked through the rear window for one last glimpse of the depot. Dad had left the upstairs light on, and the small window glowed. I thought of all those other families of miners and prospectors who had come to Battle Mountain hoping to find gold and who had to leave town like us when their luck ran out. Dad said he didn't believe in luck, but I did. We'd had a streak of it in Battle Mountain, and I wished it had held.

We passed the Green Lantern, with the Christmas lights twinkling over its door, and the Owl Club, with the winking neon owl in a chef's hat, and then we were out in the desert, the lights of Battle Mountain disappearing behind us. In the pitch-black night, there was nothing to look at but the road ahead, lit by the car's headlights.

GRANDMA SMITH'S BIG white house had green shutters and was surrounded by eucalyptus trees. Inside were tall French doors and Persian carpets and a huge grand piano that would practically dance when Grandma played her honky-tonk music. Whenever we stayed with Grandma Smith, she brought me into her bedroom and sat me down at the vanity table, which was covered with little pastel-colored bottles of perfumes and powders. While I opened the bottles and sniffed them, she'd try to run her long metal comb through my hair, cursing out of the corner of her mouth because it was so tangled. "Doesn't that goddamn lazy-ass mother of yours ever comb your hair?" she once said. I explained that Mom believed children should be responsible for their own grooming. Grandma told me my hair was too long anyway. She put a bowl on my head, cut off all the hair beneath it, and told me I looked like a flapper.

That was what Grandma used to be. But after she had her two children, Mom and our uncle Jim, she became a teacher because she didn't trust anyone else to educate them. She taught in a one-room schoolhouse in a town called Yampi. Mom hated being the teacher's daughter. She also hated the way her mother constantly corrected her both at home and at school. Grandma Smith had strong opinions about the way things ought to be done—how to dress, how to talk, how to organize your time, how to cook and keep house, how to manage your finances—and she and Mom fought each other from the beginning. Mom felt that Grandma Smith nagged and badgered, setting rules and punishments for breaking the rules. It drove Mom crazy, and it was the reason she never set rules for us.

But I loved Grandma Smith. She was a tall, leathery, broad-shouldered woman with green eyes and a strong jaw. She told me I was her favorite grandchild and that I was going to grow up to be something special. I even liked all of her rules. I liked how she woke us up every morning at dawn, shouting, "Rise and shine, everybody!" and insisted we wash our hands and comb our hair before eating breakfast. She made us hot Cream of

Wheat with real butter, then oversaw us while we cleared the table and washed the dishes. Afterward, she took us all to buy new clothes, and we'd go to a movie like *Mary Poppins*.

Now, on the way to Phoenix, I stood up in the back of the car and leaned over the front seat between Mom and Dad. "Are we going to go stay with Grandma?" I asked.

"No," Mom said. She looked out the window, but not at anything in particular. Then she said, "Grandma's dead."

"What?" I asked. I'd heard her, but I was so thrown I felt like I hadn't.

Mom repeated herself, still looking out the window. I glanced back at Lori and Brian, but they were sleeping. Dad was smoking, his eyes on the road. I couldn't believe I'd been sitting there thinking of Grandma Smith, looking forward to eating Cream of Wheat and having her comb my hair and cuss, and all along she'd been dead. I started hitting Mom on the shoulder, hard, and asking why she hadn't told us. Finally, Dad held down my fists with his free hand, the other holding both his cigarette and the steering wheel, and said, "That's enough, Mountain Goat."

Mom seemed surprised that I was so upset.

"Why didn't you tell us?" I asked.

"There didn't seem any point," she said.

"What happened?" Grandma had been only in her sixties, and most people in her family lived until they were about a hundred.

The doctors said she'd died from leukemia, but Mom thought it was radioactive poisoning. The government was always testing nuclear bombs in the desert near the ranch, Mom said. She and Jim used to go out with a Geiger counter and find rocks that ticked. They stored them in the basement and used some to make jewelry for Grandma.

"There's no reason to grieve," Mom said. "We've all got to go someday, and Grandma had a life that was longer and fuller than most." She paused. "And now we have a place to live."

Mom explained that Grandma Smith had owned two houses, the one she lived in with the green shutters and French doors, and an older house, made of adobe, in downtown Phoenix. Since Mom was the older of the two children, Grandma Smith had asked her which house she wanted to inherit. The house with the green shutters was more valuable, but Mom had chosen the adobe house. It was near Phoenix's business district, which made it a perfect place for Mom to start an art studio.

She'd also inherited some money, so she could give up teaching and buy all the art supplies she wanted.

She'd been thinking we should move to Phoenix ever since Grandma died a few months back, but Dad had refused to leave Battle Mountain because he was so close to a breakthrough in his cyanide-leaching process.

"And I was," Dad said.

Mom gave a snort of a laugh. "So the trouble you kids got into with Billy Deel was actually a blessing in disguise," she said. "My art career is going to flourish in Phoenix. I can just feel it." She turned around to look at me. "We're off on another adventure, Jeannettie-kins. Isn't this wonderful?" Mom's eyes were bright. "I'm such an excitement addict!"

WHEN WE PULLED UP in front of the house on North Third Street, I could not believe we were actually going to live there. It was a mansion, practically, so big that Grandma Smith had had two families living in it, both paying her rent. We had the entire place to ourselves. Mom said that it had been built almost a hundred years ago as a fort. The outside walls, covered with white stucco, were three feet thick. "These sure would stop any Indians' arrows," I said to Brian.

We kids ran through the house and counted fourteen rooms, including the kitchens and bathrooms. They were filled with the things Mom had inherited from Grandma Smith: a dark Spanish dining table with eight matching chairs, a hand-carved upright piano, sideboards with antique silver serving sets, and glass-fronted cabinets filled with Grandma's bone china, which Mom demonstrated was the finest quality by holding a plate up to the light and showing us the clear silhouette of her hand through it.

The front yard had a palm tree, and the backyard had orange trees that grew real oranges. We'd never lived in a house with trees. I particularly loved the palm tree, which made me think I had arrived at some kind of oasis. There were also hollyhocks and oleander bushes with pink and white flowers. Behind the yard was a shed as big as some of the houses we had lived in, and next to the shed was a parking space big enough for two cars. We were definitely moving up in the world.

The people living on North Third Street were mostly Mexicans and Indians who had moved into the neighborhood after the whites left for the suburbs and subdivided the big old houses into apartments. There seemed to be a couple of dozen people in each house, men drinking beers from paper bags, young mothers nursing babies, old ladies sunning themselves on the sagging, weathered porches, and hordes of kids.

All the kids around North Third Street went to the Catholic school at St. Mary's Church, about five blocks away. Mom, however, said nuns were killjoys who took the fun out of religion. She wanted us to go to a public school called Emerson. Although we lived outside the district, Mom begged and cajoled the principal until he allowed us to enroll.

We were not on the bus route, and it was a bit of a hike to school, but none of us minded the walk. Emerson was in a fancy neighborhood with streets canopied by eucalyptus trees, and the school building looked like a Spanish hacienda, with a red terra-cotta roof. It was surrounded by palm trees and banana trees, and, when the bananas ripened, the students all got free bananas at lunch. The playground at Emerson was covered with lush green grass watered by a sprinkler system, and it had more equipment than I'd ever seen: seesaws, swings, a merry-go-round, a jungle gym, tether balls, and a running track.

Miss Shaw, the teacher in the third-grade class I was assigned to, had steely gray hair and pointy-rimmed glasses and a stern mouth. When I told her I'd read all the Laura Ingalls Wilder books, she raised her eyebrows skeptically, but after I read aloud from one of them, she moved me into a reading group for gifted children.

Lori's and Brian's teachers also put them in gifted reading groups. Brian hated it, because the other kids were older and he was the littlest guy in the class, but Lori and I were secretly thrilled to be called special. Instead of letting on that we felt that way, however, we made light of it. When we told Mom and Dad about our reading groups, we paused before the word "gifted," clasping our hands beneath our chins, fluttering our eyelids, and pretending to look angelic.

"Don't make a mockery of it," Dad said. "'Course you're special. Haven't I always told you that?"

Brian gave Dad a sideways look. "If we're so special," he said slowly, "why don't you . . ." His words petered out.

"What?" Dad asked. "What?"

Brian shook his head. "Nothing," he said.

Emerson had its very own nurse who gave the three of us ear and eye exams, our first ever. I aced the tests—"Eagle eyes and elephant ears," the nurse said—but Lori struggled trying to read the eye chart. The nurse declared her severely shortsighted and sent Mom a note saying she needed glasses.

"Nosiree," Mom said. She didn't approve of glasses. If you had weak eyes, Mom believed, they needed exercise to get strong. The way she saw it, glasses were like crutches. They prevented people with feeble eyes from learning to see the world on their own. She said people had been trying to get her to wear glasses for years, and she had refused. But the nurse sent another note saying Lori couldn't attend Emerson unless she wore glasses, and the school would pay for them, so Mom gave in.

When the glasses were ready, we all went down to the optometrist. The lenses were so thick they made Lori's eyes look big and bugged out, like fish eyes. She kept swiveling her head around and up and down.

"What's the matter?" I asked. Instead of answering, Lori ran outside. I followed her. She was standing in the parking lot, gazing in awe at the trees, the houses, and the office buildings behind them.

"You see that tree over there?" she said, pointing at a sycamore about a hundred feet away. I nodded.

"I can not only see that tree, I can see the individual leaves on it." She looked at me triumphantly. "Can you see them?"

I nodded.

She didn't seem to believe me. "The individual leaves? I mean, not just the branches but each little leaf?"

I nodded. Lori looked at me and then burst into tears.

On the way home, she kept seeing for the first time all these things that most everyone else had stopped noticing because they'd seen them every day. She read street signs and billboards aloud. She pointed out starlings perched on the telephone wires. We went into a bank and she stared up at the vaulted ceiling and described the octagonal patterns.

At home, Lori insisted that I try on her glasses. They would blur my vision as much as they corrected hers, she said, so I'd be able to see things as she always had. I put on the glasses, and the world dissolved into fuzzy, blotchy shapes. I took a few steps and banged my shin on the coffee table, and then I realized why Lori didn't like to go exploring as much as Brian and I did. She couldn't see.

Lori wanted Mom to try on the glasses, too. Mom slipped them on and, blinking, looked around the room. She studied one of her own paintings quietly, then handed the glasses back to Lori.

"Did you see better?" I asked.

"I wouldn't say better," Mom answered. "I'd say different."

"Maybe you should get a pair, Mom."

"I like the world just fine the way I see it," she said.

But Lori loved seeing the world clearly. She started compulsively drawing and painting all the wondrous things she was discovering, like the way each curved tile on Emerson's roof cast its own curved shadow on the tile below, and the way the setting sun painted the underbellies of the clouds pink but left the piled-up tops purple.

Not long after Lori got her glasses, she decided she wanted to be an artist, like Mom.

As soon as we'd settled into the house, Mom threw herself into her art career. She erected a big white sign in the front yard on which she had carefully painted, in black letters with gold outlines, R. M. WALLS ART STUDIO. She turned the two front rooms of the house into a studio and gallery, and she used two bedrooms in the back to warehouse her collected works. An art supplies store was three blocks away, on North First Street, and thanks to Mom's inheritance, we were able to make regular shopping expeditions to the store, bringing home rolls of canvas that Dad stretched and stapled onto wooden frames. We also brought back oil paints, watercolors, acrylics, gesso, a silk-screening frame, india ink, paintbrushes and pen nibs, charcoal pencils, pastels, fancy rag paper for pastel drawings, and even a wooden mannequin with movable joints whom we named Edward and who, Mom said, would pose for her when we kids were off at school.

Mom decided that before she could get down to any serious painting, she needed to compile a thorough art reference library. She bought dozens of big loose-leaf binders and lots of packs of lined paper. Every subject was given its own binder: dogs, cats, horses, farm animals, woodland animals, flowers, fruits and vegetables, rural landscapes, urban landscapes, men's faces, women's faces, men's bodies, women's bodies, and hands-feet-bottoms-and-other-miscellaneous body parts. We spent hours and hours going through old magazines, looking for interesting pictures, and when we spotted one we thought might be a worthy subject of a painting, we held it up to Mom for approval. She studied it for a second and okayed or nixed it. If the photo made the grade, we cut it out, glued it on a piece of lined paper, and reinforced the holes in the paper with adhesive Os so the page wouldn't tear out. Then we got out the appropriate three-ringed binder, added the new photograph, and snapped the rings shut. In exchange for our help on her reference library, Mom gave us all art lessons.

Mom was also hard at work on her writing. She bought several type-writers—manuals and electrics—so she'd have backups should her favorite break down. She kept them in her studio. She never sold any-thing she wrote, but from time to time she received an encouraging rejec-tion letter, and she thumbtacked those to the wall. When we kids came home from school, she'd usually be in her studio working. If it was quiet, she was painting or contemplating potential subjects. If the typewriter keys were clattering away, she was at work on one of her novels, poems, plays, short stories, or her illustrated collection of pithy sayings—one was "Life is a bowl of cherries, with a few nuts thrown in"—which she'd titled "R. M. Walls's Philosophy of Life."

Dad joined the local electricians' union. Phoenix was booming, and he landed a job pretty quickly. He left the house in the morning wearing a yellow hard hat and big steel-toed boots, which I thought made him look extra handsome. Because of the union, he was making steadier money than we'd ever seen. On his first payday, he came home and called us all into the living room. We kids had left our toys out in the yard, he declared.

"No, sir, we didn't," I said.

"I think you did," he said. "Go out and take a look."

We ran to the front door. Outside in the yard, parked in a row, were three brand-new bicycles—a big red one and two smaller ones, a blue boy's bike and a purple girl's bike.

I thought at first that some other kids must have left them there. When Lori pointed out that Dad had obviously bought them for us, I didn't believe her. We had never had bicycles—we had learned to ride on other kids' bikes—and it had never occurred to me that one day I might actually own one myself. Especially a new one.

I turned around. Dad was standing in the doorway with his arms crossed and a sly grin on his face. "Those bikes aren't for us, are they?" I asked.

"Well, they're too damn small for your mother and me," he said.

Lori and Brian had climbed on their bikes and were riding up and down the sidewalk. I stared at mine. It was shiny purple and had a white banana seat, wire baskets on the side, chrome handlebars that swept out like steer horns, and white plastic handles with purple-and-silver tassels. Dad knelt beside me. "Like it?" he asked.

I nodded.

"You know, Mountain Goat, I still feel bad about making you leave your rock collection back in Battle Mountain," he said. "But we had to travel light."

"I know," I said. "It was more than one thing, anyway."

"I'm not so sure," Dad said. "Every damn thing in the universe can be broken down into smaller things, even atoms, even protons, so theoretically speaking, I guess you had a winning case. A collection of things should be considered one thing. Unfortunately, theory don't always carry the day."

We rode our bicycles everywhere. Sometimes we attached playing cards to the forks with clothespins, and they flapped against the spokes when the wheels turned. Now that Lori could see, she was the navigator. She got a city map from a gas station and plotted out our routes in advance. We pedaled past the Westward Ho Hotel, down Central Avenue where square-faced Indian women sold beaded necklaces and moccasins on rainbow-colored serapes they'd spread on the sidewalk. We pedaled to Woolworth's, which was bigger than all the stores in Battle Mountain put together, and played tag in the aisles until the manager chased us out. We got Grandma Smith's old wooden tennis rackets and pedaled off to Phoenix University, where we tried to play tennis with the dead balls other people had left behind. We pedaled to the Civic Center, which had a library where the librarians recognized us because we went there so much. They helped us find books they thought we'd like, and we filled up the wire baskets on our bicycles and pedaled home right down the middle of the sidewalks, as if we owned the place.

Since Mom and Dad had all this money, we got our own telephone. We had never owned a telephone before, and whenever it rang, we kids all scrambled for it. Whoever got there first summoned up a super-snooty

English accent: "Walls residence, the butler speaking, may I help you?" while the rest of us cracked up.

We also had a big record player in a wooden cabinet that had been Grandma's. You could put a stack of records on it, and when one was finished playing, the needle arm automatically swung out and the next record dropped down with a happy slap. Mom and Dad loved music, especially rousing stuff that made you want to get up and dance, or at least sway your head or tap your foot. Mom was always going to thrift stores and coming back with old albums of polka music, Negro spirituals, German marching bands, Italian operas, and cattle roundup songs. She also bought boxes of used high heels that she called her dancing shoes. She'd slip on a pair of dancing shoes, put a stack of records on the phonograph, and crank the volume way up. Dad danced with her if he was there; otherwise she'd dance alone, waltzing or jitterbugging or doing the Texas two-step from room to room, the house filled with the sounds of Mario Lanza, or oompahing tubas, or some mournful cowboy singing "The Streets of Laredo."

Mom and Dad also bought an electric washing machine that we kept out on the patio. It was a white enamel tub up on legs, and we filled it with water from the garden hose. A big agitator twisted back and forth, making the entire machine dance around on the cement patio. It had no cycles, so you waited until the water got dirty, then put the clothes through the wringer—two rubber rolling pins rigged above the tub that were turned by a motor. To rinse the clothes, you'd repeat the process without soap, then let the water drain into the yard to help the grass grow.

Despite our wondrous appliances, life in Phoenix wasn't total luxury. We had about a gazillion cockroaches, big, strong things with shiny wings. We had just a few at first, but since Mom was not exactly a compulsive cleaner, they multiplied. After a while, entire armies were scuttling across the walls and the floors and the kitchen counters. In Battle Mountain, we'd had lizards to eat the flies and cats to eat the lizards. We couldn't think of any animal that liked to eat roaches, so I suggested we buy roach spray, like all our neighbors did, but Mom was opposed to chemical warfare. It was like with those Shell No-Pest strips, she said; we'd end up poisoning ourselves, too.

Mom decided hand-to-hand combat was the best tactic. We conducted roach massacres in the kitchen at night, because that was when they came out in force. We armed ourselves with rolled-up magazines or shoes—even though I was only nine, I already wore size-ten shoes that Brian called "roach killers"—and sneaked into the kitchen. Mom threw the light switch, and we kids all started the assault. You didn't even have to aim. We had so many roaches that if you hit any flat surface, you were sure to take out at least a few.

The house also had termites. We discovered this a few months after we moved in, when Lori's foot crashed through the spongy wood floor in the living room. After inspecting the house, Dad decided that the termite infestation was so severe nothing could be done about it. We'd have to coexist with the critters. So we walked around the hole in the living room floor.

But the wood was chewed through everywhere. We kept stepping on soft spots in the floorboards, crashing through, and creating new holes. "Damned if this floor isn't starting to look like a piece of Swiss cheese," Dad said one day. He told me to fetch him his wire cutters, a hammer, and some roofing nails. He finished off the beer he was drinking, snipped the can open with his wire cutters, hammered it flat, and nailed it over the hole. He needed more patches, he said, so he had to go out and buy another six-pack. After he polished off each beer, he used the can to repair one of the holes. And whenever a new hole appeared, he'd get out his hammer, down a beer, and do another patch job.

A LOT OF OUR NEIGHBORS on North Third Street were kind of weird. A clan of Gypsies lived down the block in a big, falling-apart house with plywood nailed over the porch to create more indoor space. They were always stealing our stuff, and one time, after Brian's pogo stick had disappeared, he saw one of the old Gypsy women bouncing down the sidewalk on it. She wouldn't give it back, so Mom got into a big argument with the head of the clan, and the next day we found a chicken with its throat cut on our doorstep. It was some kind of Gypsy hex. Mom decided, as she put it, to fight magic with magic. She took a ham bone out of the beans and went down to the Gypsies' house, waving it in the air. Standing on the sidewalk, she held up the bone like a crucifix at an exorcism, and called down a curse on the entire Gypsy clan and their house, vowing that it would collapse with the lot of them in it and that the bowels of the earth would open up and swallow them forever if they bothered us again. The next morning Brian's pogo stick was lying in the front yard.

The neighborhood also had its share of perverts. Mostly, they were shabby, hunched men with wheedling voices who hung around on street corners and followed us to and from school, trying to give us boosts when we climbed a fence, offering us candy and loose change if we would go play with them. We called them creeps and hollered at them to leave us alone, but I worried about hurting their feelings because I couldn't help wondering if maybe they were telling the truth, that all they wanted was to be our friends.

At night Mom and Dad always left the front door and the back door and all the windows open. Since we had no air-conditioning, they explained, we needed to let the air circulate. From time to time, a vagrant or a wino would wander through the front door, assuming the house was deserted. When we woke up in the morning, we'd find one asleep in a front room. As soon as we roused them, they shambled off apologetically. Mom always assured us they were just harmless drunks.

Maureen, who was four and had a terrible fear of bogeymen, kept dreaming that intruders in Halloween masks were coming through the open doors to get us. One night when I was almost ten, I was awakened by someone running his hands over my private parts. At first it was confusing. Lori and I slept in the same bed, and I thought maybe she was moving in her sleep. I groggily pushed the hand away.

"I just want to play a game with you," a man's voice said.

I recognized the voice. It belonged to a scraggly guy with sunken cheeks who had been hanging around North Third Street recently. He'd tried to walk us home from school and had given Brian a magazine called *Kids on a Farm*, with pictures of boys and girls wearing only underpants.

"Pervert!" I yelled and kicked at the man's hand. Brian came running into the room with a hatchet he kept by his bed, and the man bolted out the door. Dad was out that night, and when Mom slept, she was dead to the world, so Brian and I ran after the man ourselves. As we got to the sidewalk, lit by the purplish glow from the streetlights, he disappeared around the corner. We searched for him for a few blocks, Brian whacking at the bushes with his hatchet, but we couldn't find him. On our way home, we were slapping each other's hands and pumping our fists in the air, as if we'd won a boxing match. We decided we had been Pervert Hunting, which was just like Demon Hunting except the enemy was real and dangerous instead of being the product of a kid's overactive imagination.

The next day, when Dad came home and we told him what had happened, he said he was going to kill that lowlife sonofabitch. He and Brian and I went out on a serious Pervert Hunt. Our blood up, we searched the streets for hours, but we never did find the guy. I asked Mom and Dad if we should close the doors and windows when we went to sleep. They wouldn't consider it. We needed the fresh air, they said, and it was essential that we refuse to surrender to fear.

So the windows stayed open. Maureen kept having nightmares of men in Halloween masks. And every now and then, when Brian and I were feeling revved up, he'd get a machete and I'd get a baseball bat and we'd go Pervert Hunting, clearing the streets of the creeps who preyed on kids.

Mom and Dad liked to make a big point about never surrendering to fear or to prejudice or to the narrow-minded conformist sticks-in-the-mud who tried to tell everyone else what was proper. We were supposed to ignore those benighted sheep, as Dad called them. One day Mom went with us kids to the library at the Civic Center. Since the weather was sweltering, she suggested we cool off by jumping into the fountain in front of the building. The water was too shallow to swim in, but we paddled around pretending to be crocodiles until we attracted a small crowd of people who kept insisting to Mom that swimming was forbidden in the fountain.

"Mind your own beeswax," Mom replied. I was feeling kind of embarrassed and started to climb out. "Ignore the fuddy-duddies!" Mom told me, and to make it clear she paid no nevermind to such people or their opinions, she clambered into the fountain and plopped down beside us, sending gallons of water sloshing over the sides.

It never bothered Mom if people turned and stared at her, even in church. Although she thought nuns were killjoys and she didn't follow all the Church's rules word for word—she treated the Ten Commandments more like the Ten Suggestions—Mom considered herself a devout Catholic and took us to mass most Sundays. St. Mary's was the biggest, most beautiful church I had ever seen. It was made of sand-colored adobe and had two soaring steeples, a gigantic circular stained-glass window, and, leading up to the two main doors, a pair of sweeping staircases covered with pigeons. The other mothers dressed up for mass, wearing black lace mantillas on their heads and clutching green or red or yellow handbags that matched their shoes. Mom thought it was superficial to worry about how you looked. She said God thought the same way, so she'd go to church in torn or paint-splattered clothes. It was your inner spirit and not your outward appearance that mattered, she said, and come hymn time, she showed the whole congregation her spirit, belting out the words in such a powerful voice that people in the pews in front of us would turn around and stare.

Church was particularly excruciating when Dad came along. Dad had been raised Baptist, but he didn't like religion and didn't believe in God. He believed in science and reason, he said, not superstition and voodoo. But Mom had refused to have children unless Dad agreed to raise them as Catholics and to attend church himself on holy days of obligation.

Dad sat in the pew fuming and shifting around and trying to bite his tongue while the priest carried on about Jesus resurrecting Lazarus from the dead and the communicants filed up to eat the body and drink the blood of Christ. Finally, when Dad was unable to stand it any longer, he'd shout out something to challenge the priest. He didn't do it to be hostile. He hollered out his point in a friendly tone: "Yo, Padre!" he'd say. The priest usually ignored Dad and tried to go on with his sermon, but Dad persisted. He'd challenge the priest about the scientific impossibility of the miracles, and when the priest continued to ignore him, he'd get mad and yell out something about Pope Alexander VI's bastard children, or Pope Leo X's hedonism, or Pope Nicholas III's simony, or the murders committed in the name of the Church during the Spanish Inquisition. But what could you expect, he'd say, from an institution run by celibate men who wore dresses. At that point the ushers would tell us we'd have to leave.

"Don't worry, God understands," Mom said. "He knows that your father is a cross we must bear."

CITY LIFE WAS GETTING to Dad. "I'm starting to feel like a rat in a maze," he told me. He hated the way everything in Phoenix was so organized, with time cards, bank accounts, telephone bills, parking meters, tax forms, alarm clocks, PTA meetings, and pollsters knocking on the door and prying into your affairs. He hated all the people who lived in air-conditioned houses with the windows permanently sealed, and drove air-conditioned cars to nine-to-five jobs in air-conditioned office buildings that he said were little more than gussied-up prisons. Just the sight of those people on their way to work made him feel hemmed in and itchy. He began complaining that we were all getting too soft, too dependent on creature comforts, and that we were losing touch with the natural order of the world.

Dad missed the wilderness. He needed to be roaming free in open country and living among untamed animals. He felt it was good for your soul to have buzzards and coyotes and snakes around. That was the way man was meant to live, he'd say, in harmony with the wild, like the Indians, not this lords-of-the-earth crap, trying to rule the entire goddamn planet, cutting down all the forests and killing every creature you couldn't bring to heel.

One day we heard on the radio that a woman in the suburbs had seen a mountain lion behind her house and had called the police, who shot the animal. Dad got so angry he put his fist through a wall. "That mountain lion had as much right to his life as that sour old biddy does to hers," he said. "You can't kill something just because it's wild."

Dad stewed for a while, sucking on a beer, and then he told us all to get in the car.

"Where are we going?" I asked. We hadn't been on a single expedition since we moved to Phoenix. I missed them.

"I'm going to show you," he said, "that no animal, no matter how big or wild, is dangerous as long as you know what you're doing."

We all piled into the car. Dad drove, nursing another beer and cussing under his breath about that innocent mountain lion and the chickenshit suburbanite. We turned in at the city zoo. None of us kids had ever been to a zoo before, and I didn't really know what to expect. Lori said she thought zoos should be outlawed. Mom, who had Maureen in one arm and her sketch pad under the other, pointed out that the animals had traded freedom for security. She said that when she looked at them, she would pretend not to see the bars.

At the entrance gate, Dad bought our tickets, muttering about the idiocy of paying money to look at animals, and led us down the walk. Most of the cages were patches of dirt surrounded by iron bars, with for-lorn gorillas or restless bears or irritable monkeys or anxious gazelles huddled in the corners. A lot of the kids were having fun, gawking and laughing and throwing peanuts at the animals, but the sight of those poor creatures made my throat swell up.

"I've got half a mind to sneak in here some night and free these crit-ters," Dad said.

"Can I help?" I asked.

He mussed my hair. "Me and you, Mountain Goat," he said. "We'll carry out our own animal prison break."

We stopped at a bridge. Below it, in a deep pit, alligators sunned themselves on rocks surrounding a pond. "The biddy who got that mountain lion shot didn't understand animal psychology," Dad said. "If you let them know you're not afraid, they'll leave you alone."

Dad pointed to the biggest, scaliest alligator. "Me and that nasty-looking bastard's going to have us a staring contest." Dad stood on the bridge glowering at the alligator. At first it seemed to be asleep, but then it blinked and looked up at Dad. Dad continued staring, his eyes in a fierce squint. After a minute the alligator thrashed its tail, looked away, and slid into the water. "See, you just have to communicate your posi-tion," Dad said.

"Maybe he would have gone for a swim anyway," Brian whispered.

"What do you mean?" I asked. "Didn't you see how nervous that gator got? Dad made him do it."

We followed Dad to the lion's den, but the lions were sleeping, so Dad said we should leave them alone. The aardvark was busy Hoovering up ants, and Dad said you shouldn't disturb eating animals, so we passed it by and went on to the cheetah's cage, which was about as big as our living room and surrounded by a chain fence. The lone cheetah paced back and forth, the muscles in his shoulders shifting with each step. Dad folded his arms on his chest and studied the cheetah. "He's a good animal— fastest four-footed creature on the planet," he declared. "Not happy about being in this damn cage, but he's resigned to it, and he's no longer angry. Let's see if he's hungry."

Dad took me to the concession stand. He told the lady running it that he had a rare medical condition and couldn't eat cooked meat so he'd like to buy a raw hamburger. "Yeah, right," the salesclerk said. She told Dad the zoo did not allow the sale of uncooked meat, because foolish people tried to feed it to the animals.

"I'd like to feed her lard ass to the animals," Dad muttered. He bought me a bag of popcorn, and we returned to the cheetah cage. Dad squatted outside the fence opposite the cheetah. The animal came closer to the bars and studied him curiously. Dad kept looking at him, but not in the angry-eyed way he had stared down the alligator. The cheetah looked back. Finally, he sat down. Dad stepped over the chain fence and knelt right next to the bars where the cheetah was sitting. The cheetah remained still, looking at Dad.

Dad slowly raised his right hand and put it up against the cage. The cheetah looked at Dad's hand but didn't move. Dad calmly put his hand between the iron bars of the cage and rested it on the cheetah's neck. The cheetah moved the side of his face against Dad's hand, as if asking to be petted. Dad gave the cheetah the kind of hardy, vigorous petting you'd give a big dog.

"Situation under control," Dad said and beckoned us over.

We climbed under the chain fence and knelt around Dad while he petted the cheetah. By then a few people had begun to gather. One man was calling to us to get back behind the chain fence. We ignored him. I knelt close to the cheetah. My heart was beating fast, but I wasn't scared, only excited. I could feel the cheetah's hot breath on my face. He looked right at me. His amber eyes were steady but sad, as if he knew he'd never see the plains of Africa again.

"May I pet him, please?" I asked Dad.

Dad took my hand and slowly guided it to the side of the cheetah's neck. It was soft but also bristly. The cheetah turned his head and put his moist nose up against my hand. Then his big pink tongue unfolded from his mouth, and he licked my hand. I gasped. Dad opened my hand and held my fingers back. The cheetah licked my palm, his tongue warm and rough, like sandpaper dipped in hot water. I felt all tingly.

"I think he likes me," I said.

"He does," Dad said. "He also likes the popcorn salt and butter on your hand."

There was a small crowd around the cage now, and one particularly frantic woman grabbed my shirt and tried to pull me over the chain. "It's all right," I told her. "My dad does stuff like this all the time."

"He should be arrested!" she shouted.

"Okay, kids," Dad said, "the civilians are revolting. We better ske-daddle."

We climbed over the chain. When I looked back, the cheetah was following us along the side of the cage. Before we could make our way through the crowd, a heavy man in a navy blue uniform came running toward us. He was holding on to the gun and nightstick on his belt, which made him look like he was running with his hands on his hips. He was shouting about regulations and how idiots had been killed climbing into cages and how we all had to leave immediately. He grabbed Dad by the shoulder, but Dad pushed him off and assumed a fighting stance. Some of the men in the crowd clutched Dad's arms, and Mom asked Dad to please do what the guard had ordered.

Dad nodded and held out his hands in a peace gesture. He led us through the crowd and toward the exit, chuckling and shaking his head to let us kids know that these fools were not worth the time it would take to kick their butts. I could hear people around us whispering about the crazy drunk man and his dirty little urchin children, but who cared what they thought? None of them had ever had their hand licked by a cheetah.

IT WAS AROUND this time that Dad lost his job. He said there was nothing to worry about, because Phoenix was so big and growing so fast that he could find another job at a site where they hadn't spread lies about him. Then he got fired from his second job and from his third, and was kicked out of the electricians' union and started doing odd jobs and day work. Whatever money Mom had inherited from Grandma Smith had disappeared, and once again we started scraping by.

I didn't go hungry. Hot lunch at school cost a quarter, and we could usually afford that. When we couldn't and I told Mrs. Ellis, my fourth-grade teacher, that I had forgotten my quarter, she said her records indicated that someone had already paid for me. Even though it seemed awfully coincidental, I didn't want to push my luck by asking too many questions about who this someone was. I ate the hot lunch. Sometimes that lunch was all I had to eat all day, but I could get by just fine on one meal.

One afternoon when Brian and I had come home to an empty fridge, we went out to the alley behind the house looking for bottles to redeem. Down the alley was the delivery bay of a warehouse. A big green Dumpster stood in the parking lot. When no one was looking, Brian and I pushed open the lid, climbed up, and dived inside to search for bottles. I was afraid it might be full of yucky garbage. Instead, we found an astonishing treasure: cardboard boxes filled with loose chocolates. Some of them were whitish and dried-out-looking, and some were covered with a mysterious green mold, but most of them were fine. We pigged out on chocolates, and from then on, whenever Mom was too busy to make dinner or we were out of food, we'd go back to the Dumpster to see if any new chocolate was waiting for us. From time to time, it was.

For some reason, there were no kids Maureen's age on North Third Street. She was too young to run around with me and Brian, so she spent most of her time riding up and down on the red tricycle Dad had bought for her, and playing with her imaginary friends. They all had names, and she would talk to them for hours. They'd laugh together, carry on detailed conversations, even argue. One day she came home in tears, and when I asked her why she was crying, she said she'd gotten into a fight with Suzie Q., one of the imaginary friends.

Maureen was five years younger than Brian, and Mom said that since she didn't have any allies in the family around her age, she needed special treatment. Mom decided Maureen needed to enroll in preschool, but she said she didn't want her youngest daughter dressed in the thrift-store clothes the rest of us wore. Mom told us we would have to go shoplifting.

"Isn't that a sin?" I asked Mom.

"Not exactly," Mom said. "God doesn't mind you bending the rules a little if you have a good reason. It's sort of like justifiable homicide. This is justifiable pilfering."

Mom's plan was for her and Maureen to go into the dressing room of a store with an armful of new clothes for Maureen to try on. When they came out, Mom would tell the clerk she didn't like any of the dresses. At that point Lori, Brian, and I would create a ruckus to distract the clerk while Mom hid a dress under a raincoat she would be carrying on her arm.

We got three or four nice dresses for Maureen that way, but on one excursion, when Brian and I were pretending to punch each other out and Mom was in the process of slipping a dress under her raincoat, the saleslady turned to Mom and asked if she intended to buy that dress she was holding. Mom had no choice but to pay for it. "Fourteen dollars for a child's dress!" she said as we left the store. "It's highway robbery!"

Dad devised an ingenious way to come up with extra cash. He figured out that when you made a withdrawal from the drive-through window at the bank, it took a few minutes for the transaction to register in the computer. So he would open a bank account, and a week or so later, he would withdraw all the money from a teller inside the bank while Mom withdrew the same amount from the drive-through window. Lori said it sounded outright felonious, but Dad said all he was doing was outsmarting the fat-cat bank owners who shylocked the common man by charging usurious interest rates.

"Wear innocent expressions," Mom told us kids the first time we dropped Dad off in front of the bank.

"Will we have to go to a juvenile-delinquent center if we get busted?" I asked.

Mom assured me it was all perfectly legal. "People overdraw their accounts all the time," she said. "If we get caught, we'll just pay a little overdraft fee." She explained that it was sort of like taking out a loan without all the messy paperwork. But as we drove up to the teller's window, Mom seemed to get edgy and giggled nervously as she passed the withdrawal slip through the bulletproof window. I think she was enjoying the thrill of taking from the rich.

After the woman inside passed us the cash, Mom drove around to the front of the bank. In a minute, Dad strolled out. He climbed into the front of the car, turned around, and, with a wicked grin, held up a stack of bills and riffled them with his thumb.

The reason Dad was having a tough time getting steady work—as he kept trying to tell us—was that the electricians' union in Phoenix was corrupt. It was run by the mob, he said, which controlled all the construction projects in the city, so before he could get a decent job, he had to run organized crime out of town. That required a lot of undercover research, and the best place to gather information was at the bars the mobsters owned. So Dad started spending most of his time in those joints.

Mom rolled her eyes whenever Dad mentioned his research. I began to have my own doubts about what he was up to. He came home in such a drunken fury that Mom usually hid while we kids tried to calm him down. He broke windows and smashed dishes and furniture until he'd spent all his anger; then he'd look around at the mess and at us kids standing there. When he recognized what he'd done, he hung his head in weariness and shame. Then he'd sink to his knees and pitch forward face-first on the floor.

After Dad had collapsed, I would try to pick up the place, but Mom always made me stop. She'd been reading books on how to cope with an alcoholic, and they said that drunks didn't remember their rampages, so if you cleaned up after them, they'd think nothing had happened. "Your father needs to see the mess he's making of our lives," Mom said. But when Dad got up, he'd act as if all the wreckage didn't exist, and no one discussed it with him. The rest of us had to get used to stepping over broken furniture and shattered glass.

Mom had taught us to pick Dad's pocket when he passed out. We got pretty good at it. Once, after I'd rolled Dad and collected a handful of change, I pried his fingers loose from the bottle in his hand. It was three quarters empty. I stared at the amber liquid. Mom never touched the stuff, and I wondered what Dad found so irresistible. I opened the bottle and sniffed. The awful smell stung my nose, but after working up my courage, I took a swig. It had a hideously thick taste, smoky, and so hot it burned my tongue. I ran to the bathroom, spat it out, and rinsed my mouth.

"I just took a swig of booze," I told Brian. "It's the worst thing I've ever tasted in my life."

Brian grabbed the bottle out of my hand. He emptied it into the kitchen sink, then led me out to the shed and opened up a wooden trunk in the back marked TOY BOX. It was filled with empty liquor bottles. Whenever Dad passed out, Brian said, he took the bottle Dad had been drinking, emptied it, and hid it in the trunk. He'd wait until he had ten or twelve, then tote them to a garbage can a few blocks away, because if Dad saw the empty bottles, he would get furious.

"I have a really good feeling about this Christmas," Mom announced in early December. Lori pointed out that the last few months hadn't gone so well.

"Exactly," Mom said. "This is God's way of telling us to take charge of our own fates. God helps those who help themselves."

She had such a good feeling that she'd decided that this year we were going to celebrate Christmas on Christmas Day, instead of a week later.

Mom was an expert thrift-store shopper. She read the labels on the clothes and turned over dishes and vases to study the markings on the bottom. She had no qualms about telling a saleslady that a dress marked at twenty-five cents was worth only a dime, and she usually got it at that price. Mom took us thrift-store shopping for weeks before that Christmas, giving us each a dollar to spend on presents. I got a red glass bud vase for Mom, an onyx ashtray for Dad, a model-car kit for Brian, a book about elves for Lori, and a stuffed tiger with a loose ear that Mom helped me sew back in place for Maureen.

On Christmas morning, Mom took us down to a gas station that sold Christmas trees. She selected a tall, dark, but slightly dried-out Douglas fir. "This poor old tree isn't going to sell by the end of the day, and it needs someone to love it," she told the man and offered him three dollars. The man looked at the tree and looked at Mom and looked at us kids. My dress had buttons missing. Holes were appearing along the seams of Maureen's T-shirt. "Lady, this one's been marked down to a buck," he said.

We carried the tree home and decorated it with Grandma's antique ornaments: ornate colored balls, fragile glass partridges, and lights with long tubes of bubbling water. I couldn't wait to open my presents, but Mom insisted that we celebrate Christmas in the Catholic fashion, getting to the gifts only after we'd attended midnight mass. Dad, knowing that all the bars and liquor stores would be closed on Christmas, had stocked up in advance. He'd popped open the first Budweiser before breakfast, and by the time midnight mass rolled around, he was having trouble standing up.

I suggested that maybe this once, Mom should let Dad off the hook about going to mass, but she said stopping by God's house for a quick hello was especially important at times like this, so Dad staggered and lurched into the church with us. During the sermon, the priest discussed the miracle of Immaculate Conception and the Virgin Birth.

"Virgin, my ass!" Dad shouted. "Mary was a sweet Jewish broad who got herself knocked up!"

The service came to a dead halt. Everyone was staring. The choir had swiveled around in unison and were gaping openmouthed. Even the priest was speechless.

Dad had a satisfied grin on his face. "And Jesus H. Christ is the world's best-loved bastard!"

The ushers grimly escorted us to the street. On the way home, Dad put his arm around my shoulder for support. "Baby girl, if your boyfriend ever gets into your panties and you find yourself in a family way, swear that it was Immaculate Conception and start mouthing off about miracles," he said. "Then just pass around the collection plate come Sunday."

I didn't like Dad when he talked like that, and I tried to move away from him, but he just held me tighter.

Back at home, we tried to calm Dad down. Mom gave him one of his presents, a brass cigarette lighter from the nineteen twenties in the shape of a Scottish terrier. Dad flicked it a couple of times, swaying back and forth; then he held it up to the light and studied it.

"Let's really light up this Christmas," Dad said and thrust the lighter into the Douglas fir. The dried-out needles caught fire immediately. Flames leaped through the branches with a crackling noise. Christmas ornaments exploded from the heat.

For a few moments, we were too stunned to do anything. Mom called for blankets and water. We were able to put the fire out, but only by knocking down the tree, smashing most of the ornaments, and ruining all our presents. Dad sat on the sofa the whole time, laughing and telling Mom that he was doing her a favor because trees were pagan symbols of worship.

Once the fire was out and the sodden, burned tree lay smoldering on the floor, we all just stood there. No one tried to wring Dad's neck or yell at him or even point out that he'd ruined the Christmas his family had spent weeks planning—the Christmas that was supposed to be the best we'd ever had. When Dad went crazy, we all had our own ways of shutting down and closing off, and that was what we did that night.

I TURNED TEN THAT spring, but birthdays were not a big deal around our house. Sometimes Mom stuck a few candles in some ice cream and we all sang "Happy Birthday." Mom and Dad might get us a little present—a comic book or a pair of shoes or a package of underwear—but at least as often, they forgot our birthdays altogether.

So I was surprised when, on the day I turned ten, Dad took me outside to the back patio and asked what I wanted most in the world. "It's a special occasion, seeing as how it puts you into double digits," he said. "You're growing up damn fast, Mountain Goat. You'll be on your own in no time, and if there's anything I can do for you now, before you're gone, I want to do it."

I knew Dad wasn't talking about buying me some extravagant present, like a pony or a dollhouse. He was asking what he could do, now that I was almost a grown-up, to make my last years as a kid everything I hoped they'd be. There was only one thing I truly wanted, something that I knew would change all our lives, but I was afraid to ask for it. Just thinking about saying the words out loud made me nervous.

Dad saw my hesitation. He knelt so that he was looking up at me. "What is it?" he said. "Ask away."

"It's big."

"Just ask, baby."

"I'm scared."

"You know if it's humanly possible, I'll get it for you. And if it ain't humanly possible, I'll die trying."

I looked up at the thin swirls of clouds high in the blue Arizona sky. Keeping my eyes fastened on those distant clouds, I took a breath and said, "Do you think you could maybe stop drinking?"

Dad said nothing. He was staring down at the cement patio, and when he turned to me, his eyes had a wounded look, like a dog who's been kicked. "You must be awfully ashamed of your old man," he said.

"No," I said quickly. "It's just I think Mom would be a lot happier. Plus, we'd have the extra money."

"You don't have to explain," Dad said. His voice was barely a whisper. He stood up and walked into the yard and sat down under the orange trees. I followed and sat down next to him. I was going to take his hand, but before I could reach for it, he said, "If you don't mind, honey, I think I'd like to sit here by myself for a while."

In the morning Dad told me that for the next few days, he was going to keep to himself in his bedroom. He wanted us kids to steer clear of him, to stay outside all day and play. Everything went fine for the first day. On the second day, when I came home from school, I heard a terrible groaning coming from the bedroom.

"Dad?" I called. There was no answer. I opened the door.

Dad was tied to the bed with ropes and belts. I don't know if he had done it himself or if Mom helped him, but he was thrashing about, bucking and pulling at the restraints, yelling *"No!"* and *"Stop!"* and *"Oh my God!"* His face was gray and dripping with sweat. I called out to him again, but he didn't see or hear me. I went into the kitchen and filled an empty orange-juice jug with water. I sat with the jug next to Dad's door in case he got thirsty. Mom saw me and told me to go outside and play. I told her I wanted to help Dad. She said there was nothing I could do, but I stayed by the door anyway.

Dad's delirium continued for days. When I came home from school, I'd get the jug of water, take up my position by the door, and wait there until bedtime. Brian and Maureen played outside, and Lori kept to the far side of the house. Mom painted in her studio. No one talked much about what was going on. One night when we were eating dinner, Dad let out a particularly hideous cry. I looked at Mom, who was stirring her soup as if it were an ordinary evening, and that was when I lost it.

"Do something!" I yelled at her. "You've got to do something to help Dad!"

"Your father's the only one who can help himself," Mom said. "Only he knows how to fight his own demons."

After the better part of a week, Dad's delirium stopped, and he asked us to come talk to him in the bedroom. He was propped up on a pillow, paler and thinner than I'd ever seen him. He took the water jug I offered him. His hands were shaking so badly that he had trouble holding it, and water dribbled down his chin as he drank.

A few days later, Dad was able to walk around, but he had no appetite, and his hands still trembled. I told Mom that maybe I had made a terrible mistake, but Mom said sometimes you have to get sicker before you can get better. Within a few more days, Dad seemed almost normal, except that he'd become tentative, even kind of shy. He smiled at us kids a lot and squeezed our shoulders, sometimes leaning on us to steady himself.

"I wonder what life will be like now," I said to Lori.

"The same," she said. "He tried stopping before, but it never lasted."

"This time it will."

"How do you know?"

"It's his present to me."

Dad spent the summer recuperating. For days on end, he'd sit under the orange trees reading. By early fall, he had recovered most of his strength. To celebrate his new life on the wagon, and to put some distance between himself and his drinking haunts, he decided that the Walls clan should take a long camping trip to the Grand Canyon. We'd avoid the park rangers and find a cave somewhere along the river. We'd swim and fish and cook our catch over an open fire. Mom and Lori could paint, and Dad and Brian and I could climb the cliffs and study the canyon's geological strata. It would be like old times. We kids didn't need to be going to school, he said. He and Mom could instruct us better than any of those shit-for-brains teachers. "You, Mountain Goat, can put together a rock collection the likes of which has never been seen," Dad told me.

Everyone loved the idea. Brian and I were so excited we did a jig right there on the living room floor. We packed blankets, food, canteens, fishing line, the lavender blanket Maureen took everywhere, Lori's paper and pencils, Mom's easel and canvases and brushes and paints. What couldn't fit in the trunk of the car, we tied to the top. We also took along Mom's fancy archery set, the one made of inlaid fruitwood, because Dad said you never know what wild game we might find in those canyon recesses. He promised Brian and me that we'd be shooting that bow and arrow like a couple of full-blooded Indian kids by the time we came back. If we ever came back. Hell, we might decide to live in the Grand Canyon permanently.

We started out early the next morning. Once we got north of Phoenix, past all the tract-house suburbs, the traffic thinned, and Dad started going faster and faster. "There ain't no better feeling than being on the move," he said.

We were out in the desert now, the telephone poles snapping past. "Hey, Mountain Goat," he hollered. "How fast do you think I can make this car go?"

"Faster than the speed of light!" I said. I leaned over the front seat and watched the needle on the speedometer creep up. We were doing ninety miles an hour.

"You're gonna see that little needle go all the way off the dial," Dad said.

I could see his leg move as he stepped on the gas. We'd rolled down the windows, and maps and art paper and cigarette ashes were whipping around our heads. The speedometer needle crept past one hundred, the last number on the dial, and pushed into the empty space beyond. The car started shuddering, but Dad didn't let up on the accelerator. Mom covered her head with her arms and told Dad to slow down, but that only made him press on the gas even harder.

Suddenly, there was a clattering noise under the car. I looked back to make sure no important part had fallen off, and saw a cone of gray smoke billowing behind us. Just then white steam that smelled like iron started pouring out from the sides of the hood and blowing past the windows. The shuddering increased, and with a terrible coughing, clunking noise, the car began to slow. Soon it was going at no more than a crawl. Then the engine died altogether. We coasted for a few yards in silence before the car stopped.

"Now you've done it," Mom said.

We kids and Dad got out and pushed the car to the side of the road while Mom steered. Dad lifted the hood. I watched while he and Brian studied the smoking, grease-encrusted engine and discussed the parts by name. Then I went to sit in the car with Mom, Lori, and Maureen.

Lori gave me a disgusted look, as if she thought it was my fault that the car had broken down. "Why do you always encourage him?" she asked.

"Don't worry," I said. "Dad will fix it."

We sat there for a long time. I could see buzzards circling high in the distance, which reminded me of that ingrate Buster. Maybe I should have cut him some slack. With his broken wing and lifetime of eating road-kill, he probably had a lot to be ungrateful about. Too much hard luck can create a permanent meanness of spirit in any creature.

Finally, Dad shut the hood.

"You can fix it, can't you?" I asked.

"Of course," he said. "If I had the proper tools."

We'd have to temporarily postpone our expedition to the Grand Canyon, he told us. Our first priority now was to head back to Phoenix so he could get his hands on the right tools.

"How?" Lori asked.

Hitchhiking was one option, Dad said. But it might be hard finding a car with enough room to accommodate four kids and two adults. Since we were all so athletic, and since none of us were whiners, walking home would be no problem.

"It's almost eighty miles," Lori said.

"That's right," Dad said. If we covered three miles an hour for eight hours a day, we could make it in three days. We had to leave everything behind except Maureen's lavender blanket and the canteens. That included Mom's fruitwood archery set. Since Mom was attached to that archery set, which her father had given her, Dad had Brian and me hide it in an irrigation ditch. We could come back and retrieve it later.

Dad carried Maureen. To keep our spirits up, he called out *hup, two, three, four,* but Mom and Lori refused to march along in step. Eventually, Dad gave up, and it was quiet except for the sound of our feet crunching on the sand and rocks and the wind whipping off the desert. After walking for what seemed like a couple of hours, we reached a motel billboard that we had passed only a minute or so before the car broke down. The occasional car whizzed by, and Dad stuck out his thumb, but none of them stopped. Around midday, a big blue Buick with gleaming chrome bumpers slowed down and pulled onto the shoulder in front of us. A lady with a beauty-parlor hairdo rolled down the window.

"You poor people!" she exclaimed. "Are you okay?"

She asked us where we were going, and when we told her Phoenix, she offered us a ride. The air-conditioning in the Buick was so cold that goose bumps popped up on my arms and legs. The lady had Lori and me pass around Coca-Colas and sandwiches from a cooler in the foot well. Dad said he wasn't hungry.

The lady kept talking about how her daughter had been driving down the highway and had seen us and, when she got to the lady's house, had told her about this poor family walking along the side of the road. "And I said to her, I said to my daughter, 'Why, I can't leave those poor people out there.' I told my daughter, 'Those poor kids must be dying of thirst, poor things.'"

"We're not poor," I said. She had used that word one too many times.

"Of course you're not," the lady quickly replied. "I didn't mean it that way."

But I could tell that she had. The lady grew quiet, and for the rest of the trip, no one said much. As soon as she dropped us off, Dad disappeared. I waited on the front steps until bedtime, but he didn't come home.

THREE DAYS LATER, while Lori and I were sitting at Grandma's old upright piano trying to teach each other to play, we heard heavy, uneven footsteps at the front door. We turned and saw Dad. He tripped on the coffee table. When we tried to help him, he cursed and lurched at us, swinging his fist. He wanted to know where that goddamn sorry-assed mother of ours was, and he got so mad when we didn't tell him that he pulled over Grandma's china closet, sending her fine bone china crashing to the floor. Brian came running in. He tried to grab Dad's leg, but Dad kicked him off.

Dad yanked out the silverware drawer and hurled the forks and spoons and knives across the room, then picked up one of the chairs and smashed it on Grandma's table. "Rose Mary, where the goddamn hell are you, you stinking bitch?" he yelled. "Where is that whore hiding?"

He found Mom in the bathroom, crouched in the tub. As she darted past him, he grabbed her dress, and she started flailing. They fought their way into the dining room, and he knocked her to the floor. She reached into the pile of kitchen utensils that Dad had thrown there, grabbed a butcher knife, and slashed it through the air in front of him.

Dad leaned back. "A knife fight, eh?" He grinned. "Okay, if that's what you want." He picked up a knife, too, tossing it from hand to hand. Then he knocked the knife out of Mom's hand, dropped his own knife, and wrestled her to the floor. We kids pounded on Dad's back and begged him to stop, but he ignored us. At last, he pinned Mom's hands behind her head.

"Rose Mary, you're one hell of a woman," Dad said. Mom told him he was a stinking rotten drunk. "Yeah, but you love this old drunk, don't you?" Dad said. Mom at first said no, she didn't, but Dad kept asking her again and again, and when she finally said yes, the fight disappeared from both of them. Vanished as if it had never existed. Dad started laughing and hugging Mom, who was laughing and hugging him. It was as if they were so happy they hadn't killed each other that they had fallen in love all over again.

I didn't feel like celebrating. After all he'd put himself through, I couldn't believe Dad had gone back to the booze.

With Dad drinking again, and no money coming in, Mom began to talk about moving east, to West Virginia, where Dad's parents lived. Maybe his parents would help keep him in line. If nothing else, they could help us out financially, like Grandma Smith had done from time to time.

We'd love it in West Virginia, she told us. We'd live in the forest in the mountains with the squirrels and the chipmunks. We could meet our grandma and grandpa Walls, who were genuine hillbillies.

Mom made living in West Virginia sound like another great adventure, and pretty soon all us kids had signed on for the trip. Dad hated the idea, however, and refused to help Mom, so she plotted on her own. Since we had never retrieved the car—or any of our stuff—from the failed Grand Canyon expedition, the first thing Mom needed was a set of wheels. She said that God works in mysterious ways, and it just so happened that she had inherited some land in Texas when Grandma died. She waited until she received a check for several hundred dollars from the company that was leasing the drilling rights. Then she went to buy a used car.

A local radio station had a promotional broadcast once a week from a car lot that we passed on our way to school. Every Wednesday the DJs and used-car salesmen would rave on-air about the incredible deals and the lowest prices around; to prove their point, they'd announce the Piggy Bank Special: some car priced under a thousand dollars that they'd sell to the first lucky caller. Mom set her sights on a Piggy Bank Special. She wasn't taking any chances on being the first caller; she went down with her cash and sat in the dealership office while we kids waited on a park bench across the street, listening to the broadcast on a transistor radio.

The Piggy Bank Special that Wednesday was a 1956 Oldsmobile, which Mom bought for two hundred dollars. We listened as she took to the airwaves to tell the radio audience she knew a heck of a bargain when she saw one.

Mom was not allowed to test-drive the Piggy Bank Special before buying it. The car lurched and stalled several times on the way home. It was impossible to tell whether it was Mom's driving or whether we had bought a lemon.

We kids were not all that thrilled about the idea of Mom driving us cross-country. She didn't have a valid driver's license, for one thing, and she'd always been a terrible driver. If Dad got too drunk, she ended up behind the wheel, but cars never seemed to run right for Mom. Once we were driving through downtown Phoenix and she couldn't get the brakes to work and she had Brian and me stick our heads out the windows and scream, "No brakes! No brakes!" as we rolled through intersections and she looked for something relatively soft to crash into. We ended up plowing into a Dumpster behind a supermarket and walking home.

Mom said that anyone critical of her driving could help with the task. Now that we had a car, she continued, we could leave the next morning. It was October, and we had been in school for just over a month, but Mom said we had no time to tell our teachers we were withdrawing or to get any of our school records. When we enrolled in West Virginia, she'd vouch for our scholastic achievement, and once our new teachers heard us read, they'd realize we were all gifted.

Dad was still refusing to come with us. When we left, he said, he was going to head out into the desert on his own, to become a prospector. I asked Mom if we were going to sell the house on North Third Street or rent it out. "Neither," she said. "It's my house." She explained that it was nice to own something for a change, and she saw no point in selling it just because we were moving. She didn't want to rent it, either, since she was opposed to anyone else living in her house. We'd leave it as it was. To prevent burglars and vandals from breaking in, we'd hang laundry on the clothesline and put dirty dishes in the sink. That way, Mom pointed out, potential intruders would think the house was occupied and would be fooled into believing that the people who lived there might come home any second.

The following morning, we packed up the car while Dad sat in the living room sulking. We tied Mom's art supplies to the roof and filled the trunk with pots and pans and blankets. Mom had bought each of us a warm coat at a thrift store so we'd have something to wear in West Virginia, where it got so cold in the winter that it snowed. Mom said we could each take only one thing, like the time we left Battle Mountain. I wanted to bring my bike, but Mom said it was too big, so I brought my geode.

I ran into the backyard and said goodbye to the orange trees, and then

I ran out front to get in the Oldsmobile. I had to crawl over Brian and sit in the middle because he and Lori had already staked out the window seats. Maureen was in the front seat with Mom, who had started the engine and was practicing her gear shifts. Dad was still in the house, so I leaned over Brian and shouted at the top of my voice. Dad appeared in the doorway, his arms folded across his chest.

"Dad, please come, we need you!" I hollered.

Lori and Brian and Mom and Maureen all chimed in. "We need you!" we shouted. "You're the head of the family! You're the dad! Come on!"

Dad stood there looking at us for a minute. Then he flicked the cigarette he was smoking into the yard, closed the front door, loped over to the car, and told Mom to move aside—he was driving.

III

WELCH

Back in Battle Mountain, we had stopped naming the Walls family cars, because they were all such heaps that Dad said they didn't deserve names. Mom said that when she was growing up on the ranch, they never named the cattle, because they knew they would have to kill them. If we didn't name the car, we didn't feel as sad when we had to abandon it.

So the Piggy Bank Special was just the Oldsmobile, and we never said the name with any fondness or even pity. That Oldsmobile was a clunker from the moment we bought it. The first time it conked out, we were still an hour shy of the New Mexico border. Dad stuck his head under the hood, tinkered with the engine, and got it going, but it broke down again a couple of hours later. Dad got it running—"More like limping," he said—but it never went any faster than fifteen or twenty miles an hour. Also, the hood kept popping up, so we had to tie it down with a rope.

We steered clear of tollbooths by taking two-lane back roads, where we usually had a long line of drivers behind us, honking in exasperation. When one of the Oldsmobile's windows stopped rolling up in Oklahoma, we taped garbage bags over it. We slept in the car every night, and after arriving late in Muskogee and parking on an empty downtown street, we woke up to find a bunch of people surrounding the car, little kids pressing their noses against the windows and grown-ups shaking their heads and grinning.

Mom waved at the crowd. "You know you're down and out when Okies laugh at you," she said. With our garbage-bag-taped window, our roped-down hood, and the art supplies tied to the roof, we'd out-Okied the Okies. The thought gave her a fit of the giggles.

I pulled a blanket over my head and refused to come out until we were beyond the Muskogee city limits. "Life is a drama full of tragedy and comedy," Mom told me. "You should learn to enjoy the comic episodes a little more."

*　*　*

It took us a month to cross the country. We might as well have been traveling in a Conestoga wagon. Mom also kept insisting that we make scenic detours to broaden our horizons. We drove down to see the Alamo—"Davy Crockett and James Bowie got what was coming to them," Mom said, "for stealing this land from the Mexicans"—and over to Beaumont, where the oil rigs bobbed like giant birds. In Louisiana, Mom had us climb up on the roof of the car and pull down tufts of Spanish moss hanging from the tree branches.

After crossing the Mississippi, we swung north toward Kentucky, then east. Instead of the flat desert edged by craggy mountains, the land rolled and dipped like a sheet when you shook it clean. Finally, we entered hill country, climbing higher and deeper into the Appalachian Mountains, stopping from time to time to let the Oldsmobile catch its breath on the steep, twisting roads. It was November. The leaves had turned brown and were falling from the trees, and a cold mist shrouded the hillsides. There were streams and creeks everywhere, instead of the irrigation ditches you saw out west, and the air felt different. It was very still, heavier and thicker, and somehow darker. For some reason, it made us all grow quiet.

At dusk, we approached a bend where hand-painted signs advertising auto repairs and coal deliveries had been nailed to trees along the roadside. We rounded the bend and found ourselves in a deep valley. Wooden houses and small brick buildings lined the river and rose in uneven stacks on both hillsides.

"Welcome to Welch!" Mom declared.

We drove along dark, narrow streets, then stopped in front of a big, worn house. It was on the downhill side of the street, and we had to descend a set of stairs to get to it. As we clattered onto the porch, a woman opened the door. She was enormous, with pasty skin and about three chins. Bobby pins held back her lank gray hair, and a cigarette dangled from her mouth.

"Welcome home, son," she said and gave Dad a long hug. She turned to Mom. "Nice of you to let me see my grandchildren before I die," she said without a smile.

Without taking the cigarette out of her mouth, she gave us each a quick, stiff hug. Her cheek was tacky with sweat.

"Pleased to meet you, Grandma," I said.

"Don't call me Grandma," she snapped. "Name's Erma."

"She don't like it none 'cause it makes her sound old," said a man who appeared beside her. He looked fragile, with short white hair that stood straight up. His voice was so mumbly I could hardly understand him. I didn't know if it was his accent or if maybe he wasn't wearing his dentures. "Name's Ted, but you can call me Grandpa," he went on. "Don't bother me none being a grandpa."

Behind Grandpa was a ruddy-faced man with a wild swirl of red hair pushing out from under his baseball cap, which had a Maytag logo. He wore a red-and-black-plaid coat but had no shirt on underneath it. He kept announcing over and over again that he was our uncle Stanley, and he wouldn't stop hugging and kissing me, as though I was someone he truly loved and hadn't seen in ages. You could smell the whiskey on his breath, and when he talked, you could see the pink ridges of his toothless gums.

I stared at Erma and Stanley and Grandpa, searching for some feature that reminded me of Dad, but I saw none. Maybe this was one of Dad's pranks, I thought. Dad must have arranged for the weirdest people in town to pretend they were his family. In a few minutes he'd start laughing and tell us where his real parents lived, and we'd go there and a smiling woman with perfumed hair would welcome us and feed us steaming bowls of Cream of Wheat. I looked at Dad. He wasn't smiling, and he kept pulling at the skin of his neck as if he were itchy.

We followed Erma and Stanley and Grandpa inside. It was cold in the house, and the air smelled of mold and cigarettes and unwashed laundry. We huddled around a potbellied cast-iron coal stove in the middle of the living room and held out our hands to warm them. Erma pulled a bottle of whiskey from the pocket of her housedress, and Dad looked happy for the first time since we'd left Phoenix.

Erma ushered us into the kitchen, where she was fixing dinner. A bulb dangled from the ceiling, casting harsh light on the yellowed walls, which were coated with a thin film of grease. Erma stuck a curved steel handle into an iron disk on top of an old coal cooking stove, lifted it, and with her other hand grabbed a poker from the wall and jabbed at the hot orange coals inside. She stirred a potful of green beans stewing in fatback and poured in a big handful of salt. Then she set a tray of Pillsbury biscuits on the kitchen table and ladled out a plate of the beans for each of us kids.

The beans were so overcooked that they fell apart when I stuck my fork in them and so salty that I could barely force myself to swallow. I pinched my nose closed, which was the way Mom had taught us to get down things that had gone a little bit rotten. Erma saw me and slapped my hand away. "Beggars can't be choosers," she said.

There were three bedrooms upstairs, Erma said, but no one had been to the second floor in nigh on ten years, because the floorboards were rotted through. Uncle Stanley volunteered to give us his room in the basement and sleep on a cot in the foyer while we were there. "We'll only be staying a few days," Dad said, "until we find a place of our own."

After dinner, Mom and us kids went down into the basement. It was a big dank room, with cinder-block walls and a green linoleum floor. There was another coal stove, a bed, a pullout couch where Mom and Dad could sleep, and a chest of drawers painted fire-engine red. It held hundreds of dog-eared comic books—Little Lulu, Richie Rich, Beetle Bailey, Archie and Jughead—that Uncle Stanley had collected over the years. Under the chest of drawers were jugs of genuine moonshine.

We kids climbed into Stanley's bed. To make it less crowded, Lori and I lay down with our heads at one end, and Brian and Maureen lay down with theirs at the other. Brian's feet were in my face, so I grabbed him by the ankles and started chewing on his toes. He laughed and kicked and started chewing on my toes in retaliation, and that made me laugh. We heard a loud *thunk thunk thunk* from above.

"What's that?" Lori asked.

"Maybe the roaches here are bigger than in Phoenix," Brian said. We all laughed and heard the *thunk thunk thunk* again. Mom went upstairs to investigate, then came down and explained that Erma was hitting the floor with a broom handle to signal that we were making too much noise. "She asked that you kids don't laugh while you're in her house," Mom said. "It gets on her nerves."

"I don't think Erma likes us very much," I said.

"She's just an old woman who's had a tough life," Mom said.

"They're all sort of weird," Lori said.

"We'll adapt," Mom said.

Or move on, I thought.

THE NEXT DAY WAS Sunday. When we got up, Uncle Stanley was leaning against the refrigerator and staring intently at the radio. It made strange noises, not static but a combination of shrieking and wailing. "That there's tongues," he said. "Only the Lord can understand it."

The preacher started talking in actual English, more or less. He spoke with a hillbilly accent so thick it was almost as hard to understand as the tongues. He asked all them good folk out there who'd been helped by this here channeling of the Lord's spirit to send contributions. Dad came into the kitchen and listened. "It's the sort of soul-curdling voodoo," he said, "that turned me into an atheist."

Later that day, we got into the Oldsmobile, and Mom and Dad took us for a tour of the town. Welch was surrounded on all sides by such steep mountains that you felt like you were looking up from the bottom of a bowl. Dad said the hills around Welch were too steep for cultivating much of anything. Couldn't raise a decent herd of sheep or cattle, couldn't even till crops except maybe to feed your family. So this part of the world was left pretty much alone until around the turn of the century, when robber barons from the North laid a track into the area and brought in cheap labor to dig out the huge fields of coal.

We stopped under a railroad bridge and got out of the car to admire the river that ran through the town. It moved sluggishly, with barely a ripple. The river's name, Dad said, was the Tug. "Maybe in the summer we can go fishing and swimming," I said. Dad shook his head. The county had no sewer system, he explained, so when people flushed their johns, the discharge went straight into the Tug. Sometimes the river flooded and the water rose as high as the treetops. Dad pointed to the toilet paper up in the branches along the river's banks. The Tug, Dad said, had the highest level of fecal bacteria of any river in North America.

"What's fecal?" I asked.

Dad watched the river. "Shit," he said.

Dad led us along the main road through town. It was narrow, with old brick buildings crowding in close on both sides. The stores, the signs, the sidewalks, the cars were all covered with a film of black coal dust, giving the town an almost monochromatic look, like an old hand-tinted photograph. Welch was shabby and worn out, but you could tell it had once been a place on its way up. On a hill stood a grand limestone courthouse with a big clock tower. Across from it was a handsome bank with arched windows and a wrought-iron door.

You could also tell that the people of Welch were still trying to maintain some pride of place. A sign near the town's only stoplight announced that Welch was the county seat of McDowell County and that for years, more coal had been mined in McDowell County than any comparable spot in the world. Next to it, another sign boasted that Welch had the largest outdoor municipal parking lot in North America.

But the cheerful advertisements painted on the sides of buildings like the Tic Toc diner and the Pocahontas movie theater were faded and nearly illegible. Dad said bad times had come in the fifties. They hit hard and stayed. President John F. Kennedy had come to Welch not long after he was elected and personally handed out the nation's first food stamps here on McDowell Street, to prove his point that—though ordinary Americans might find it hard to believe—starvation-level poverty existed right in their own country.

The road through Welch, Dad told us, led only farther up into the wet, forbidding mountains and on to other dying coal towns. Few strangers passed through Welch these days, and almost all who did came to inflict one form of misery or another—to lay off workers, to shut down a mine, to foreclose on someone's house, to compete for the rare job opening. The townspeople didn't care much for outsiders.

The streets were mostly silent and deserted that morning, but every now and then we'd pass a woman wearing curlers or a group of men in T-shirts with motor-oil decals, loitering in a doorway. I tried to catch their eyes, to give them a nod and a smile to let them know we had only good intentions, but they never nodded or spoke a word or even glanced our way. As soon as we passed, however, I could feel eyes following us up the street.

Dad had brought Mom to Welch for a brief visit fifteen years earlier, right after they were married. "Gosh, things have gone downhill a little bit since we were here last," she said.

Dad gave a short snort of a laugh. He looked at her like he was about to say *What the hell did I tell you?* Instead he just shook his head.

Suddenly, Mom grinned broadly. "I'll bet there aren't any other artists living in Welch," she said. "I won't have any competition. My career could really take off here."

THE NEXT DAY MOM took Brian and me to Welch Elementary, near the outskirts of town. She marched confidently into the principal's office with us in tow and informed him that he would have the pleasure of enrolling two of the brightest, most creative children in America in his school.

The principal looked at Mom over his black-rimmed glasses but remained seated behind his desk. Mom explained that we'd left Phoenix in a teensy bit of a hurry, you know how that goes, and unfortunately, in all the commotion, she forgot to pack stuff like school records and birth certificates.

"But you can take my word for it that Jeannette and Brian are exceptionally bright, even gifted." She smiled at him.

The principal looked at Brian and me, with our unwashed hair and our thin desert clothes. His face took on a sour, skeptical expression. He focused on me, pushed his glasses up his nose, and said something that sounded like "Wuts et tahm sebm?"

"Excuse me?" I said.

"*Et tahm sebm!*" he said louder.

I was completely bewildered. I looked at Mom.

"She doesn't understand your accent," Mom told the principal. He frowned. Mom turned to me. "He's asking you what's eight times seven."

"Oh!" I shouted. "Fifty-six! Eight times seven is fifty-six!" I started spouting out all sorts of mathematical equations.

The principal looked at me blankly.

"He can't make out what you're saying," Mom told me. "Try to talk slowly."

The principal asked me a few more questions I couldn't understand. With Mom translating, I gave answers that he couldn't understand. Then he asked Brian some questions, and they couldn't understand each other, either.

The principal decided that Brian and I were both a bit slow and had speech impediments that made it difficult for others to understand us. He placed us both in special classes for students with learning disabilities.

"You'll have to impress them with your intelligence," Mom said as Brian and I headed off to school the next day. "Don't be afraid to be smarter than they are."

It had rained the night before our first day of school. When Brian and I stepped off the bus at Welch Elementary, our shoes got soaked in the water that filled the muddy tire ruts left by the school buses. I looked around for the playground equipment, figuring I could win some new friends with the fierce tetherball skills I'd picked up at Emerson, but I didn't see a single seesaw or jungle gym, not to mention any tetherball poles.

It had been cold ever since we arrived in Welch. The day before, Mom had unpacked the thrift-shop coats she'd bought us in Phoenix. When I'd pointed out that all the buttons had been torn from mine, she said that minor flaw was more than offset by the fact that the coat was imported from France and made of 100-percent lamb's wool. As we waited for the opening bell, I stood with Brian at the edge of the playground, my arms crossed to keep my coat closed. The other kids stared at us, whispering among themselves, but they also kept their distance, as if they hadn't decided whether we were predators or prey. I had thought West Virginia was all white hillbillies, so I was surprised by how many black kids there were. I saw one tall black girl with a strong jaw and almond eyes smiling at me. I nodded and smiled back, then I realized there was something malicious in her smile. I locked my arms tighter across my chest.

I was in the fifth grade, so my day was divided into periods, with different teachers and classrooms for each. For the first period, I had West Virginia history. History was one of my favorite subjects. I was coiled and ready to raise my hand as soon as the teacher asked a question I could answer, but he stood at the front of the room next to a map of West Virginia, with all fifty-five counties outlined, and spent the entire class pointing to counties and asking students to identify them. In my second period, we passed the hour watching a film of the football game that Welch High had played several days earlier. Neither of those teachers introduced me to the class; they seemed as uncertain as the kids about how to act around a stranger.

My next class was English for students with learning disabilities. Miss Caparossi started out by informing the class that it might surprise them to learn some people in this world thought they were better than other people. "They're convinced they're so special that they don't need to follow the rules other people have to follow," she said, "like presenting their school records when they enroll in a new school." She looked at me and raised her eyebrows meaningfully. "Who thinks that's not fair?" she asked the class.

All the kids except me raised their hands.

"I see our new student doesn't agree," she said. "Perhaps you'd like to explain yourself?"

I was sitting in the second-to-last row. The students in front of me swiveled their heads around to stare. I decided to dazzle them with the answer from the Ergo Game.

"Insufficient information to draw a conclusion," I said.

"Oh, really?" Miss Caparossi asked. "Is that what they say in a big city like Phoenix?" She pronounced it "Feeeeenix." Then she turned to the class and said in a high, mocking voice, "Insufficient information to draw a conclusion."

The class laughed violently.

I felt something sharp and painful between my shoulder blades and turned around. The tall black girl with the almond eyes was sitting at the desk behind me. Holding up the sharp pencil she had jabbed into my back, she smiled the same malicious smile I'd seen in the playground.

I looked for Brian in the cafeteria at lunchtime, but fourth-graders were on a different schedule, so I sat by myself and bit into the sandwich Erma had made for me that morning. It was tasteless and greasy. I pulled apart the two slices of Wonder bread. Inside was a thin smear of lard. That was it. No meat, no cheese, not even a slice of pickle. Even so, I chewed slowly, staring intently at my bite marks in the bread to delay as long as possible the moment I would have to leave the cafeteria and go out to the playground. When I was the last student left in the cafeteria, the janitor, who was putting the chairs on the tabletops so the floor could be mopped, told me it was time to go.

Outside, a thin mist hung in the still air. I pulled the sides of my lamb's wool coat together. Three black girls, led by the one with the almond eyes, started moving toward me as soon as they saw me. A half-dozen other girls followed. Within moments, I was surrounded.

"You think you better than us?" the tall girl asked.

"No," I said. "I think we're all equal."

"You think you as good as me?" She punched at me. When, instead of raising my hands in defense, I kept clutching my coat closed, she realized it had no buttons. "This girl ain't got no buttons on her coat!" she shouted. That seemed to give her the license she needed. She pushed me in the chest, and I fell backward. I tried to get up, but all three girls started kicking me. I rolled away into a puddle, shouting for them to quit and hitting back at the feet coming at me from all sides. The other girls had closed in a circle around us and none of the teachers could see what was going on. There was no stopping those girls until they'd had their fill.

WHEN WE ALL GOT home that afternoon, Mom and Dad were eager to hear about our first day.

"It was good," I said. I didn't want to tell Mom the truth. I was in no mood to hear one of her lectures about the power of positive thinking.

"See?" she said. "I told you you'd fit right in."

Brian shrugged off Mom and Dad's questions, and Lori didn't want to talk about her day at all.

"How were the other kids?" I asked her later.

"Okay," she said, but she turned away, and that was the end of the conversation.

The bullying continued every day for weeks. The tall girl, whose name was Dinitia Hewitt, watched me with her smile while we all waited on the asphalt playground for classes to start. At lunch, I ate my lard sandwiches with paralytic slowness, but sooner or later, the janitor started putting the chairs up on the tables. I walked outside trying to hold my head high, and Dinitia and her gang surrounded me and it began.

As we fought, they called me poor and ugly and dirty, and it was hard to argue the point. I had three dresses to my name, all hand-me-downs or from a thrift store, which meant each week I had to wear two of them twice. They were so worn from countless washings that the threads were beginning to separate. We were also always dirty. Not dry-dirty like we'd been in the desert, but grimy-dirty and smudged with oily dust from the coal-burning stove. Erma allowed us only one bath a week in four inches of water that had been heated on the kitchen stove and that all of us kids had to share.

I thought of discussing the fighting with Dad, but I didn't want to sound like a whiner. Also, he'd rarely been sober since we had arrived in Welch, and I was afraid that if I told him, he'd show up at school snockered and make things even worse.

I did try to talk to Mom. I couldn't bring myself to tell her about the beatings, fearing that if I did, she'd try to butt in and she'd also only make things worse. I did say that these three black girls were giving me a hard time because we were so poor. Mom told me I should tell them there was nothing wrong with being poor, that Abraham Lincoln, the greatest president this country had ever seen, came from a dirt-poor family. She also said I should tell them Martin Luther King, Jr., would be ashamed of their behavior. Even though I knew these high-minded arguments would get me nowhere, I tried them anyway—*Martin Luther King would be ashamed!*—and they made the three girls shriek with laughter as they pushed me to the ground.

Lying in Stanley's bed at night with Lori, Brian, and Maureen, I concocted revenge scenarios. I imagined myself like Dad in his air force days, whupping the entire lot of them. After school, I'd go out to the woodpile next to the basement and practice karate chops and dropkicks on the kindling while laying down some pretty wicked curse words. But I also kept thinking about Dinitia, trying to make sense of her. I hoped for a while to befriend her. I'd seen Dinitia smile a few times with genuine warmth, and it transformed her face. With a smile like that, she had to have some good in her, but I couldn't figure out how to get her to shine it my way.

About a month after I'd started school, I was walking up some steps to a park at the top of the hill when I heard a low, furious barking coming from the other side of the World War I memorial. I ran up the stairs and saw a big, lathered-up mongrel cornering a little black kid of about five or six against the monument. The kid kept giving kicks at the dog as it barked and lunged at him. The kid was looking over at the tree line on the far side of the park, and I could tell he was calculating the chances of making it over there.

"Don't run!" I shouted.

The boy looked up at me. So did the dog, and in that instant, the kid took off in a hopeless dash for the trees. The dog bounded after him, barking, then caught up with him and snapped at his legs.

Now, there are mad dogs and wild dogs and killer dogs, and any one of them would go for your throat and hold on until you or it was dead, but I could tell this dog was not truly bad. Instead of tearing into the kid, it was having fun terrifying him, growling and pulling on his pant leg but doing no real damage. It was just a mutt who had been kicked around too much and was happy to find a creature who was afraid of it.

I picked up a stick and raced toward them. "Go on, now!" I shouted at the dog. When I raised the stick, it whimpered and slunk off.

The dog's teeth had not broken the boy's skin, but his pant leg was torn, and he was trembling as if he had palsy. I offered to take him home, and I ended up carrying him piggyback. He was feather-light. I couldn't get a word out of him except the most minimal directions—"up there," "that way"—in a voice I could hardly hear.

The houses in the neighborhood were old but freshly painted, some in bright colors like lavender or kelly green. "This here," the boy whispered when we came to a house with blue shutters. It had a neat yard but was so small that dwarves could have lived there. When I put the kid down, he dashed up the steps and through the door. I turned to go.

Dinitia Hewitt was standing on the porch across the street, looking at me curiously.

The next day when I went out to the playground after lunch, the gang of girls started toward me, but Dinitia hung back. Without their leader, the others lost their sense of purpose and stopped short of me. The following week, Dinitia asked me for help on an English assignment. She never said she was sorry for the bullying, or even mentioned it, but she thanked me for bringing her neighbor home that night, and I figured that her request for help was as close to an apology as I would get. Erma had made it clear how she felt about black people, so instead of inviting Dinitia to our house to work on her assignment, I suggested that on the upcoming Saturday, I'd go to hers.

That day I was leaving the house at the same time as Uncle Stanley. He never had the wherewithal to learn to drive, but someone from the appliance store where he worked was picking him up. He asked if I wanted a ride, too. When I told him where I was headed, he frowned. "That's Niggerville," he said. "What you going there for?"

Stanley didn't want his friend to drive me there, so I walked. When I got back home later in the afternoon, the house was empty except for

Erma, who never set foot outside. She stood in the kitchen, stirring a pot of green beans and taking swigs from the bottle of hooch in her pocket.

"So, how was Niggerville?" she asked.

Erma was always going on about "the niggers." Her and Grandpa's house was on Court Street, on the edge of the black neighborhood. It galled her when they started moving into that section of town, and she always said it was their fault that Welch had gone downhill. When you were sitting in the living room, where Erma always kept the shades drawn, you could hear groups of black people walking into town, talking and laughing. "Goddamn niggers," Erma always muttered. "The reason I have not gone out of this house in fifteen years is because I do not want to see or be seen by a nigger." Mom and Dad had always forbidden us to use that word. It was much worse than any curse word, they told us. But since Erma was my grandmother, I never said anything when she used it.

Erma kept stirring the beans. "Keep this up and people are going to think you're a nigger lover," she said.

She gave me a serious look, as if imparting a meaningful life lesson I should ponder and absorb. She unscrewed the cap from her bottle of hooch and took a long, contemplative swallow.

As I watched her drinking, I felt this pressure building in my chest and I had to let it out. "You're not supposed to use that word," I said.

Erma's face went slack with astonishment.

"Mom says they're just like us," I continued, "except they have different complexions."

Erma glared at me. I thought she was going to backhand me, but instead she said, "You ungrateful little shit. I'll be damned if you're eating my food tonight. Get your worthless ass down to the basement."

Lori gave me a hug when she heard I'd told off Erma. Mom was upset, though. "We may not agree with all of Erma's views," she said, "but we have to remember that as long as we're her guests, we have to be polite."

That didn't seem like Mom. She and Dad happily railed against anyone they disliked or disrespected: Standard Oil executives, J. Edgar Hoover, and especially snobs and racists. They'd always encouraged us to be outspoken about our opinions. Now we were supposed to bite our tongues. But she was right; Erma would boot us. Situations like these, I realized, were what turned people into hypocrites.

"I hate Erma," I told Mom.

"You have to show compassion for her," Mom said. Erma's parents had died when she was young, Mom explained, and she had been shipped off to one relative after another who had treated her like a servant. Scrubbing clothes on a washboard until her knuckles bled—that was the preeminent memory of Erma's childhood. The best thing Grandpa did for her when they got married was buy her an electric washing machine, but whatever joy it had once given her was long gone.

"Erma can't let go of her misery," Mom said. "It's all she knows." She added that you should never hate anyone, even your worst enemies. "Everyone has something good about them," she said. "You have to find the redeeming quality and love the person for that."

"Oh yeah?" I said. "How about Hitler? What was his redeeming quality?"

"Hitler loved dogs," Mom said without hesitation.

IN LATE WINTER, Mom and Dad decided to drive the Oldsmobile back to Phoenix. They said they were going to fetch our bikes and all the other stuff we'd had to leave behind, pick up copies of our school records, and see if they could rescue Mom's fruitwood archery set from the irrigation ditch alongside the road to the Grand Canyon. We kids were to remain in Welch. Since Lori was the oldest, Mom and Dad said she was in charge. Of course, we were all answerable to Erma.

They left one morning during a thaw. I could tell by the high color in Mom's cheeks that she was excited about the prospect of an adventure. Dad was also clearly itching to get out of Welch. He had not found a job, and we were dependent on Erma for everything. Lori had suggested that Dad go to work in the mines, but he said the mines were controlled by the unions, and the unions were controlled by the mob, and the mob had blackballed him for investigating corruption in the electricians' union back in Phoenix. Another reason for him to return to Phoenix was to gather his research on corruption, because the only way he could get a job in the mines was by helping reform the United Mine Workers of America.

I wished we were all going together. I wanted to be back in Phoenix, sitting under the orange trees behind our adobe house, riding my bike to the library, eating free bananas in a school where the teachers thought I was smart. I wanted to feel the desert sun on my face and breathe in the dry desert air and climb the steep rock mountains while Dad led us on one of the long hikes that he called geological survey expeditions.

I asked if we could all go, but Dad said he and Mom were making a quick trip, strictly business, and we kids would only get in the way. Besides, he couldn't go taking us out of school in the middle of the year. I pointed out that it had never bothered him before. Welch wasn't like those other places we had lived, he said. There were rules that had to be followed, and people didn't take it kindly when you flouted them.

"Do you think they'll come back?" Brian asked as Mom and Dad drove off.

"Of course," I said, though I had been wondering the same thing. These days we seemed more of an inconvenience than we used to be. Lori was already a teenager, and in a couple of years, Brian and I would be, too. They couldn't toss us into the back of a U-Haul or put us in cardboard boxes at night.

Brian and I started running after the Oldsmobile. Mom turned once and waved, and Dad stuck his hand out the window. We followed them all the way down Court Street, where they picked up speed and then turned the corner. I had to believe they'd come back, I told myself. If I didn't believe, then they might not return. They might leave us forever.

After Mom and Dad left, Erma became even more cantankerous. If she didn't like the look on our faces, she would hit us on the head with a serving spoon. Once she pulled out a framed photograph of her father and told us he was the only person who had ever loved her. She talked on and on about how much she'd suffered as an orphan at the hands of her aunts and uncles who hadn't treated her half as kindly as she was treating us.

About a week after Mom and Dad left, we kids were all sitting in Erma's living room watching TV. Stanley was sleeping in the foyer. Erma, who'd been drinking since before breakfast, told Brian that his britches needed mending. He started to take them off, but Erma said she didn't want him running around the house in his skivvies or with a towel wrapped around him looking like he was wearing a goddamn dress. It would be easier for her to mend the britches while he was still wearing them. She ordered him to follow her into Grandpa's bedroom, where she kept her sewing kit.

They'd been gone for a minute or two when I heard Brian weakly protesting. I went into Grandpa's bedroom and saw Erma kneeling on the floor in front of Brian, grabbing at the crotch of his pants, squeezing and kneading while mumbling to herself and telling Brian to hold still, goddammit. Brian, his cheeks wet with tears, was holding his hands protectively between his legs.

"Erma, you leave him alone!" I shouted.

Erma, still on her knees, twisted around and glared at me. "Why, you little bitch!" she said.

Lori heard the commotion and came running. I told Lori that Erma was touching Brian in a way she ought not to be. Erma said she was merely mending Brian's inseam and that she shouldn't have to defend herself against some lying little whore's accusations.

"I know what I saw," I said. "She's a pervert!"

Erma reached over to slap me, but Lori caught her hand. "Let's all calm down," Lori said in the same voice she used when Mom and Dad got carried away, arguing. "Everybody. Calm down."

Erma jerked her hand out of Lori's grasp and slapped her so hard that Lori's glasses went flying across the room. Lori, who had turned thirteen, slapped her back. Erma hit Lori again, and this time Lori struck Erma a blow in the jaw. Then they flew at each other, tussling and flailing and pulling hair, locked together, with Brian and me cheering on Lori until we woke up Uncle Stanley, who staggered into the room and pushed them apart.

Erma relegated us to the basement after that. A door in the basement led directly outside, so we never went upstairs. We weren't even allowed to use Erma's bathroom, which meant we either had to wait for school or go outside after dark. Uncle Stanley sometimes sneaked down beans he'd boiled for us, but he was afraid if he stayed talking, Erma would think he'd taken our side and get mad at him, too.

The following week, a storm hit. The temperature dropped, and a foot of snow fell on Welch. Erma wouldn't let us use any coal—she said we didn't know how to operate the stove and would burn the house down—and it was so cold in the basement that Lori, Brian, Maureen, and I were glad we all shared one bed. As soon as we got home from school, we'd climb under the covers with our clothes on and do our homework there.

We were in bed the night Mom and Dad came back. We didn't hear the sound of the car pulling up. All we heard was the front door opening upstairs, then Mom and Dad's voices and Erma beginning the long narrative of her grievances against us. That was followed by the sound of Dad stomping down the stairs into the basement, furious at all of us, me for back-talking Erma and making wild accusations, and Lori even more for daring to strike her own grandmother, and Brian for being such a pussy and starting the whole thing. I thought Dad would come around to our side once he'd heard what had happened, and I tried to explain.

"I don't care what happened!" he yelled.

"But we were just protecting ourselves," I said.

"Brian's a man, he can take it," he said. "I don't want to hear another word of this. Do you hear me?" He was shaking his head, but wildly, almost as if he thought he could keep out the sound of my voice. He wouldn't even look at me.

After Dad had gone back upstairs to tie into Erma's hooch and we kids were all in bed, Brian bit my toe to try to make me laugh, but I kicked him away. We all lay there in the silent darkness.

"Dad was really weird," I said, because someone had to say it.

"You'd be weird, too, if Erma was your mom," Lori said.

"Do you think she ever did something to Dad like what she did to Brian?" I asked.

No one said a thing.

It was gross and creepy to think about, but it would explain a lot. Why Dad left home as soon as he could. Why he drank so much and why he got so angry. Why he never wanted to visit Welch when we were younger. Why he at first refused to come to West Virginia with us and only at the last possible moment overcame his reluctance and jumped into the car. Why he was shaking his head so hard, almost like he wanted to put his hands over his ears, when I tried to explain what Erma had been doing to Brian.

"Don't think about things like that," Lori told me. "It'll make you crazy."

And so I put it out of my mind.

MOM AND DAD TOLD us how they'd made it to Phoenix only to find that Mom's laundry-on-the-clothesline ploy hadn't kept out intruders. Our house on North Third Street had been looted. Pretty much everything was gone, including, of course, our bikes. Mom and Dad had rented a trailer to carry back what little was left—Mom said those foolish thieves had overlooked some good stuff, such as a pair of Grandma Smith's riding breeches from the thirties that were of the highest quality—but the Oldsmobile's engine had seized up in Nashville, and they'd had to abandon it along with the trailer and Grandma Smith's riding breeches and take the bus the rest of the way to Welch.

I thought that once Mom and Dad returned, they'd be able to make peace with Erma. But she said she could never forgive us kids and didn't want us in her house any longer, even if we stayed in the basement and kept as quiet as church mice. We were banished. That was the word Dad used. "You did wrong," he said, "and now we've all been banished."

"This isn't exactly the Garden of Eden," Lori said.

I was more upset about the bike than I was about Erma banishing us. "Why don't we just move back to Phoenix?" I asked Mom.

"We've already been there," she said. "And there are all sorts of opportunities here that we don't even know about."

She and Dad set out to find us a new place to live. The cheapest rental in Welch was an apartment over a diner on McDowell Street that cost seventy-five dollars a month, which was out of our price range. Also, Mom and Dad wanted outdoor space we could call our own, so they decided to buy. Since we had no money for a down payment and no steady income, our options were pretty limited, but within a couple of days, Mom and Dad told us they had found a house we could afford. "It's not exactly palatial, so there's going to be a lot of togetherness," Mom said. "And it's on the rustic side."

"How rustic?" Lori asked.

Mom paused. I could see her debating how to phrase her answer. "It doesn't have indoor plumbing," she said.

Dad was still looking for a car to replace the Olds—our budget was in the high two figures—so that weekend we all hiked over for our first look at the new place. We walked down the valley through the center of town and around a mountainside, past the small, tidy brick houses put up after the mines were unionized. We crossed a creek that fed into the Tug River and started up a barely paved one-lane road called Little Hobart Street. It climbed through several switchbacks and, for a stretch, rose at an angle so steep you had to walk on your toes; if you tried walking flatfooted, you stretched your calves till they hurt.

The houses up here were shabbier than the brick houses lower down in the valley. They were made of wood, with lopsided porches, sagging roofs, rusted-out gutters, and balding tar paper or asphalt shingles slowly but surely parting from the underwall. In almost every yard, a mutt or two was chained to a tree or to a clothesline post, and they barked furiously as we walked by. Like most houses in Welch, these were heated by coal. The more prosperous families had coal sheds; the poorer ones left their coal in a pile out front. The porches were every bit as furnished as the insides of most houses, with rust-stained refrigerators, folding card tables, hook rugs, couches or car seats for serious porch-sitting, and maybe a battered armoire with a hole cut in the side so the cat would have a cozy place to sleep.

We followed the road almost to the end, where Dad pointed up at our new house.

"Well, kids, welcome to Ninety-three Little Hobart Street!" Mom said. "Welcome to home sweet home."

We all stared. The house was a dinky thing perched high up off the road on a hillside so steep that only the back of the house rested on the ground. The front, including a drooping porch, jutted precariously into the air, supported by tall, spindly cinder-block pillars. It had been painted white a long time ago, but the paint, where it hadn't peeled off altogether, had turned a dismal gray.

"It's good we raised you young 'uns to be tough," Dad said. "Because this is not a house for the faint of heart."

Dad led us up the lower steps, which were made of rocks slapped together with cement. Because of settling and erosion and downright slipshod construction, they tilted dangerously toward the street. Where the stone steps ended, a rickety set of stairs made from two-by-fours—more like a ladder than a staircase—took you up to the front porch.

Inside were three rooms, each about ten feet by ten feet, facing onto the front porch. The house had no bathroom, but underneath it, behind one of the cinder-block pillars, was a closet-sized room with a toilet on a cement floor. The toilet wasn't hooked up to any sewer or septic system. It just sat atop a hole about six feet deep. There was no running water indoors. A water spigot rose a few inches above the ground near the toilet, so you could get a bucket and tote water upstairs. While the house was wired for electricity, Dad confessed that we could not at the moment afford to have it turned on.

On the upside, Dad said, the house had cost only a thousand dollars, and the owner had waived the down payment. We were supposed to pay him fifty dollars a month. If we could make the payments on time, we'd own the place outright in under two years.

"Hard to believe that one day this will all be ours," said Lori. She was developing what Mom called a bit of a sarcastic streak.

"Count your blessings," Mom said. "There are people in Ethiopia who would kill for a place like this." She pointed out that the house did have some attractive features. For example, in the living room was a cast-iron potbellied coal stove for heating and cooking. It was big and handsome, with heavy bear-claw feet, and she was certain it was valuable, if you took it to a place where people appreciated antiques. But since the house had no chimney, the stovepipe vented out a back window. Someone had replaced the glass in the upper part of the window with plywood, and wrapped tinfoil around the opening to keep the coal smoke from leaking into the room. The tinfoil had not done its job too well, and the ceiling was black with soot. Someone—probably the same someone—had also made the mistake of trying to clean the ceiling in a few spots, but had ended up only smudging and smearing the soot, creating whitish patches that made you realize how black the rest of the ceiling was.

"The house itself isn't much," Dad apologized, "but we won't be living in it long." The important thing, the reason he and Mom had decided to acquire this particular piece of property, was that it came with plenty of land to build our new house. He planned to get to work on it right away. He intended to follow the blueprints for the Glass Castle, but he had to do some serious reconfiguring and increase the size of the solar cells to take into account that since we were on the north face of the mountain, and enclosed by hills on both sides, we'd hardly ever get any sun.

We moved in that afternoon. Not that there was much to move. Dad borrowed a pickup from the appliance store where Uncle Stanley worked, and brought back a sofa bed that a friend of Grandpa's was throwing out. Dad also scavenged a couple of tables and chairs, and he built some makeshift closets—which were actually kind of nifty—by hanging lengths of pipe from the ceiling with wires.

Mom and Dad took over the room with the stove, and it became a combined living room, master bedroom, art studio, and writer's study. We put the sofa bed there, though once we opened it, it never went back to being a sofa. Dad built shelves all along the upper walls to store Mom's art supplies. She set up her easel under the stovepipe, right next to the back window, because she said it got natural sunlight—which it did, relatively speaking. She put her typewriters under another window, with shelves for her manuscripts and works in progress, and she immediately started thumbtacking index cards with story ideas to the walls.

We kids all slept in the middle room. At first we shared one big bed that had been left by the previous owner, but Dad decided we were getting a tad old for that. We were also too big to sleep in cardboard boxes, and there wasn't enough room on the floor for them, anyway, so we helped Dad build two sets of bunk beds. We made the frames with two-by-fours; then we drilled holes in the sides and threaded ropes through. For mattresses, we laid cardboard over the ropes. When we finished, our bunk beds looked sort of plain, so we spray-painted the sides with ornate red and black curlicues. Dad came home with a discarded four-drawer dresser, one drawer for each of us. He also built each of us a wooden box with sliding doors for personal stuff. We nailed them on the wall above our beds, and that was where I kept my geode.

The third room at 93 Little Hobart Street, the kitchen, was in a category all its own. It had an electric stove, but the wiring was not exactly up to code, with faulty connectors, exposed lines, and buzzing switches. "Helen Keller must have wired this damn house," Dad declared. He decided it was too convoluted to bother fixing.

We called the kitchen the loose-juice room, because on the rare occasions that we had paid the electricity bill and had power, we'd get a wicked electric shock if we touched any damp or metallic surface in the room. The first time I got zapped, it knocked my breath out and left me twitching on the floor. We quickly learned that whenever we ventured into the kitchen, we needed to wrap our hands in the driest socks or rags we could find. If we got a shock, we'd announce it to everyone else, sort of like giving a weather report. "Big jolt from touching the stove today," we'd say. "Wear extra rags."

One corner of the kitchen ceiling leaked like a sieve. Every time it rained, the plasterboard ceiling would get all swollen and heavy, with water streaming steadily from the center of the bulge. During one particularly fierce rainstorm that spring, the ceiling grew so fat it burst, and water and plasterboard came crashing down onto the floor. Dad never repaired it. We kids tried patching the roof on our own with tar paper, tinfoil, wood, and Elmer's glue, but no matter what we did, the water found its way through. Eventually we gave up. So every time it rained outside, it rained in the kitchen, too.

At first Mom tried to make living at 93 Little Hobart Street seem like an adventure. The woman who had lived there before us left behind an old-fashioned sewing machine that you operated with a foot treadle. Mom said it would come in handy because we could make our own clothes even when the electricity was turned off. She also claimed you didn't need patterns to sew, you could get creative and wing it. Shortly after we moved in, Mom, Lori, and I measured one another and tried to make our own dresses.

It took forever, and they came out baggy and lopsided, with sleeves that were different lengths and armholes in the middle of our backs. I couldn't get mine over my head until Mom snipped out a few stitches. "It's stunning!" she said. But I told her I looked like I was wearing a big pillowcase with elephant trunks sticking out of the sides. Lori refused to wear hers outdoors, or even indoors, and Mom had to agree that sewing wasn't the best use of our creative energy—or our money. The cheapest cloth we could find cost seventy-nine cents a yard, and you needed more than two yards for a dress. It made more sense to buy thrift-store clothes, and they had the armholes in the right places.

Mom also tried to make the house cheerful. She decorated the living room walls with her oil paintings, and soon every square inch was covered, except for the space above her typewriter reserved for index cards. We had vivid desert sunsets, stampeding horses, sleeping cats, snow-covered mountains, bowls of fruit, blooming flowers, and portraits of us kids.

Since Mom had more paintings than we had wall space, Dad nailed long shelf brackets to the wall, and she hung one picture in front of another until they were three or four deep. Then she'd rotate the paintings. "Just a little redecorating to perk the place up," she'd say. But I believed she thought of her paintings as children and wanted them to feel that they were all being treated equally.

Mom also built rows of shelves in the windows and arranged brightly colored bottles to catch the light. "Now it looks like we have stained glass," she announced. It did, sort of, but the house was still cold and dank. Every night for the first few weeks, lying on my cardboard mattress and listening to the sound of rainwater dripping in the kitchen, I dreamed of the desert and the sun and the big house in Phoenix with the palm tree in the front and the orange trees and oleanders in the back. We had owned that house outright. Still owned it, I kept thinking. It was ours, the one true home we'd ever had.

"Are we ever going home?" I asked Dad one day.

"Home?"

"Phoenix."

"This is home now."

Seeing as how Welch was our new home, Brian and I figured we'd make the best of it. Dad had shown us the spot near the house where we were going to put the foundation and basement for the Glass Castle. He'd measured it off and marked it with stakes and string. Since Dad was hardly ever home—he was out making contacts and investigating the UMW, he told us—and never got around to breaking ground, Brian and I decided to help. We found a shovel and pickax at an abandoned farm and spent just about every free minute digging a hole. We knew we had to dig it big and deep. "No point in building a good house unless you put down the right foundation," Dad always said.

It was hard work, but after a month we'd dug a hole deep enough for us to disappear in. Even though we hadn't squared the edges or smoothed the floor, we were still pretty darn proud of ourselves. Once Dad had poured the foundation, we could help him on the frame.

But since we couldn't afford to pay the town's trash-collection fee, our garbage was really piling up. One day Dad told us to dump it in the hole.

"But that's for the Glass Castle," I said.

"It's a temporary measure," Dad told me. He explained that he was going to hire a truck to cart the garbage to the dump all at once. But he never got around to that, either, and as Brian and I watched, the hole for the Glass Castle's foundation slowly filled with garbage.

Around that time, probably because of all the garbage, a big, nasty-looking river rat took up residence at 93 Little Hobart Street. I first saw him in the sugar bowl. This rat was too big to fit into an ordinary sugar bowl, but since Mom had a powerful sweet tooth, putting at least eight teaspoons in a cup of tea, we kept our sugar in a punch bowl on the kitchen table.

This rat was not just eating the sugar. He was bathing in it, wallowing in it, positively luxuriating in it, his flickering tail hanging over the side of the bowl, flinging sugar across the table. When I saw him, I froze, then backed out of the kitchen. I told Brian, and we opened the kitchen door cautiously. The rat had climbed out of the sugar bowl and leaped up onto the stove. We could see his teeth marks on the pile of potatoes, our dinner, on a plate on the stove. Brian threw the cast-iron skillet at the rat. It hit him and clanged on the floor, but instead of fleeing, the rat hissed at us, as if we were the intruders. We ran out of the kitchen, slammed the door, and stuffed rags in the gap beneath it.

That night Maureen, who was five, was too terrified to sleep. She kept on saying that the rat was coming to get her. She could hear it creeping nearer and nearer. I told her to stop being such a wuss.

"I really do hear the rat," she said. "I think he's close to me."

I told her she was letting fear get the best of her, and since this was one of those times that we had electricity, I turned on the light to prove it. There, crouched on Maureen's lavender blanket, a few inches away from her face, was the rat. She screamed and pushed off her covers, and the rat jumped to the floor. I got a broom and tried to hit the rat with the handle, but it dodged me. Brian grabbed a baseball bat, and we maneuvered it, hissing and snapping, into a corner.

Our dog, Tinkle, the part–Jack Russell terrier who had followed Brian home one day, caught the rat in his jaws and banged it on the floor until it was dead. When Mom ran into the room, Tinkle was strutting around, all pumped up like the proud beast-slayer that he was. Mom said she felt a little sorry for the rat. "Rats need to eat, too," she pointed out. Even though it was dead, it deserved a name, she went on, so she christened it Rufus. Brian, who had read that primitive warriors placed the body parts of their victims on stakes to scare off their enemies, hung Rufus by the tail from a poplar tree in front of our house the next morning. That afternoon we heard the sound of gunshots. Mr. Freeman, who lived next door, had seen the rat hanging upside down. Rufus was so big, Mr. Freeman thought he was a possum, went and got his hunting rifle, and blew him clean away. There was nothing left of Rufus but a mangled piece of tail.

After the Rufus incident, I slept with a baseball bat in my bed. Brian slept with a machete in his. Maureen could barely sleep at all. She kept dreaming that she was being eaten by rats, and she used every excuse she could to spend the night at friends' houses. Mom and Dad shrugged off the

Rufus incident. They told us that we had done battle with fiercer adversaries in the past, and we would again someday.

"What are we going to do about the garbage pit?" I asked. "It's almost filled up."

"Enlarge it," Mom said.

"We can't keep dumping garbage out there," I said. "What are people going to think?"

"Life's too short to worry about what other people think," Mom said. "Anyway, they should accept us for who we are."

I was convinced that people might be more accepting of us if we made an effort to improve the way 93 Little Hobart Street looked. There were plenty of things we could do, I felt, that would cost almost nothing. Some people around Welch cut tires into two semicircles, painted them white, and used them as edging for their gardens. Maybe we couldn't afford to build the Glass Castle quite yet, but certainly we could put painted tires around our front yard to spruce it up. "It would make us fit in a little bit," I pleaded with Mom.

"It sure would," Mom said. But when it came to Welch, she had no interest in fitting in. "I'd rather have a yard filled with genuine garbage than with trashy lawn ornaments."

I kept looking for other ways to make improvements. One day Dad brought home a five-gallon can of house paint left over from some job he'd worked on. The next morning I pried the can open. It was nearly full of bright yellow paint. Dad had brought some paintbrushes home, too. A layer of yellow paint, I realized, would completely transform our dingy gray house. It would look, at least from the outside, almost like the houses other people lived in.

I was so excited by the prospect of living in a perky yellow home that I could barely sleep that night. I got up early the next day and tied my hair back, ready to begin the housepainting. "If we all work together, we can get it done in a day or two," I told everyone.

But Dad said 93 Little Hobart Street was such a dump that we shouldn't waste time or energy on it that we could be devoting to the Glass Castle. Mom said she thought bright yellow houses were tacky. Brian and Lori said we didn't have the ladders and scaffolding we needed.

Dad was making no visible progress on the Glass Castle, and I knew that the can of yellow paint would sit on the porch unless I undertook the job myself. I'd borrow a ladder or make one, I decided. I was certain that once everyone saw the amazing transformation of the house begin, they'd all join in.

Out on the porch, I opened the can and stirred the paint with a stick, blending in the oil that had risen to the surface until the paint, which was the color of buttercups, had turned creamy. I dipped in a fat brush and spread the paint along the old clapboard siding in long, smooth strokes. It went on bright and glossy and looked even better than I had hoped. I started on the far side of the porch, around the door that went into the kitchen. In a few hours, I had covered everything that could be reached from the porch. Parts of the front were still unpainted, and so were the sides, but I had used less than a quarter of the paint. If everyone else helped, we could paint all the areas I couldn't reach, and in no time we would have a cheerful yellow house.

But neither Mom nor Dad nor Brian nor Lori nor Maureen was impressed. "So part of the front of the house is yellow now," Lori said. "That's really going to turn things around for us."

I was going to have to finish the job myself. I tried to make a ladder from bits of scrap wood, but it kept collapsing whenever I put my weight on it. I was still trying to build a sturdy ladder when, during a cold snap a few days later, my can of paint froze solid. When it got warm enough for the paint to thaw, I opened the can. During the freeze, the chemicals had separated and the once-smooth liquid was as lumpy and runny as curdled milk. I stirred it as hard as I could and kept stirring even after I knew the paint was ruined, because I also knew that we'd never get more, and instead of a freshly painted yellow house, or even a dingy gray one, we now had a weird-looking half-finished patch job—one that announced to the world that the people inside the house wanted to fix it up but lacked the gumption to get the work done.

LITTLE HOBART STREET led up into one of those hollows so deep and narrow that people joked you had to pipe in the sunlight. The neighborhood did have lots of kids—Maureen had real friends for the first time—and we all tended to hang out at the National Guard armory at the foot of the hill. The boys played tackle football on the training field. Most of the girls my age spent their afternoons sitting on the brick wall surrounding the armory, combing their hair and touching up their lip gloss and pretending to get all indignant but secretly loving it if a crew-cut reservist wolf-whistled at them. One of the girls, Cindy Thompson, made a special effort to befriend me, but it turned out that what she really wanted was to recruit me for the junior Ku Klux Klan. Neither putting on makeup nor wearing a sheet had much appeal for me, so I played football with the boys, who would waive their guys-only rule and let me join a team if they were short a player.

The better-off folk of Welch had not exactly flocked to our part of town. A few miners lived along the street, but most of the grown-ups didn't work at all. Some of the moms had no husbands, and some of the dads had black lung. The rest were either too distracted by their troubles or just plain unmotivated, so pretty much everyone grudgingly accepted some form of public aid. Although we were the poorest family on Little Hobart Street, Mom and Dad never applied for welfare or food stamps, and they always refused charity. When teachers gave us bags of clothes from church drives, Mom made us take them back. "We can take care of our own," Mom and Dad liked to say. "We don't accept handouts from anyone."

If things got tight, Mom kept reminding us that some of the other kids on Little Hobart Street had it tougher than we did. The twelve Grady kids had no dad—he'd either died in a mine cave-in or run off with a whore, depending on whom you listened to—and their mom spent her days in bed suffering from migraines. As a result, the Grady boys ran completely wild. It was hard to tell them apart, because they all wore blue

159

jeans and torn T-shirts and had their heads shaved bald to keep away lice. When the oldest boy found their dad's old pump-action shotgun under their mom's bed, he decided to get in some target practice on Brian and me, firing buckshot at us as we ran for our lives through the woods.

And then there were the Halls. All six of the Hall children had been born mentally retarded, and although they were now middle-aged, they all still lived at home with their mom and dad. When I was friendly to the oldest, Kenny Hall, who was forty-two, he developed a powerful crush on me. The other kids in the neighborhood teased Kenny by telling him that if he gave them a dollar or stripped down to his skivvies and showed them his wanker, they'd arrange for me to go on a date with him. On a Saturday night, if he'd been set up like that, he'd come stand on the street in front of our house, sobbing and hollering about me not keeping our date, and I'd have to go down and explain to him that the other kids had played a trick on him and that, although he did have many admirable qualities, I had a policy against dating older men.

The family who had it the toughest on Little Hobart Street, I would have to say, was the Pastors. The mother, Ginnie Sue Pastor, was the town whore. Ginnie Sue Pastor was thirty-three years old and had eight daughters and one son. Their names all ended with Y. Her husband, Clarence Pastor, had black lung and sat on the front porch of their huge sagging house all day long, but he never smiled or waved at passersby. Just sat there like he was frozen. Everyone in town said he'd been impotent for years and none of the Pastor kids was his.

Ginnie Sue Pastor pretty much kept to herself. At first I wondered if she lay around in a lacy negligee all day, smoking cigarettes and waiting for gentlemen callers. Back in Battle Mountain, the women lounging on the front porch of the Green Lantern—I'd long since figured out what they really did—wore white lipstick and black mascara and partially unbuttoned blouses that showed the tops of their brassieres. But Ginnie Sue Pastor didn't look like a whore. She was a blowsy woman with dyed yellow hair, and from time to time we saw her out in the front yard, chopping wood or filling a scuttle from the coal pile. She usually wore the same kinds of aprons and canvas farm coats worn by the rest of the women on Little Hobart Street. She looked like any other mom.

I also wondered how she did her whoring with all those kids to look after. One night I saw a car pull up in front of the Pastor house and blink its headlights twice. After a minute, Ginnie Sue came running out the door and climbed into the front seat. Then the car drove off.

Kathy was Ginnie Sue Pastor's oldest daughter. The other kids treated her like a total pariah, crowing that her mother was a "hoor" and calling her "lice girl." Truth was, she did have a pretty advanced case of head lice. She kept trying to befriend me. One afternoon on the way home from school, when I told her we'd lived for a while in California, she lit up. She said her mama had always wanted to go there. She asked if maybe I'd come over to her place and tell her mama all about life in California.

Of course I went. I'd never gotten inside the Green Lantern, but now I'd get an up-close look at a genuine prostitute. There were lots of things I wanted to know: Was whoring easy money? Was it ever any fun, or was it just gross? Did Kathy and her sisters and her father all know Ginnie Sue Pastor was a whore? What did they think of it? I didn't plan on flat out asking these questions, but I did think that by getting inside the Pastors' house and meeting Ginnie Sue, I'd come away with some idea of the answers.

Clarence Pastor, sitting on the porch, ignored Kathy and me as we walked by. Inside, there were all these tiny rooms connected together like boxcars. Because of the way the house was settling on the eroding hillside, the floors and ceilings and windows tilted at different angles. There were no paintings on the walls, but the Pastors had taped up pictures of smartly dressed women torn from Sears Roebuck catalogs.

Kathy's little sisters scampered around noisily, half dressed. None of them looked alike; one was redheaded, one a blonde, one had black hair, and there were all different shades of brown. Sweet Man, the youngest, crawled along the living room floor, sucking on a fat dill pickle. Ginnie Sue Pastor sat at the table in the kitchen. At her elbow was the carcass of a big expensive roaster, the kind we could hardly ever afford. She had a tired, lined face, but her smile was cheerful and open. "Pleased to meet you," she said to me, wiping her hands on her shirttail. "We ain't used to getting visitors."

Ginnie Sue offered us seats at the table. She had heavy breasts that swayed when she moved, and her blond hair was dark at the roots. "You-all help me with this bird, and I'll fix you a couple of Ginnie Sue's special chicken rolls." She turned to me. "You know how to pick a chicken clean?"

"I sure do," I said. I hadn't had anything to eat all day.

"Well, show me, then," Ginnie Sue said.

I went for a wing first, pulling apart the spindly double bones and getting all the meat trapped there. Then I set to work on the leg and thigh bones, snapping them at the joints and peeling off the tendons and digging out the marrow. Kathy and Ginnie Sue were also working on the bird, but soon they stopped to watch me. From the tail, I pulled that nice piece of meat that everybody misses. I turned the carcass upside down and scraped off the jellied fat and meat flecks with my fingernails. I stuck my arm elbow-deep into the bird to excavate any meat clinging to the rib cage.

"Girl," Ginnie Sue said, "in all my days, I have never seen no one pick a chicken clean like you."

I held up the spear-shaped cartilage in the breast bone, which most people don't eat, and bit down with a satisfying crunch.

Ginnie Sue scraped the meat into a bowl, mixed it with mayonnaise and Cheez Whiz, then crushed a handful of potato chips and added them. She spread the mixture onto two slices of Wonder bread, then rolled each slice into a cylinder and passed them to us. "Birds in a blanket," she said. They tasted great.

"Mama, Jeannette lived in California," Kathy said.

"That so?" Ginnie Sue said. "Live in California and be a stewardess, that was my dream." She sighed. "Never got beyond Bluefield."

I told her and Kathy about life in California. It quickly became clear they had no interest in desert mining towns, so I told them about San Francisco and then about Las Vegas, which wasn't exactly in California, but they didn't seem to care. I made the days we had spent there seem like years, and the showgirls I'd seen from a distance seem like close friends and neighbors. I described the glittering casinos and the glamorous high rollers, the palm trees and the swimming pools, the hotels with ice-cold air-conditioning and the restaurants where hostesses with long white gloves lit flaming desserts.

"It don't get no better than that!" Ginnie Sue said.

"No, ma'am, it sure don't," I told her.

Sweet Man came in crying, and Ginnie Sue picked him up and let him suck some mayonnaise off her finger. "You did good on that bird," Ginnie Sue told me. "You strike me as the kind of girl who's one day going to be eating roast chicken and those on-fire desserts just as much as you want." She winked.

It was only on the way home that I realized I hadn't gotten answers to any of my questions. While I was sitting there talking to Ginnie Sue, I'd even forgotten she was a whore. One thing about whoring: It put a chicken on the table.

WE FOUGHT A LOT in Welch. Not just to fend off our enemies but to fit in. Maybe it was because there was so little to do in Welch; maybe it was because life there was hard and it made people hard; maybe it was because of all the bloody battles over unionizing the mines; maybe it was because mining was dangerous and cramped and dirty work and it put all the miners in bad moods and they came home and took it out on their wives, who took it out on their kids, who took it out on other kids. Whatever the reason, it seemed that just about everyone in Welch—men, women, boys, girls—liked to fight.

There were street brawls, bar stabbings, parking-lot beatings, wife slappings, and toddler whalings. Sometimes it was simply a matter of someone throwing a stray punch, and it would all be over before you knew it had started. Other times it would be more like a twelve-round prizefight, with spectators cheering on the bloody, sweating opponents. Then there were the grudges and feuds that went on for years, a couple of brothers beating up some guy because back in the fifties his father had beaten up their father, a woman shooting her best friend for sleeping with her husband and the best friend's brother then stabbing the husband. You'd walk down McDowell Street, and half the people you passed seemed to be nursing an injury sustained in local combat. There were shiners, split lips, swollen cheekbones, bruised arms, scraped knuckles, and bitten earlobes. We had lived in some pretty scrappy places back in the desert, but Mom said Welch was the fightingest town she'd ever seen.

Brian and Lori and Maureen and I got into more fights than most kids. Dinitia Hewitt and her friends were only the first in a whole line of little gangs who did battle with one or more of us. Other kids wanted to fight us because we had red hair, because Dad was a drunk, because we wore rags and didn't take as many baths as we should have, because we lived in a falling-down house that was partly painted yellow and had a pit filled with garbage, because they'd go by our dark house at night and see that we couldn't even afford electricity.

But we always fought back, usually as a team. Our most spectacular fight, and our most audacious tactical victory—the Battle of Little Hobart Street—took place against Ernie Goad and his friends when I was ten and Brian was nine. Ernie Goad was a pug-nosed, thick-necked kid who had little eyes set practically on the sides of his head, like a whale. He acted as if it was his sworn mission to drive the Walls family out of town. It started one day when I was playing with some other kids on the tank parked next to the armory. Ernie Goad appeared and began throwing rocks at me and yelling that the Wallses should all leave Welch because we were stinking it up so bad.

I threw a couple of rocks back and told him to leave me alone.

"Make me," Ernie said.

"I don't make garbage," I shouted. "I burn it." This was usually a foolproof comeback, making up in scorn what it lacked in originality, but on this occasion it backfired.

"Y'all Wallses don't burn garbage!" Ernie yelled back. "Y'all throw it in a hole next to your house! You live in it!"

I tried to think of a comeback to his comeback, but my mind seized up because what Ernie had said was true: We did live in garbage.

Ernie stuck his face in mine. "Garbage! You live in garbage 'cause you *are* garbage!"

I shoved him good and hard, then turned to the other kids, hoping for backup, but they were easing away and looking down, as if they were ashamed to have been caught playing with a girl who had a garbage pit next to her house.

That Saturday, Brian and I were reading on the sofa bed when one of the windowpanes shattered and a rock landed on the floor. We ran to the door. Ernie and three of his friends were pedaling their bikes up and down Little Hobart Street, whooping madly. "Garbage! Garbage! Y'all are a bunch of garbage!"

Brian went out on the porch. One of the kids hurled another rock that hit Brian in the head. He staggered back, then ran down the steps, but

Ernie and his friends pedaled away, shrieking. Brian came back up the stairs, blood trickling down his cheek and onto his T-shirt and a pump knot already swelling up above his eyebrow. Ernie's gang returned a few minutes later, throwing stones and shouting that they had actually seen the pigsty where the Walls kids lived and that they were going to tell the whole school it was even worse than everyone said.

This time both Brian and I chased after them. Even though they outnumbered us, they were enjoying the game of taunting us too much to make a stand. They rode down to the first switchback and got away.

"They'll be back," Brian said.

"What are we going to do?" I asked.

Brian sat thinking, then told me he had a plan. He found some rope under the house and led me up to a clearing in the hillside above Little Hobart Street. A few weeks earlier, Brian and I had dragged an old mattress up there because we were thinking of camping out. Brian explained how we could make a catapult, like the medieval ones we'd read about, by piling rocks on the mattress and rigging it with ropes looped over tree branches. We quickly assembled the contraption and tested it once, jerking back on the ropes at the count of three. It worked—a minor avalanche of rocks rained onto the street below. It was, we were convinced, enough to kill Ernie Goad and his gang, which was what we fully intended to do: kill them and commandeer their bikes, leaving their bodies in the street as a warning to others.

We piled the rocks back on the mattress, rerigged the catapult, and waited. After a couple of minutes, Ernie and his gang reappeared at the switchback. Each of them rode one-handed and carried an egg-sized rock in his throwing hand. They were proceeding single file, like a Pawnee war party, a few feet apart. We couldn't get them all at once, so we aimed for Ernie, who was at the head of the pack.

When he came within range, Brian gave the word, and we jerked back on the ropes. The mattress shot forward, and our arsenal of rocks flew through the air. I heard them thud against Ernie's body and clatter on the road. He screamed and cursed as his bike skidded. The kid behind Ernie ran into him, and they both fell. The other two turned around and sped off. Brian and I started hurling whatever rocks were at hand. Since they were downhill, we had a good line of fire and scored several direct hits, the rocks dinging off their bikes, nicking the paint and denting the fenders.

Then Brian yelled, "Charge!" and we came barreling down the hill. Ernie and his friend jumped back on their bikes and furiously pedaled off before we could reach them. As they disappeared around the bend, Brian and I did a victory dance in the rock-strewn street, giving our own war whoops.

As the weather warmed, a sort of rough beauty overtook the steep hillsides around Little Hobart Street. Jack-in-the-pulpits and bleeding hearts sprouted wild. White Queen Anne's lace and purple phlox and big orange daylilies blossomed along the road. During the winter you could see abandoned cars and refrigerators and the shells of deserted houses in the woods, but in the spring the vines and weeds and moss grew over them, and in no time they disappeared altogether.

One benefit of summer was that each day we had more light to read by. Mom really piled up on books. She came home from the Welch public library every week or two with a pillowcase full of novels, biographies, and histories. She snuggled into bed with them, looking up from time to time, saying she was sorry, she knew she should be doing something more productive, but like Dad, she had her addictions, and one of them was reading.

We all read, but I never had the feeling of togetherness I'd had in Battle Mountain when we all sat around in the depot with our books. In Welch, people drifted off to different corners of the house. Once night came, we kids all lay in our rope-and-cardboard beds, reading by flashlight or a candle we'd set on our wooden boxes, each of us creating our own little pool of dim light.

Lori was the most obsessive reader. Fantasy and science fiction dazzled her, especially *The Lord of the Rings*. When she wasn't reading, she was drawing orcs or hobbits. She tried to get everyone in the family to read the books. "They transport you to a different world," she'd say.

I didn't want to be transported to another world. My favorite books all involved people dealing with hardships. I loved *The Grapes of Wrath*, *Lord of the Flies*, and especially *A Tree Grows in Brooklyn*. I thought Francie Nolan and I were practically identical, except that she had lived fifty years earlier in Brooklyn and her mother always kept the house clean. Francie Nolan's father sure reminded me of Dad. If Francie saw the good in her father, even though most people considered him a shiftless drunk, maybe I wasn't a complete fool for believing in mine. Or trying to believe in him. It was getting harder.

One night that summer, when I was lying in bed and everyone else was asleep, I heard the front door open and the sound of someone muttering and stumbling around in the darkness. Dad had come home. I went into the living room, where he was sitting at the drafting table. I could see by the moonlight coming through the window that his face and hair were matted with blood. I asked him what had happened.

"I got in a fight with a mountain," he said, "and the mountain won."

I looked at Mom asleep on the sofa bed, her head buried under a pillow. She was a deep sleeper and hadn't stirred. When I lit the kerosene lamp, I saw that Dad also had a big gash in his right forearm and a cut on his head so deep that I could see the white of his skull. I got a toothpick and tweezers and picked the rocky grit out of the gash. Dad didn't wince when I poured rubbing alcohol on the wound. Because of all his hair, I had no way to put on a bandage, and I told Dad I should shave the area around the cut. "Hell, honey, that would ruin my image," he said. "A fellow in my position's got to look presentable."

Dad studied the gash on his forearm. He tightened a tourniquet around his upper arm and told me to fetch Mom's sewing box. He fumbled around in it for silk thread but, unable to find any, decided that cotton would be fine. He threaded a needle with black thread, handed it to me, and pointed at the gash. "Sew it up," he said.

"Dad! I can't do that."

"Oh, go ahead, honey," he said. "I'd do it myself, except I can't do diddly with my left hand." He smiled. "Don't worry about me. I'm so thoroughly pickled, I won't feel a thing." Dad lit a cigarette and placed his arm on the table. "Go ahead," he said.

I pressed the needle up against Dad's skin and shuddered.

"Go ahead," he said again.

I pushed the needle and felt a slight tug when it pierced the skin. I wanted to close my eyes, but I needed to see. I pushed a little harder and felt the resistance of Dad's flesh. It was like sewing meat. It *was* sewing meat.

"I can't, Dad, I'm sorry, I just can't do it," I said.

"We'll do it together," Dad said.

Using his left hand, he guided my fingers as they pushed the needle all the way in through his skin and out the other side. A few droplets of blood appeared. I pulled the needle out and then gave the thread a gentle jerk to tighten it. I tied the two ends of the thread together, like Dad told me to, and then, to put in a second stitch, did it again. The gash was pretty big and could have used a few more stitches, but I couldn't bring myself to stick that needle in Dad's arm one more time.

We both looked at the two dark, slightly sloppy stitches.

"That's some fine handiwork," Dad said. "I'm mighty proud of you, Mountain Goat."

When I left the house the next morning, Dad was still asleep. When I came home in the evening, he was gone.

DAD HAD TAKEN TO disappearing for days at a time. When I asked him where he'd been, his explanations were either so vague or so improbable that I stopped asking. Whenever he did come home, he usually brought a bag of groceries in each arm. We'd gobble deviled-ham sandwiches with thick slices of onion while he told us about the progress of his investigation into the UMW and his latest moneymaking schemes. People were always offering him jobs, he'd explain, but he wasn't interested in work for hire, in saluting and sucking up and brownnosing and taking orders. "You'll never make a fortune working for the boss man," he said. He was focused on striking it rich. There might not be gold in West Virginia, but there were plenty of other ways to make your pile. For instance, he was working on a technology to burn coal more efficiently, so that even the lowest-grade coal could be mined and sold. There was a big market for that, he said, and it was going to make us rich beyond our dreams.

I listened to Dad's plans and tried to encourage him, hoping that what he was saying was true but also pretty certain it wasn't. Money would come in—and with it, food—on the rare occasion that Dad landed an odd job or Mom received a check from the oil company leasing the drilling rights on her land in Texas. Mom was always vague about how big the land was and where exactly it was, and she refused to consider selling it. All we knew was that every couple of months, this check would show up and we'd have plenty of food for days at a time.

When the electricity was on, we ate a lot of beans. A big bag of pinto beans cost under a dollar and would feed us for days. They tasted especially good if you added a spoonful of mayonnaise. We also ate a lot of rice mixed with jack mackerel, which Mom said was excellent brain food. Jack mackerel was not as good as tuna but was better than cat food, which we ate from time to time when things got really tight. Sometimes Mom popped up a big batch of popcorn for dinner. It had lots of fiber, she pointed out, and she had us salt it heavily because the iodine would keep us from getting goiters. "I don't want my kids looking like pelicans," she said.

Once, when an extra-big royalty check came in, Mom bought us a whole canned ham. We ate off it for days, cutting thick slices for sandwiches. Since we had no refrigerator, we left the ham on a kitchen shelf. After it had been there for about a week, I went to saw myself a slab at dinnertime and found it crawling with little white worms.

Mom was sitting on the sofa bed, eating the piece she'd cut. "Mom, that ham's full of maggots," I said.

"Don't be so picky," she told me. "Just slice off the maggoty parts. The inside's fine."

Brian and I became expert foragers. We picked crab apples and wild blackberries and pawpaws during the summer and fall, and we swiped ears of corn from Old Man Wilson's farm. The corn was tough—Old Man Wilson grew it as feed for his cattle—but if you chewed it enough, you could get it down. Once we caught a wounded blackbird by throwing a blanket over it and figured we could make a blackbird pie, like in the nursery rhyme. But we couldn't bring ourselves to kill the bird, and anyway, it looked too scrawny to eat.

We'd heard of a dish called poke salad, and since a big patch of pokeweed grew behind our house, Brian and I thought we'd give it a try. If it was any good, we'd have a whole new supply of food. We first tried eating the pokeweed raw, but it was awfully bitter, so we boiled it—singing "Poke Salad Annie" in anticipation—but it still tasted sour and stringy, and our tongues itched for days afterward.

One day, hunting for food, we climbed through the window of an abandoned house. The rooms were tiny, and it had dirt floors, but in the kitchen we found shelves lined with rows of canned food.

"Bo-nanza!" Brian cried out.

"Feast time!" I said.

The cans were coated with dust and starting to rust, but we figured the food was still safe to eat, since the whole point of canning was to preserve. I passed a can of tomatoes to Brian, who took out his pocketknife. When he punctured the tin, the contents exploded in his face, covering us with a fizzy brown juice. We tried a few more, but they exploded, too, and we walked home without having eaten anything, our shirts and faces stained with rotten tomatoes.

When I started sixth grade, the other kids made fun of Brian and me because we were so skinny. They called me spider legs, skeleton girl, pipe cleaner, two-by-four, bony butt, stick woman, bean pole, and giraffe, and they said I could stay dry in the rain by standing under a telephone wire.

At lunchtime, when other kids unwrapped their sandwiches or bought their hot meals, Brian and I would get out books and read. Brian told everyone he had to keep his weight down because he wanted to join the wrestling team when he got to high school. I told people that I had forgotten to bring my lunch. No one believed me, so I started hiding in the bathroom during lunch hour. I'd stay in one of the stalls with the door locked and my feet propped up so that no one would recognize my shoes.

When other girls came in and threw away their lunch bags in the garbage pails, I'd go retrieve them. I couldn't get over the way kids tossed out all this perfectly good food: apples, hard-boiled eggs, packages of peanut-butter crackers, sliced pickles, half-pint cartons of milk, cheese sandwiches with just one bite taken out because the kid didn't like the pimentos in the cheese. I'd return to the stall and polish off my tasty finds.

There was, at times, more food in the wastebasket than I could eat. The first time I found extra food—a bologna-and-cheese sandwich—I stuffed it into my purse to take home for Brian. Back in the classroom, I started worrying about how I'd explain to Brian where it came from. I was pretty sure he was rooting through the trash, too, but we never talked about it.

As I sat there trying to come up with ways to justify it to Brian, I began smelling the bologna. It seemed to fill the whole room. I became terrified that the other kids could smell it, too, and that they'd turn and see my overstuffed purse, and since they all knew I never ate lunch, they'd figure out that I had pinched it from the trash. As soon as class was over, I ran to the bathroom and shoved the sandwich back in the garbage can.

Maureen always had plenty to eat, since she had made friends throughout the neighborhood and would show up at their houses around dinnertime. I had no idea what Mom and Lori were doing to fend for themselves. Mom, weirdly, was getting heavier. One evening when Dad was away and we had nothing to eat and we were all sitting around the living room trying not to think of food, Mom kept disappearing under the blanket on the sofa bed. At one point Brian looked over.

"Are you chewing something?" he asked.

"My teeth hurt," Mom said, but she was getting all shifty-eyed, glancing around the room and avoiding our stares. "It's my bad gums. I'm working my jaw to increase the circulation."

Brian yanked the covers back. Lying on the mattress next to Mom was one of those huge family-sized Hershey chocolate bars, the shiny silver wrapper pulled back and torn away. She'd already eaten half of it.

Mom started crying. "I can't help it," she sobbed. "I'm a sugar addict, just like your father is an alcoholic."

She told us we should forgive her the same way we always forgave Dad for his drinking. None of us said a thing. Brian snatched up the chocolate bar and divided it into four pieces. While Mom watched, we wolfed them down.

WINTER CAME HARD that year. Just after Thanksgiving, the first big snow started with fat wet flakes the size of butterflies. They floated down lazily but were followed by smaller, drier flakes that kept coming for days. At first I loved winter in Welch. The blanket of snow hid the soot and made the entire town seem clean and cozy. Our house looked almost like all the others along Little Hobart Street.

It was so cold that the youngest, most fragile branches snapped in the frigid air, and very quickly, I started feeling it. I still had only my thin wool coat with the buttons missing. I felt almost as cold in the house; while we had the coal stove, we had no coal. There were forty-two coal retailers listed in the Welch phone book. A ton of coal, which would last most of the winter, cost about fifty dollars—including delivery—or even as little as thirty dollars for the lower-grade stuff. Mom said she was sorry, but there was no room in our budget for coal. We'd have to devise other ways to stay warm.

Pieces of coal were always falling off the trucks when they made their deliveries, and Brian suggested that he and I get a bucket and collect some. We were walking along Little Hobart Street, picking up pieces of coal, when our neighbors the Noes drove by in their station wagon. The Noe girls, Karen and Carol, were sitting in the backward-facing jump seat, looking out the rear window. "We're working on our rock collection!" I shouted.

The pieces we found were so small that after an hour we'd filled only half the bucket. We needed at least a bucket to keep a fire going for one evening. So while we made occasional coal-collecting expeditions, we used mostly wood. We couldn't afford wood any more than we could afford coal, and Dad wasn't around to chop and split any, which meant it was up to us kids to gather dead branches and logs from the forest.

Finding good, dry wood was a challenge. We trekked along the mountainside, looking for pieces that weren't waterlogged or rotten, shaking the snow off branches. But we went through the wood awfully quickly, and while a coal fire burns hot, a wood fire doesn't throw off much heat. We all huddled around the potbellied stove, wrapped in blankets, holding out our hands toward the weak, smoky heat. Mom said we should be thankful because we had it better than pioneers, who didn't have modern conveniences like window glass and cast-iron stoves.

One day we got a roaring fire going, but even then we could still see our breath, and there was ice on both sides of the windows. Brian and I decided we needed to make the fire even bigger and went out to collect more wood. On the way back, Brian stopped and looked at our house. "There's no snow on our roof," he said. He was right. It had completely melted. "Every other house has snow on its roof," he said. He was right about that, too.

"This house doesn't have a lick of insulation," Brian told Mom when we got back inside. "All the heat's going right through the roof."

"We may not have insulation," Mom said as we all gathered around the stove, "but we have each other."

It got so cold in the house that icicles hung from the kitchen ceiling, the water in the sink turned into a solid block of ice, and the dirty dishes were stuck there as if they'd been cemented in place. Even the pan of water that we kept in the living room to wash up in usually had a layer of ice on it. We walked around the house wearing our coats and wrapped in blankets. We wore our coats to bed, too. There was no stove in the bedroom, and no matter how many blankets I piled on top of myself, I still felt cold. I lay awake at night, rubbing my feet with my hands, trying to warm them.

We fought over who got to sleep with the dogs—Tinkle, the Jack Russell terrier, and Pippin, a curly-haired mutt who had wandered down through the woods one day—because they kept us warm. They usually ended up in a heap with Mom, because she had the bigger body, and they were cold, too. Brian had bought an iguana at G. C. Murphy, the five-and-dime on McDowell Street, because it reminded him of the desert. He named the lizard Iggy and slept with it against his chest to keep it warm, but it froze to death one night.

We had to leave the faucet under the house dripping or the water froze in the pipe. When it got really cold, the water froze anyway, and we'd wake up to find a big icicle hanging from the faucet. We tried to thaw the pipe by running a burning piece of wood along it, but it would be frozen so solid there was nothing to do but wait for the next warm spell. When the pipe froze like that, we got our water by melting snow or icicles in the tin pan on the potbellied stove.

A couple of times when there wasn't enough snow on the ground, Mom sent me next door to borrow a pail of water from Mr. Freeman, a retired miner, who lived in the house with his grown son and daughter, Peanut and Prissy. He never turned me down outright, but he would look at me for a minute in silence, then shake his head and disappear into the house. When he passed out the bucket, he would give me another disgusted head-shake, even after I assured him that he could have as much water from us as he wanted come spring.

"I hate winter," I told Mom.

"All seasons have something to offer," she said. "Cold weather is good for you. It kills the germs."

That seemed to be true, because none of us kids ever got sick. But even if I'd woken up one morning with a raging fever, I never would have admitted it to Mom. Being sick might have meant staying home in our freezing house instead of spending the day in a toasty classroom.

Another good thing about the cold weather was that it kept odors to a minimum. By New Year's we had washed our clothes only once since that first November snowfall. In the summer, Mom had bought a wringer washing machine like the one we'd had in Phoenix, and we kept it in the kitchen. When we had electricity, we washed the clothes and hung them on the front porch to dry. Even when the weather was warm, they'd have to stay out there for days, because it was always so damp in that hollow on the north side of the mountain. But then it got cold, and the one time we did our laundry, it froze on the porch. We brought the clothes inside—the socks had hardened into the shape of question marks, and the pants were so stiff you could lean them against the wall—and we banged them against the stove, trying to soften them up. "At least we don't need to buy starch," Lori said.

Even with the cold, by January we were all so rank that Mom decided it was time to splurge: We would go to the Laundromat. We loaded our dirty clothes into pillowcases and lugged them down the hill and up Stewart Street.

Mom put the loaded bag on her head, the way women in Africa do, and tried to get us to do the same. She said it was better for our posture and easier on our spines, but there was no way we kids were going to be caught dead walking through Welch with laundry bags on our heads. We followed Mom with our bags over our shoulders, rolling our eyes when we passed people to show we agreed with them: The lady with the bag on her head looked pretty peculiar.

The Laundromat, with its windows completely steamed up, was as warm and damp as a Turkish bath. Mom let us put the coins in the washers, then we climbed up and sat on them. The heat from the rumbling machines warmed our behinds and spread up through our bodies. When the wash was done, we heaved the armfuls of wet clothes into the dryers and watched them tumbling around as if they were on some fun carnival ride. Once the cycle was over, we pulled out the scorching-hot clothes and buried our faces in them. We spread them on the tables and folded them carefully, lining up the sleeves of the shirts and the seams on the pants and balling the paired-up socks. We never folded our clothes at home, but that Laundromat was so warm and cozy, we were looking for any excuse to extend our stay.

A warm spell in January seemed like good news, but then the snow started melting, and the wood in the forest became totally soaked. We couldn't get a fire to do anything but sputter smoke. If the wood was wet, we'd douse it with the kerosene that we used in the lamps. Dad was disdainful of a fire starter like kerosene. No true frontiersman would ever stoop to use it. It wasn't cheap, and since it didn't burn hot, it took a lot to make the wood catch fire. Also, it was dangerous. Dad said that if you got sloppy with kerosene, it could explode. But still, if the wood was wet and didn't want to catch and we were all freezing, we would pour a little kerosene on it.

One day Brian and I climbed the hillside to try to find some dry wood while Lori stayed in the house, stoking the fire. As Brian and I were shaking the snow off some promising branches, we heard a loud boom from the house. I turned and saw flames leap up inside the windows.

We dropped our wood and ran back down the hill. Lori was lurching around the living room, her eyebrows and bangs all singed off and the smell of burned hair in the air. She had used kerosene to try to get the fire going better, and it had exploded, just like Dad had said it would. Nothing in the house except Lori's hair had caught on fire, but the explosion had blown back her coat and skirt, and the flames had scorched her thighs. Brian went out and got some snow, and we packed it on Lori's legs, which were dark pink. The next day she had blisters the length of her thighs.

"Just remember," Mom said after examining the blisters, "what doesn't kill you will make you stronger."

"If that was true, I'd be Hercules by now," Lori said.

Days later, when the blisters burst, the clear liquid inside ran down to her feet. For weeks, the fronts of her legs were open sores, so sensitive that she had trouble sleeping under blankets. But by then the temperature had fallen again, and if she kicked off the blankets, she froze.

One day that winter, I went to a classmate's house to work on a school project. Carrie Mae Blankenship's father was an administrator at the McDowell County hospital, and her family lived in a solid brick house on McDowell Street. The living room was decorated in shades of orange and brown, and the plaid pattern of the curtains matched the couch upholstery. On the wall was a framed photo of Carrie Mae's older sister in her high school graduation gown. It was lit with its own tiny lamp, just like in a museum.

There was also a small plastic box on the wall near the living room door. A row of tiny numbers ran along the top, under a lever. Carrie Mae's father saw me studying the box while she was out of the room. "It's a thermostat," he told me. "You move the lever to make the house warmer or cooler."

I thought he was pulling my leg, but he moved the lever, and I heard a muffled roar kick on in the basement.

"That's the furnace," he said.

He led me over to a vent in the floor and had me hold my hand above it and feel the warm air wafting upward. I didn't want to say anything to show how impressed I was, but for many nights afterward, I dreamed that we had a thermostat at 93 Little Hobart Street. I dreamed that all we had to do to fill our house with that warm, clean furnace heat was to move a lever.

ERMA DIED DURING the last hard snowfall at the end of our second winter in Welch. Dad said her liver simply gave out. Mom took the position that Erma drank herself to death. "It was suicide every bit as much as if she had stuck her head in the oven," Mom said, "only slower."

Whatever the cause, Erma had made detailed preparations for the occasion of her death. For years she had read *The Welch Daily News* only for the obituaries and black-bordered memorial notices, clipping and saving her favorites. They provided inspiration for her own death announcement, which she'd worked and reworked. She had also written pages of instructions on how she wanted her funeral conducted. She had picked out all the hymns and prayers, chosen her favorite funeral home, ordered a lavender lace nightgown from JCPenney that she wanted to be buried in, and selected a two-toned lavender casket with shiny chrome handles from the mortician's catalog.

Erma's death brought out Mom's pious side. While we were waiting for the preacher, she took out her rosary and prayed for Erma's soul, which she feared was in jeopardy since, as she saw it, Erma had committed suicide. She also tried to make us kiss Erma's corpse. We flat out refused, but Mom went up in front of the mourners, genuflected with a grand sweep, and then kissed Erma's cheek so vigorously that you could hear the puckering sound throughout the chapel.

I was sitting next to Dad. It was the first time in my life I'd ever seen him wearing a necktie, which he always called a noose. His face was tight and closed, but I could tell he was distraught. More distraught than I'd ever seen him, which surprised me, because Erma had seemed to have some sort of an evil hold over Dad, and I thought he'd be relieved to be free of it.

As we walked home, Mom asked us kids if we had anything nice to say about Erma now that she had passed. We took a couple of steps in silence, then Lori said, "Ding-dong, the witch is dead."

Brian and I started snickering. Dad wheeled around and gave Lori such a cold, angry look that I thought he might wallop her. "She was my mother, for God's sake," he said. He glared at us. "You kids. You make me ashamed. Do you hear me? Ashamed!"

He turned down the street to Junior's bar. We all watched him go. "*You're* ashamed of *us*?" Lori called after him.

Dad just kept walking.

Four days later, when Dad still hadn't come home, Mom sent me to go find him. "Why do I always have to get Dad?" I asked.

"Because he likes you the best," she said. "And he'll come home if you tell him to."

The first step in tracking down Dad was going next door to the Freemans, who let us use their phone if we paid a dime, and calling Grandpa to ask if Dad was there. Grandpa said he had no idea where Dad was.

"When y'all gonna get your own telephone?" Mr. Freeman asked after I hung up.

"Mom disapproves of telephones," I said as I placed the dime on his coffee table. "She thinks they're an impersonal means of communication."

My first stop, as always, was Junior's. It was the fanciest bar in Welch, with a picture window, a grill that served hamburgers and french fries, and a pinball machine.

"Hey!" one of the regulars called out when I walked in. "It's Rex's little girl. How ya doin', sweetheart?"

"I'm fine, thank you. Is my dad here?"

"Rex?" He turned to the man next to him. "Where's that old polecat Rex?"

"I seen him this morning at the Howdy House."

"Honey, you look like you could use a rest," the bartender said. "Sit down and have a Coca-Cola on the house."

"No, thank you. I've got kites to fly and fish to fry."

I went to the Howdy House, which was a notch below Junior's. It was smaller and darker, and the only food it served was pickled eggs. The bartender told me Dad had gone to the Pub, which was a notch below the Howdy House—almost pitch black, with a sticky bar top and no food at all. There he was, in the midst of a few other regulars, telling one of his air force stories.

When Dad saw me, he stopped talking and looked at me the way he did every time I had to track him down in a bar. It was always an awkward moment for us both. I didn't want to be fetching him any more than he wanted his ragamuffin daughter summoning him home like a wayward schoolboy. He looked at me in this cold, strange way for just a moment, then broke into a hearty grin.

"Hey, Mountain Goat!" he shouted. "What the hell are you doing in this dive?"

"Mom says you have to come home," I said.

"She does, does she?" He ordered a Coca-Cola for me and another shot of whiskey for himself. I kept telling Dad it was time to go, but he kept putting me off and ordering more shots, as if he had to gulp a whole bunch of them down before he could face home. He staggered off to the bathroom, came back, ordered one for the road, slammed the shot glass down on the bar, and walked to the door. He lost his footing trying to open it and sprawled on the floor. I tried to help him up, but he kept falling over.

"Honey, you ain't getting him nowhere like that," a man behind me said. "Here, let me give you a lift home."

"I'd appreciate that, sir," I said. "If it's not out of your way."

Some of the other regulars helped the man and me load Dad into the bay of the man's pickup. We propped Dad up against a tool chest. It was late afternoon in early spring, the light was beginning to fade, and people on McDowell Street were locking up their shops and heading home. Dad started singing one of his favorite songs.

Swing low, sweet chariot
Coming for to carry me home.

Dad had a fine baritone, with strength and timbre and range, and despite being tanked, he sang that hymn like the roof-raiser it is.

I looked over Jordan, and what did I see
Coming for to carry me home?
A band of angels coming after me
Coming for to carry me home.

I climbed in next to the driver. On the way home—with Dad still singing away in the back, extending the word "low" so long he sounded like a mooing cow—the man asked me about school. I told him I was studying hard because I wanted to become either a veterinarian or a geologist specializing in the Miocene period, when the mountains out west were formed. I was telling him how geodes were created from bubbles in lava when he interrupted me. "For the daughter of the town drunk, you sure got big plans," he said.

"Stop the truck," I said. "We can make it on our own from here."

"Aw, now, I didn't mean nothing by that," he said. "And you know you ain't getting him home on your own."

Still, he stopped. I opened the pickup's tailgate and tried to drag Dad out, but the man was right. I couldn't do it. So I climbed back in next to the driver, folded my arms across my chest, and stared straight ahead. When we reached 93 Little Hobart Street, he helped me pull Dad out.

"I know you took offense at what I said," the man told me. "Thing is, I meant it as a compliment."

Maybe I should have thanked him, but I just waited until he drove off, and then I called Brian to help me get Dad up the hill and into the house.

A couple of months after Erma died, Uncle Stanley fell asleep in the basement while reading comic books and smoking a cigarette. The big clapboard house burned to the ground, but Grandpa and Stanley got out alive, and they moved into a windowless two-room apartment in the basement of an old house around the hill. The drug dealers who'd lived there before had spray-painted curse words and psychedelic patterns on the walls and the ceiling pipes. The landlord didn't paint over them, and neither did Grandpa and Stanley.

Grandpa and Uncle Stanley did have a working bathroom, so every weekend some of us went over to take a bath. One time I was sitting next to Uncle Stanley on the couch in his room, watching *Hee Haw* and waiting for my turn in the tub. Grandpa was off at the Moose Lodge, where he spent the better part of every day; Lori was taking her bath; and Mom was at the table in Grandpa's room working on a crossword puzzle. I felt Stanley's hand creeping onto my thigh. I looked at him, but he was staring at the *Hee Haw* Honeys so intently that I couldn't be sure he was doing it on purpose, so I knocked his hand away without saying anything. A few minutes later, the hand came creeping back. I looked down and saw that Uncle Stanley's pants were unzipped and he was playing with himself. I felt like hitting him, but I was afraid I'd get in trouble the way Lori had after punching Erma, so I hurried out to Mom.

"Mom, Uncle Stanley is behaving inappropriately," I said.

"Oh, you're probably imagining it," she said.

"He groped me! And he's wanking off!"

Mom cocked her head and looked concerned. "Poor Stanley," she said. "He's so lonely."

"But it was gross!"

Mom asked me if I was okay. I shrugged and nodded. "Well, there you go," she said. She said that sexual assault was a crime of perception. "If you don't think you're hurt, then you aren't," she said. "So many women make such a big deal out of these things. But you're stronger than that." She went back to her crossword puzzle.

After that, I refused to go back to Grandpa's. Being strong was fine, but the last thing I needed was Uncle Stanley thinking I was coming back for more of his fooling around. I did whatever it took to wash myself at Little Hobart Street. In the kitchen, we had an aluminum tub you could fit into if you pulled your legs up against your chest. By then the weather was warm enough to fill the tub with water from the tap under the house and bathe in the kitchen. After the bath, I crouched by the side of the tub and dipped my head in the water and washed my hair. But lugging all those buckets of water up to the house was hard work, and I would put off bathing until I was feeling pretty gamy.

In the spring, the rains came, drenching the valley for days in sheets of falling water. The water ran down the hillside gullies, pulling rocks and small trees with it, and spilled across the roads, tearing off chunks of asphalt. It gushed into the creeks, which swelled up and turned a foaming light brown, like a chocolate milk shake. The creeks emptied into the Tug, which overflowed its banks and flooded the houses and stores along McDowell Street. Mud was four feet deep in some houses, and folks' pickups and mobile homes were swept away. Over in Buffalo Creek Hollow, a mine impoundment gave way, and a wave of black water thirty feet high killed 126 people. Mom said that this was how nature took her revenge on men who raped and pillaged the land, ruining nature's own drainage system by clear-cutting forests and strip-mining mountains.

Little Hobart Street was too high up in the hollow to get any flooding, but the rain washed parts of the road into the yards of the people who lived below us. The water also ate away some of the soil from around the pillars holding up our house, making it even more precarious. The hole in the kitchen ceiling widened, and then the ceiling on Brian and Maureen's side of the bedroom started leaking. Brian had the top bunk, and when it rained, he'd spread a tarp over himself to keep the dripping water off.

Everything in the house was damp. A fine green mold spread over the books and papers and paintings that were stacked so high and piled so deep you could hardly cross the room. Tiny mushrooms sprouted up in corners. The moisture ate away at the wooden stairs leading up to the house, and climbing them became a daily hazard. Mom fell through a rotted step and went tumbling down the hillside. She had bruises on her legs and arms for weeks. "My husband doesn't beat me," she'd say when anyone stared at them. "He just won't fix the stairs."

The porch had also started to rot. Most of the banisters and railing had given way, and the floorboards had turned spongy and slick with mold and algae. It became a real problem when you had to go down under the house to use the toilet at night, and each of us had slipped and fallen off the porch at least once. It was a good ten feet to the ground.

"We have to do something about the porch situation," I told Mom. "It's getting downright dangerous to go to the bathroom at night." Besides, the toilet under the house was now totally unusable. It had overflowed, and you were better off digging yourself a hole in the hillside somewhere.

"You're right," Mom said. "Something has to be done."

She bought a bucket. It was made of yellow plastic, and we kept it on the floor in the kitchen, and that was what we used whenever we had to go to the bathroom. When it filled up, some brave soul would carry it outside, dig a hole, and empty it.

ONE DAY WHILE Brian and I were out scrounging around on the edge of our property, he picked up a piece of rotting lumber, and there among the pill bugs and night crawlers was a diamond ring. The stone was big. At first we thought it was just neat junk, but we spit-polished it and scratched glass with it like Dad had shown us, and it seemed real. We figured it must have belonged to the old lady who had lived there. She had died before we moved in. Everyone had said she was a little loopy.

"What do you think it's worth?" I asked Brian.

"Probably more than the house," he said.

We figured we could sell it and buy food, pay off the house—Mom and Dad kept missing the monthly payments, and there was talk that we were going to be evicted—and maybe still have enough left over for something special, like a new pair of sneakers for each of us.

We brought the ring home and showed it to Mom. She held it up to the light, then said we needed to have it appraised. The next day she took the Trailways bus to Bluefield. When she returned, she told us it was in fact a genuine two-carat diamond.

"So what's it worth?" I asked.

"That doesn't matter," Mom said.

"How come?"

"Because we're not selling it."

She was keeping it, she explained, to replace the wedding ring her mother had given her, the one Dad had pawned shortly after they got married.

"But Mom," I said, "that ring could get us a lot of food."

"That's true," Mom said, "but it could also improve my self-esteem. And at times like these, self-esteem is even more vital than food."

Mom's self-esteem did need some shoring up. Sometimes, things just got to her. She retreated to her sofa bed and stayed there for days on end, crying and occasionally throwing things at us. She could have been a famous artist by now, she yelled, if she hadn't had children, and none of us appreciated her sacrifice. The next day, if the mood had passed, she'd be painting and humming away as if nothing had happened.

One Saturday morning not long after Mom started wearing her new diamond ring, her mood was on an upswing, and she decided we'd all clean the house. I thought this was a great idea. I told Mom we should empty out each room, clean it thoroughly, and put back only the things that were essential. That was the one way, it seemed to me, to get rid of the clutter. But Mom said my idea was too time-consuming, so all we ended up doing was straightening piles of paper into stacks and stuffing dirty clothes into the chest of drawers. Mom insisted that we chant Hail Marys while we worked. "It's a way of cleansing our souls while we're cleaning house," she said. "We're killing two birds with one stone."

The reason she had become a tad moody, she said later that day, was that she hadn't been getting enough exercise. "I'm going to start doing calisthenics," she announced. "Once you get your circulation going, it changes your entire outlook on life." She leaned over and touched her toes.

When she came up, she said she was feeling better already, and went down for another toe touch. I watched from the writing desk with my arms folded across my chest. I knew the problem was not that we all had poor circulation. We didn't need to start doing toe touches. We needed to take drastic measures. I was twelve by now, and I had been weighing our options, doing some research at the public library and picking up scraps of information about how other families on Little Hobart Street survived. I had come up with a plan and had been waiting for the opportunity to broach it to Mom. The moment seemed ripe.

"Mom, we can't go on living like this," I said.

"It's not so bad," she said. Between each toe touch, she was reaching up into the air.

"We haven't had anything to eat but popcorn for three days," I said.

"You're always so negative," she said. "You remind me of my mother—criticize, criticize, criticize."

"I'm not being negative," I said. "I'm trying to be realistic."

"I'm doing the best I can under the circumstances," she said. "How come you never blame your father for anything? He's no saint, you know."

"I know," I said. I ran a finger along the edge of the desk. Dad was always parking his cigarettes there, and it was ribbed with a row of black cigarette burns, like a decorative border. "Mom, you have to leave Dad," I said.

She stopped doing her toe touches. "I can't believe you would say that," she said. "I can't believe that you, of all people, would turn on your father." I was Dad's last defender, she continued, the only one who pretended to believe all his excuses and tales, and to have faith in his plans for the future. "He loves you so much," Mom said. "How can you do this to him?"

"I don't blame Dad," I said. And I didn't. But Dad seemed hell-bent on destroying himself, and I was afraid he was going to pull us all down with him. "We've got to get away."

"But I can't leave your father!" she said.

I told Mom that if she left Dad, she'd be eligible for government aid, which she couldn't get now because she had an able-bodied husband. Some people at school—not to mention half the people on Little Hobart Street—were on welfare, and it wasn't so bad. I knew Mom was opposed to welfare, but those kids got food stamps and clothing allowances. The state bought them coal and paid for their school lunches.

Mom wouldn't hear of it. Welfare, she said, would cause irreparable psychological damage to us kids. "You can be hungry every now and then, but once you eat, you're okay," she said. "And you can get cold for a while, but you always warm up. Once you go on welfare, it changes you. Even if you get off welfare, you never escape the stigma that you were a charity case. You're scarred for life."

"Fine," I said. "If we're not charity cases, then get a job." There was a teacher shortage in McDowell County, just like there had been in Battle Mountain. She could get work in a heartbeat, and when she had a salary, we could move into a little apartment in town.

"That sounds like an awful life," Mom said.

"Worse than this?" I asked.

Mom turned quiet. She seemed to be thinking. Then she looked up. She was smiling serenely. "I can't leave your father," she said. "It's against the Catholic faith." Then she sighed. "And anyway, you know your mom. I'm an excitement addict."

MOM NEVER TOLD Dad that I'd urged her to leave him. That summer he still thought of me as his biggest supporter, and given that there was so little competition for the job, I probably was.

One afternoon in June, Dad and I were sitting out on the porch, our legs dangling over the side, looking down at the houses below. That summer, it was so hot I could barely breathe. It seemed hotter than Phoenix or Battle Mountain, where it regularly climbed above a hundred degrees, so when Dad told me it was only ninety degrees, I said the thermometer must be broken. But he said no, we were used to dry desert heat, and this was humid heat.

It was a lot hotter, Dad pointed out, down in the valley along Stewart Street, which was lined with those cute brick houses that had their neat, square lawns and corrugated aluminum breezeways. The valleys trapped the heat. Our house was the highest on the mountainside, which made it, ergo, the coolest spot in Welch. In case of flooding—as we had seen— it was also the safest. "You didn't know I put a lot of thought into where we should live, did you?" he asked me. "Real estate's about three things, Mountain Goat. Location. Location. Location."

Dad started laughing. It was a silent laugh that made his shoulders shake, and the more he laughed, the funnier it seemed to him, which made him laugh even harder. I had to start laughing, too, and soon we were both hysterical, lying on our backs, tears running down our cheeks, slapping our feet on the porch floor. We'd get too winded to laugh any further, our sides cramping with stitches, and we'd think our fit was over, but then one of us would start chuckling, and that would get the other going, and again we'd both end up shrieking like hyenas.

The main source of relief from the heat for the kids in Welch was the public swimming pool, down by the railroad tracks near the Esso station. Brian and I had gone swimming once, but Ernie Goad and his friends were there, and they started telling everybody that we Wallses lived in garbage and would stink up the pool water something awful. This was Ernie Goad's opportunity to take revenge for the Battle of Little Hobart Street. One of his friends came up with the phrase "health epidemic," and they were going on to the parents and lifeguards that we needed to be ejected to prevent an outbreak at the pool. Brian and I decided to leave. As we were walking away, Ernie Goad came up to the chain-link fence. "Go on home to the garbage dump!" he shouted. His voice was shrill with triumph. "Go on, now, and don't come back!"

A week later, with the heat still holding, I ran into Dinitia Hewitt downtown. She had just come from the pool and had her wet hair pulled back under a scarf. "Brother, that water felt good," she said, drawing out the word "good" so it sounded like it had about fifteen Os in it. "Do you ever go swimming?"

"They don't like us to go there," I said.

Dinitia nodded, even though I hadn't explained. Then she said, "Why don't you come swimming with us in the morning?"

By "us" I knew she meant the other black people. The pool was not segregated, anyone could swim at any time—technically, at least—but the fact was that all the black people swam in the morning, when the pool was free, and all the white people swam in the afternoon, when admission was fifty cents. No one had planned this arrangement, and no rules enforced it. That was just the way it was.

I surely wanted to get back in that water, but I couldn't help but feel that if I took Dinitia up on her offer, I'd be violating some sort of taboo. "Wouldn't anybody get mad?" I asked.

"'Cause you're white?" she asked. "Your own kind might, but we won't. And your own kind won't be there."

The next morning I met Dinitia in front of the pool entrance, my thrift-shop one-piece rolled inside my frayed gray towel. The white girl clerking the entrance booth gave me a surprised look when we passed through the gate, but she said nothing. The women's locker room was dark and smelled of Pine-Sol, with cinder-block walls and a wet cement floor. A soul tune was blasting out of an eight-track tape player, and all the black women packed between the peeling wooden benches were singing and dancing to the music.

In the locker rooms I'd been in, the white women always seemed embarrassed by their nakedness and wrapped towels around their waists before slipping off their underpants, but here most of the women were buck-naked. Some of them were skinny, with angular hips and jutting collarbones. Others had big pillowy behinds and huge swinging breasts, and they were bumping their butts together and pushing their breasts up against each other as they danced.

As soon as the women saw me, they stopped dancing. One of the naked ones came over and stood in front of me, her hands on her hips, her breasts so close I was terrified her nipples were going to touch me. Dinitia explained that I was with her and that I was good people. The women looked at one another and shrugged.

I was going on thirteen and self-conscious, so I planned to slip my bathing suit on underneath my dress, but I worried this would only make me more conspicuous, so I took a deep breath and stepped out of my clothes. The scar on my ribs was about the size of my outstretched hand, and Dinitia noticed it immediately. I explained that I had gotten it when I was three, and that I'd been in the hospital for six weeks getting skin grafts, and that was why I never wore a bikini. Dinitia ran her fingers lightly over the scar tissue. "It ain't so bad," she said.

"Hey, 'Nitia!" one of the women shouted. "Your white friend's got a red bush coming in!"

"What did you expect?" Dinitia asked.

"That's right," I said. "Collar got to match the cuffs."

It was a line I'd heard Dinitia use. She smiled at it, and the women all shrieked with laughter. One of the dancers bumped her hip up against me. I felt welcome enough to give a saucy bump back.

Dinitia and I stayed in the pool all morning, splashing, practicing the backstroke and the butterfly. She flailed around in the water almost as much as I did. We stood on our hands and stuck our legs out of the water, did underwater twists, and played Marco Polo and chicken with the other kids. We climbed out to do cannonballs and watermelons off the side, making big geyserlike splashes intended to drench as many people sitting poolside as possible. The blue water sparkled and churned white with foam. By the time the free swim was over, my fingers and toes were completely wrinkled, and my eyes were red and stinging from the chlorine, which was so strong it wafted up from the pool in a vapor you could practically see. I'd never felt cleaner.

THAT AFTERNOON I WAS alone in the house, still enjoying the itchy, dry feeling of my chlorine-scoured skin and the wobbly-bone feeling you get from a lot of exercise, when I heard a knock on the door. The noise startled me. Almost no one ever visited us at 93 Little Hobart Street. I opened the door a few inches and peered out. A balding man carrying a file folder under his arm stood on the porch. Something about him said government—a species Dad had trained us to avoid.

"Is the head of the household in?" he asked.

"Who wants to know?" I said.

The man smiled the way you do to sugarcoat bad news. "I'm with child welfare, and I'm looking for either Rex or Rose Mary Walls," he said.

"They're not here," I said.

"How old are you?" he asked.

"Twelve."

"Can I come in?"

I could see he was trying to peer behind me into the house. I pulled the door all the way closed except for a crack. "Mom and Dad wouldn't want me to let you in," I said. "Until they talk to their attorney," I added to impress him. "Just tell me what it is you're after, and I'll pass on the message."

The man said that someone whose name he was not at liberty to disclose had called his office recommending an inquiry into conditions at 93 Little Hobart Street, where it was possible that dependent children might be living in a state of neglect.

"No one's neglecting us," I said.

"You sure?"

"I'm sure, mister."

"Dad work?"

"Of course," I said. "He does odd jobs. And he's an entrepreneur. He's developing a technology to burn low-grade bituminous coal safely and efficiently."

"And your mother?"

"She's an artist," I said. "And a writer and a teacher."

"Really?" The man made a note on a pad. "Where?"

"I don't think Mom and Dad would want me talking to you without them here," I said. "Come back when they're here. They'll answer your questions."

"Good," the man said. "I will come back. Tell them that."

He passed a business card through the crack in the doorway. I watched him make his way down to the ground. "Careful on those stairs now," I called. "We're in the process of building a new set."

After the man left, I was so furious that I ran up the hillside and started hurling rocks—big rocks that it took two hands to lift—into the garbage pit. Except for Erma, I had never hated anyone more than I hated that child-welfare man. Not even Ernie Goad. At least when Ernie and his gang came around yelling that we were trash, we could fight them off with rocks. But if the child-welfare man got it into his head that we were an unfit family, we'd have no way to drive him off. He'd launch an investigation and end up sending me and Brian and Lori and Maureen off to live with different families, even though we all got good grades and knew Morse code. I couldn't let that happen. No way was I going to lose Brian and Lori and Maureen.

I wished we could do the skedaddle. For a long time Brian, Lori, and I had assumed we would leave Welch sooner or later. Every couple of months we'd ask Dad if we were going to move on. He'd sometimes talk about Australia or Alaska, but he never took any action, and when we asked Mom, she'd start singing some song about how her get up and go had got up and went. Maybe coming back to Welch had killed the idea Dad used to have of himself as a man going places. The truth was, we were stuck.

When Mom got home, I gave her the man's card and told her about his visit. I was still in a lather. I said that since neither she nor Dad could be bothered to work, and since she refused to leave Dad, the government was going to do the job of splitting up the family for her.

I expected Mom to come back with one of her choice remarks, but she listened to my tirade in silence. Then she said she needed to consider her options. She sat down at her easel. She had run out of canvases and had begun painting on plywood, so she picked up a piece of wood, got out her palette, squeezed some paints onto it, and selected a brush.

"What are you doing?" I asked.

"I'm thinking," she said.

Mom worked quickly, automatically, as if she knew exactly what it was she wanted to paint. A figure took shape in the middle of the board. It was a woman from the waist up, with her arms raised. Blue concentric circles appeared around the waist. The blue was water. Mom was painting a picture of a woman drowning in a stormy lake. When she was finished, she sat for a long time in silence, staring at the picture.

"So what are we going to do?" I finally asked.

"Jeannette, you're so focused it's scary."

"You didn't answer my question," I said.

"I'll get a job, Jeannette," she snapped. She threw her paintbrush into the jar that held her turpentine and sat there looking at the drowning woman.

QUALIFIED TEACHERS were so scarce in McDowell County that two of the teachers I'd have at Welch High School had never been to college. Mom was able to land a job by the end of the week. We spent those days frantically trying to clean the house in anticipation of the return of the child-welfare man. It was a hopeless task, given all the stacks of Mom's junk and the hole in the ceiling and the disgusting yellow bucket in the kitchen. However, for some reason he never came back.

Mom's job was teaching remedial reading in an elementary school in Davy, a coal-mining camp twelve miles north of Welch. Since we still had no car, the school's principal arranged for Mom to get a ride with another teacher, Lucy Jo Rose, who had just graduated from Bluefield State College and was so fat she could barely squeeze behind the steering wheel of her brown Dodge Dart. Lucy Jo, whom the principal had more or less ordered to perform this service, took an instant dislike to Mom. She refused to say much during the trip, instead playing Barbara Mandrell tapes and smoking filter-tip Kools the entire time. As soon as Mom got out of the car, Lucy Jo made a big show of spraying Mom's seat with Lysol. Mom, for her part, felt that Lucy Jo was woefully uninformed. When Mom mentioned Jackson Pollock once, Lucy Jo said that she had Polish blood and therefore did not appreciate Mom using derogatory names for Polish people.

Mom had the same problems she'd had in Battle Mountain with organizing her paperwork and disciplining her students. At least one morning a week, she'd throw a tantrum and refuse to go to work, and Lori, Brian, and I would have to get her collected and down to the street where Lucy Jo waited with a scowl, blue smoke chugging up out of the Dart's rusted-through tailpipe.

But at least we had money. While I'd been bringing in a little extra cash babysitting, Brian was cutting other people's weeds, and Lori had a paper route, it didn't add up to much. Now Mom got paid about seven hundred dollars a month, and the first time I saw her gray-green paycheck, with its detachable stub and automated signatures, I thought our troubles were over. On paydays, Mom took us kids down to the big bank across from the courthouse to cash the check. After the cashier gave her the money, Mom went into a corner of the bank and stuffed it into a sock she'd safety-pinned to her bra. Then we all scurried around to the power company and the water authority and the landlord, paying off our bills with tens and twenties. The clerks averted their eyes as Mom fished the sock out of her bra, explaining to everyone within earshot that this was her way of making sure she was never pickpocketed.

Mom also bought some electric heaters and a refrigerator on layaway, and we'd go to the appliance store and put down a few dollars every month, figuring they'd be ours by wintertime. Mom always had at least one "extravagance" on layaway, something we really didn't need—a tasseled silk throw or a cut crystal vase—because she said the surest way to feel rich was to invest in quality nonessentials. After that, we'd go to the grocery store at the bottom of the hill and stock up on staples such as beans and rice, powdered milk, and canned goods. Mom always bought the dented cans, even if they weren't marked down, because she said they needed to be loved, too.

At home, we'd empty Mom's purse onto the sofa bed and count the remaining money. There'd be hundreds of dollars, more than enough to cover our expenses until the end of the month, I thought. But month after month, the money would disappear before the next paycheck arrived, and once more I'd find myself rooting in the garbage at school for food.

Toward the end of one month that fall, Mom announced that we had only one dollar for dinner. That was enough to buy one gallon of Neapolitan ice cream, which she said was not only delicious but had lots of calcium and would be good for our bones. We brought the ice cream home, and Brian pulled apart the carton and cut the block into five even slices. I called dibs on first choice. Mom told us to savor it because we had no money for dinner the next night.

"Mom, what happened to it all?" I asked as we ate our ice-cream slices.

"Gone, gone, gone!" she said. "It's all gone."

"But where?" Lori asked.

"I've got a houseful of kids and a husband who soaks up booze like a sponge," Mom said. "Making ends meet is harder than you think."

It couldn't be that hard, I thought. Other moms did it. I tried quizzing her. Was she spending the money on herself? Was she giving it to Dad? Was Dad stealing it? Or did we go through it quickly? I couldn't get an answer. "Give us the money," I said. "We'll work out a budget and stick to it."

"Easy for you to say," Mom replied.

Lori and I did work out a budget, and we included a generous allowance for Mom to cover luxuries such as extra-large Hershey bars and cut crystal vases. If we kept to our budget, we believed, we could afford new clothes and shoes and coats, and buy a ton of coal at the cheaper off-season price. Eventually, we could install insulation, run a water pipe into the house, and maybe even add a water heater. But Mom never turned the money over to us. So even though she had a steady job, we were living pretty much like we had before.

I'D STARTED SEVENTH grade that fall, which meant attending Welch High School. It was a big school, near the top of a hill looking down on the town, with a steep road leading up. Kids were bused in from way up in the hollows and from coal camps such as Davy and Hemphill that were too small to have their own high school. Some of the kids looked as poor as me, with home-cut hair and holes in the toes of their shoes. I found it a lot easier to fit in than at Welch Elementary.

Dinitia Hewitt was there, too. That summer morning I'd spent swimming with Dinitia at the public pool was the happiest time I'd had in Welch, but she never invited me back, and even though it was a public pool, I didn't feel I could go to the free swim unless I had an invitation from her. I saw her again only when school started, and neither of us ever mentioned that day at the pool. I guess we both knew that, given the way people in Welch thought about mixing, it would be too weird for us to try to be close friends. During lunch, Dinitia hung out with the other black kids, but we had a study hall together and passed notes to each other there.

By the time she got to Welch High, Dinitia had changed. The spark had gone out of her. She started drinking malt ale during school. She'd fill a soda can with Mad Dog 20/20 and carry it right into class. I tried to find out what was wrong, but all I could pry from her was that her mother's new boyfriend had moved in with them, and the fit was a little tight.

One day just before Christmas, Dinitia passed me a note in study hall asking for girls' names that began with D. I wrote down as many as I could think of—Diane, Donna, Dora, Dreama, Diandra—and then wrote, *Why?* She passed a note back saying, *I think I'm pregnant.*

After Christmas, Dinitia did not return to school. When a month had gone by, I walked around the mountain to her house and knocked on the door. A man opened it and stared at me. He had skin like an iron skillet and nicotine-yellow eyes. He left the storm door shut, so I had to speak through the screen.

"Is Dinitia home?" I asked.

"Why you want to know?"

"I want to see her."

"She don't want to see you," he said and shut the door.

I saw Dinitia around town once or twice after that, and we waved but never spoke again. Later, we all learned she'd been arrested for stabbing her mother's boyfriend to death.

The other girls talked endlessly among themselves about who still had their cherry and how far they would let their boyfriend go. The world seemed divided into girls with boyfriends and girls without them. It was the distinction that mattered the most, practically the only one that did matter. But I knew that boys were dangerous. They'd say they loved you, but they were always after something.

Even though I didn't trust boys, I sure did wish one would show some interest in me. Kenny Hall, the old guy down the street who was still pining away for me, didn't count. If any boy was interested in me, I wondered if I'd have the wherewithal to tell him, when he tried to go too far, that I was not that kind of girl. But the truth was, I didn't need to worry much about fending off advances, seeing how—as Ernie Goad told me on every available occasion—I was pork-chop ugly. And by that he meant so ugly that if I wanted a dog to play with me, I'd have to tie a pork chop around my neck.

I had what Mom called distinctive looks. That was one way of putting it. I was nearly six feet tall, pale as a frog's underbelly, and had bright red hair. My elbows were like flying wedges and my knees like tea saucers. But my most prominent feature—my worst—was my teeth. They weren't rotten or crooked. In fact, they were big, healthy things. But they stuck straight out. The top row thrust forward so enthusiastically that I had trouble closing my mouth completely, and I was always stretching my upper lip to try to cover them. When I laughed, I put my hand over my mouth.

Lori told me I had an exaggerated view of how bad my teeth looked. "They're just a little bucked," she'd say. "They have a certain Pippi Longstockingish charm." Mom told me my overbite gave my face character. Brian said they'd come in handy if I ever needed to eat an apple through the knothole in a fence.

What I needed, I knew, was braces. Every time I looked in the mirror, I longed for what the other kids called a barbed-wire mouth. Mom and Dad had no money for braces, of course—none of us kids had ever even been to the dentist—but since I'd been babysitting and doing other kids' homework for cash, I resolved to save up until I could afford braces myself. I had no idea how much they cost, so I approached the only girl in my class who wore braces and, after complimenting her orthodontia, casually asked how much it had set her folks back. When she said twelve hundred dollars, I almost fell over. I was getting a dollar an hour to babysit. I usually worked five or six hours a week, which meant that if I saved every penny I earned, it would take about four years to raise the money.

I decided to make my own braces.

I went to the library and asked for a book on orthodontia. The librarian looked at me kind of funny and said she didn't have one, so I realized I'd have to figure things out as I went along. The process involved some experimentation and several false starts. At first I simply used a rubber band. Before going to bed, I would stretch it all the way around the entire set of my upper teeth. The rubber band was small but thick and had a good, tight fit. But it pressed down uncomfortably on my tongue, and sometimes it would pop off during the night and I'd wake up choking on it. Usually, however, it stayed on all night, and in the morning my gums would be sore from the pressure on my teeth.

That seemed like a promising sign, but I began to worry that instead of pushing my front teeth in, the rubber band might be pulling my back teeth forward. So I got some larger rubber bands and wore them around my whole head, pressing against my front teeth. The problem with this technique was that the rubber bands were tight—they had to be, to work—so I'd wake up with headaches and deep red marks where the rubber bands had dug into the sides of my face.

I needed more advanced technology. I bent a metal coat hanger into a horseshoe shape to fit the back of my head. Then I curled the two ends outward, so when the coat hanger was around my head, the ends angled away from my face and formed hooks to hold the rubber band in place. When I tried it on, the coat hanger dug into the back of my skull, so I used a Kotex sanitary napkin for padding.

The contraption worked perfectly, except that I had to sleep flat on my back, which I always had trouble doing, especially when it was cold: I liked to snuggle down into the blankets. Also, the rubber bands still popped off in the middle of the night. Another drawback was that the device took a lot of time to put on properly. I'd wait until it was dark so no one else would see it.

One night I was lying in my bunk wearing my elaborate coat-hanger braces when the bedroom door opened. I could make out a dim figure in the darkness. "Who's there?" I called out, but because I had my braces on, it came out sounding like "Phoof der?"

"It's your old man," Dad answered. "What's with the mumbling?" He came over to my bunk, held up his Zippo, and flicked it. A flame shot up. "What the Sam Hill's that on your head?"

"My brafef," I said.

"Your what?"

I took off the contraption and explained to Dad that, because my front teeth stuck out so badly, I needed braces, but they cost twelve hundred dollars, so I had made my own.

"Put them back on," Dad said. He studied my handiwork intently, then nodded. "Those braces are a goddamn feat of engineering genius," he said. "You take after your old man."

He took my chin and pulled my mouth open. "And I think they're by God working."

THAT YEAR I STARTED working for the school newspaper, *The Maroon Wave*. I wanted to join some club or group or organization where I could feel I belonged, where people wouldn't move away if I sat down next to them. I was a good runner, and I thought of going out for the track team, but you had to pay for your uniform, and Mom said we couldn't afford it. You didn't have to buy a uniform or a musical instrument or pay any dues to work on the *Wave*.

Miss Jeanette Bivens, one of the high school English teachers, was the *Wave*'s faculty adviser. She was a quiet, precise woman who had been at Welch High School so long that she had also been Dad's English teacher. She was the first person in his life, he once told me, who'd showed any faith in him. She thought he was a talented writer and had encouraged him to submit a twenty-four-line poem called "Summer Storm" to a statewide poetry competition. When it won first prize, one of Dad's other teachers wondered aloud if the son of two lowlife alcoholics like Ted and Erma Walls could have written it himself. Dad was so insulted that he walked out of school. It was Miss Bivens who convinced him to return and earn his diploma, telling him he had what it took to be somebody. Dad had named me after her; Mom suggested adding the second N to make it more elegant and French.

Miss Bivens told me that as far as she could remember, I was the only seventh-grader who'd ever worked for the *Wave*. I started out as a proofreader. On winter evenings, instead of huddling around the stove at 93 Little Hobart Street, I'd go down to the warm, dry offices of *The Welch Daily News,* where *The Maroon Wave* was typeset, laid out, and printed. I loved the newsroom's purposeful atmosphere. Teletype machines clattered against the wall as spools of paper carrying news from around the world piled up on the floor. Banks of fluorescent lights hung down eighteen inches above the slanted, glass-topped desks where men wearing green eyeshades conferred over stacks of copy and photographs.

I'd take the *Wave* galleys and sit at one of the desks, my back firm, a pencil behind my ear, studying the pages for typos. The years I'd spent helping Mom check spelling on her students' homework had given me lots of practice for this line of work. I'd make corrections with a light blue felt marker that couldn't be picked up by the camera that photographed the pages for printing. The typesetters would retype the lines I'd corrected and print them out. I'd run the corrected lines through the hot-wax machine that made the back side sticky, then cut out the lines with an X-Acto knife and fit them over the original lines.

I tried to remain inconspicuous in the newsroom, but one of the typesetters, a crabbed, chain-smoking woman who always wore a hair-net, took a dislike to me. She thought I was dirty. When I walked by, she'd turn to the other typesetters and say loudly, "Y'all smell something funny?" Just like Lucy Jo Rose had done to Mom, she took to spraying disinfectant and air freshener in my general direction. Then she complained to the editor, Mr. Muckenfuss, that I might have head lice and could infect the entire staff. Mr. Muckenfuss conferred with Miss Bivens, and she told me that as long as I kept clean, she'd fight for me. That was when I started going back to Grandpa and Uncle Stanley's apartment for a weekly bath, though when I was there, I made sure to give Uncle Stanley a wide berth.

Whenever I was at the *Daily News,* I watched the editors and reporters at work in the newsroom. They kept a police scanner on all the time, and when an accident or fire or crime was called in, an editor would send a reporter to find out what had happened. He'd come back a couple of hours later and type up a story, and it would appear in the next day's paper. This appealed to me mightily. Until then, when I thought of writers, what first came to mind was Mom, hunched over her typewriter, clattering away on her novels and plays and philosophies of life and occasionally receiving a personalized rejection letter. But a newspaper reporter, instead of holing up in isolation, was in touch with the rest of the world. What the reporter wrote influenced what people thought about and talked about the next day; he knew what was really going on. I decided I wanted to be one of the people who knew what was really going on.

When my work was done, I read the stories on the wire services. Because we never subscribed to newspapers or magazines, I'd never known what was going on in the world, except for the skewed version of events we got from Mom and Dad—one in which every politician was a crook, every cop was a thug, and every criminal had been framed. I began to feel like I was getting the whole story for the first time, that I was being handed the missing pieces to the puzzle, and the world was making a little more sense.

AT TIMES I FELT LIKE I was failing Maureen, like I wasn't keeping my promise that I'd protect her—the promise I'd made to her when I held her on the way home from the hospital after she'd been born. I couldn't get her what she needed most—hot baths, a warm bed, steaming bowls of Cream of Wheat before school in the morning—but I tried to do little things. When she turned seven that year, I told Brian and Lori that she needed a special birthday celebration. We knew Mom and Dad wouldn't get her presents, so we saved for months, went to the Dollar General Store, and bought her a toy set of kitchen appliances that were pretty realistic: The agitator in the washing machine twisted around, and the refrigerator had metal shelves inside. We figured when she was playing, she could at least pretend to have clean clothes and regular meals.

"Tell me again about California," Maureen said after she opened the presents. Although she had been born there, she couldn't remember it. She always loved hearing our stories about life in the California desert, so we told them to her again, about how the sun shone all the time and it was so warm that we ran around barefoot even in the dead of winter, about how we ate lettuce in the farm fields and picked carloads of green grapes and slept on blankets under the stars. We told her that she was blond because she'd been born in a state where so much gold had been mined, and she had blue eyes the color of the ocean that washed onto California's beaches. "That's where I'm going to live when I grow up," Maureen said.

Although she longed for California, the magical place of light and warmth, she seemed happier than the rest of us kids in Welch. She was a storybook-beautiful girl, with long blond hair and startling blue eyes. She spent so much time with the families of her friends that she often didn't seem like a member of our family. A lot of her friends were Pentecostals whose parents held that Mom and Dad were disgracefully irresponsible and took it upon themselves to save Maureen's soul. They took her up like a surrogate daughter and brought her with them to revival meetings and to snake-handling services over in Jolo.

Under their influence, Maureen developed a powerful religious streak. She got baptized more than once and was all the time coming home proclaiming that she'd been born again. Once she insisted that the devil had taken the form of a hoop snake with its tail in its mouth, and had rolled after her down the mountain, hissing that it would claim her soul. Brian told Mom we needed to keep Maureen away from those nutty Pentecostals, but Mom said we all came to religion in our individual ways and we each needed to respect the religious practices of others, seeing as it was up to every human being to find his or her own way to heaven.

Mom could be as wise as a philosopher, but her moods were getting on my nerves. At times she'd be happy for days on end, announcing that she had decided to think only positive thoughts, because if you think positive thoughts, then positive things will happen to you. But the positive thoughts would give way to negative thoughts, and the negative thoughts seemed to swoop into her mind the way a big flock of black crows takes over the landscape, sitting thick in the trees and on the fence rails and lawns, staring at you in ominous silence. When that happened, Mom would refuse to get out of bed, even when Lucy Jo showed up to drive her to school, honking impatiently.

One morning toward the end of the school year, Mom had a complete meltdown. She was supposed to write up evaluations of her students' progress, but she'd spent every free minute painting, and now the deadline was on her and the evaluations were unwritten. The remedial reading program was going to lose its funding, and the principal would be either furious or just plain disgusted. Mom couldn't bear to face the woman. Lucy Jo, who'd been waiting for Mom in the Dart, drove off without her, and Mom lay wrapped up in blankets on the sofa bed, sobbing about how much she hated her life.

Dad wasn't there, and neither was Maureen. Brian, typically, started doing an impersonation of Mom carrying on and sobbing, but no one was laughing, so he picked up his books and walked out of the house. Lori sat next to Mom on the bed, trying to console her. I just stood in the doorway with my arms crossed, staring at her.

It was hard for me to believe that this woman with her head under the blankets, feeling sorry for herself and boohooing like a five-year-old, was my mother. Mom was thirty-eight, not young but not old, either. In twenty-five years, I told myself, I'd be as old as she was now. I had no idea what my life would be like then, but as I gathered up my schoolbooks and walked out the door, I swore to myself that it would never be like Mom's, that I would not be crying my eyes out in an unheated shack in some godforsaken holler.

I walked down Little Hobart Street. It had rained the night before, and the only sound was the gurgle of the runoff pouring down through the eroded gullies on the hillside. Thin streams of muddy water flowed across the road, seeping into my shoes and soaking my socks. The sole of my right shoe had come loose and flapped with each step.

Lori caught up with me, and we walked for a while in silence. "Poor Mom," Lori finally said. "She's got it tough."

"No tougher than the rest of us," I said.

"Yes, she does," Lori said. "She's the one who's married to Dad."

"That was her choice," I said. "She needs to be firmer, lay down the law for Dad instead of getting hysterical all the time. What Dad needs is a strong woman."

"A caryatid wouldn't be strong enough for Dad."

"What's that?"

"Pillars shaped like women," Lori said. "The ones holding up those Greek temples with their heads. I was looking at a picture of some the other day, thinking, Those women have the second toughest job in the world."

I disagreed with Lori. I thought a strong woman would be able to manage Dad. What he needed was someone who was focused and determined, someone who would set ultimatums and stick to them. I figured I was strong enough to keep Dad in line. When Mom told me I was so focused it was scary, I know she didn't mean it as a compliment, but I took it that way.

My chance to prove that Dad could be managed came that summer, once school was out. Mom had to spend eight weeks up in Charleston, taking college courses to renew her teaching certificate. Or so she said. I wondered if she was looking for a way to get away from us all for a while. Lori, because of her good grades and art portfolio, had been accepted into a government-sponsored summer camp for students with special aptitudes. That left me, at thirteen, the head of the household.

Before Mom left, she gave me two hundred dollars. That was plenty, she said, to buy food for Brian and Maureen and me for two months and pay the water and electricity bills. I did the math. It came out to twenty-five dollars a week, or a little over three-fifty a day. I worked up a budget and calculated that we could indeed squeak by if I made extra money babysitting.

For the first week, everything went according to plan. I bought food and made meals for Brian, Maureen, and me. It had been almost a year since the welfare man had scared us into cleaning the house, and it was once again an unholy mess. Mom would have had a fit if I had thrown anything out, but I spent hours straightening up and trying to organize the huge stacks of junk.

Dad usually stayed out at night until we were in bed, and he would still be asleep when we got up and left in the morning. But one afternoon about a week after Mom had gone to Charleston, he caught me alone in the house.

"Hon, I need some money," he said.

"For what?"

"Beer and cigarettes."

"I've got sort of a tight budget, Dad."

"I don't need much. Just five dollars."

That was two days' worth of food. A half gallon of milk, a loaf of bread, a dozen eggs, two cans of jack mackerel, a small bag of apples, and some popcorn. And Dad wasn't even doing me the honor of pretending he needed the money for something useful. He also didn't argue or wheedle or cajole or ratchet the charm way up. He simply waited for me to fork over the cash, as if he knew I didn't have it in me to say no. And I didn't. I took out my green plastic change purse and pulled out a crumpled five and passed it over slowly.

"You're a doll," Dad said and gave me a kiss.

I pulled my head back. Giving him that money pissed me off. I was mad at myself but even madder at Dad. He knew I had a soft spot for him the way no one else in the family did, and he was taking advantage of it.

I felt used. The girls at school always talked about how this or that guy was a user and how such and such a girl got used, and now I understood, from deep inside, the meaning of that word.

When Dad asked me for another five bucks a few days later, I gave it to him. It made me feel sick thinking I was now ten dollars off budget. In a few more days, he asked for twenty.

"Twenty dollars?" I couldn't believe Dad was pushing me this far. "Why twenty?"

"Goddammit, since when do I have to explain myself to my children?" Dad asked. In the next breath, he told me that he had borrowed a friend's car and needed to buy gas so he could drive to Gary for a business meeting. "I need money to make money. I'll pay you back." He looked at me, defying me to disbelieve him.

"I've got bills piling up," I said. I heard my voice growing shrill, but I couldn't control it. "I've got kids to feed."

"Don't you worry about food and bills," Dad said. "That's for me to worry about. Okay?"

I put my hand in my pocket. I didn't know if I was reaching for my money or trying to protect it.

"Have I ever let you down?" Dad asked.

I'd heard that question at least two hundred times, and I'd always answered it the way I knew he wanted me to, because I thought it was my faith in Dad that had kept him going all those years. I was about to tell him the truth for the first time, about to let him know that he'd let us all down plenty, but then I stopped. I couldn't do it. Dad, meanwhile, was saying he was not asking me for the money; he was telling me to give it to him. He needed it. Did I think he was a liar when he said he'd get it back to me?

I gave him the twenty dollars.

That Saturday, Dad told me that to pay me back, he had to earn the money first. He wanted me to accompany him on a business trip. He said I needed to wear something nice. He went through my dresses hanging from the pipe in the bedroom and picked out one with blue flowers that buttoned up the front. He had borrowed a car, an old pea-green Plymouth with a broken passenger-side window, and we drove through the mountains to a nearby town, stopping at a roadside bar.

The place was dark and as hazy as a battlefield from the cigarette smoke. Neon signs for Pabst Blue Ribbon and Old Milwaukee glowed on the walls. Gaunt men with creased cheeks and women with dark red lipstick sat along the bar. A couple of guys wearing steel-toed boots played pool.

Dad and I took seats at the bar. Dad ordered Buds for himself and me, even though I told him I wanted a Sprite. After a while, he got up to play pool, and no sooner had he left his stool than a man came over and sat on it. He had a black mustache that curved around the sides of his mouth and coal grime under his fingernails. He poured salt in his beer, which Dad said some guys did because they liked to make extra foam.

"Name's Robbie," he said. "That your man there?" He gestured toward Dad.

"I'm his daughter," I said.

He took a lick of foam and started asking me about myself, leaning in close as he talked. "How old are you, girl?"

"How old do you think?" I asked.

"About seventeen."

I smiled, putting my hand over my teeth.

"Know how to dance?" he asked. I shook my head. "Sure you do," he said and pulled me off the stool. I looked over at Dad, who grinned and waved.

On the jukebox, Kitty Wells was singing about married men and honky-tonk angels. Robbie held me close, with his hand on the small of my back. We danced to a second song, and when we sat down again on the stools facing the pool table, our backs against the bar, he slid his arm behind me. That arm made me tense but not entirely unhappy. No one had flirted with me since Billy Deel, unless you counted Kenny Hall.

Still, I knew what Robbie was after. I was going to tell him I wasn't that sort of girl, but then I thought he would say I was getting ahead of myself. After all, the only thing he'd done was dance me slow and put his arm around me. I caught Dad's eye. I expected him to come barreling across the room and whock Robbie with a pool cue for getting fresh with his daughter. Instead, he hollered to Robbie, "Do something worthwhile with those damned hands of yours. Get over here and play me a game of pool."

They ordered whiskeys and chalked their cues. Dad held back at first and lost some money to Robbie, then started upping the stakes and beating him. After every game, Robbie wanted to dance with me again. It went on that way for a couple of hours, with Robbie getting sloppy drunk, losing to Dad, and groping me when we danced or sat at the bar between games. All Dad said to me was "Keep your legs crossed, honey, and keep 'em crossed tight."

After Dad had taken him for about eighty bucks, Robbie started muttering angrily to himself. He snapped down the cue chalk, sending up a puff of blue powder, and missed a final shot. He flung his cue on the table and announced he'd had enough, then sat down next to me. His eyes were bleary. He kept saying he couldn't believe that old fart had beat him out of eighty bucks, as if he couldn't decide whether he was pissed off or impressed.

Then he told me he lived in an apartment over the bar. He had a Roy Acuff record that wasn't on the jukebox, and he wanted us to go upstairs and listen to it. If all he wanted to do was dance some more and maybe kiss a little, I could handle that. But I had the feeling he thought he was entitled to something in return for losing so much money.

"I'm not sure," I said.

"Aw, come on," he said and shouted at Dad, "I'm going to take your girl upstairs."

"Sure," Dad said. "Just don't do anything I wouldn't do." He pointed his pool cue at me. "Holler if you need me," he said and winked at me as if to say he knew I could take care of myself, that this was just a part of my job.

So, with Dad's blessing, I went upstairs. Inside the apartment, we pushed through a curtain made from strands of beer-can pull tabs linked together. Two men sat on a couch watching wrestling on television. When they saw me, they grinned wolfishly at Robbie, who put on the Roy Acuff record without turning down the television. He pressed me to him and started dancing again, but I knew this was not going in a direction I wanted, and I resisted him. His hands dropped down. He squeezed my bottom, pushed me onto the bed, and began kissing me. "All right!" one friend said, and the other yelled, "Get it on!"

"I'm not that kind of girl," I said, but he ignored me. When I tried rolling away, he pinned back my arms. Dad had said to holler if I needed him, but I didn't want to scream. I was so angry at Dad that I couldn't bear the idea of him rescuing me. Robbie, meanwhile, was saying something about me being too bony to screw.

"Yeah, most guys don't like me," I said. "Besides being skinny, I got these scars."

"Oh, sure," he said. But he paused.

I rolled off the bed, quickly unbuttoned my dress at the waist, and pulled it open to show him the scar on my right side. For all he knew, my entire torso was one giant mass of scar tissue. Robbie looked uncertainly at his friends. It was like seeing a gap in a fence.

"I think I hear Dad calling," I said, then made for the door.

In the car, Dad took out the money he'd won and counted off forty dollars, which he passed to me.

"We make a good team," he said.

I felt like throwing the money at him, but we kids needed it, so I put the bills in my purse. We hadn't scammed Robbie, but we'd worked him in a way that felt downright sleazy, and I'd ended up in a tight spot. If Robbie had been set up by Dad, so had I.

"You upset about something, Mountain Goat?"

For a moment I considered not telling Dad. I was afraid there'd be bloodshed, since he was always going on about how he'd kill anyone who laid a finger on me. Then I decided I wanted to see the guy pummeled. "Dad, that creep attacked me when we were upstairs."

"I'm sure he just pawed you some," Dad said as we pulled out of the parking lot. "I knew you could handle yourself."

The road back to Welch was dark and empty. The wind whistled through the broken window on my side of the Plymouth. Dad lit a cigarette. "It was like that time I threw you into the sulfur spring to teach you to swim," he said. "You might have been convinced you were going to drown, but I knew you'd do just fine."

THE NEXT EVENING Dad disappeared. After a couple of days, he wanted me to go out with him again to some bar, but I said no. Dad got ticked off and said that if I wasn't going to team up with him, the least I could do was stake him some pool-shooting money. I found myself forking over a twenty, and then another in a few days.

Mom had told me to expect a check in early July for the lease on her Texas land. She also warned me that Dad would try to get his hands on it. Dad actually waited at the foot of the hill for the mailman and took it from him on the day it arrived, but when the mailman told me what had happened, I ran down Little Hobart Street and caught Dad before he got into town. I told him Mom had wanted me to hide the check until she returned. "Let's hide it together," Dad said and suggested we stash it in the 1933 *World Book Encyclopedia* Mom got free from the library—under "currency."

The next day when I went to rehide the check, it was gone. Dad swore he had no idea what happened to it. I knew he was lying, but I also knew if I accused him, he'd deny it and there'd be a loud yelling match that wouldn't do me any good. For the first time, I had a clear idea of what Mom was up against. Being a strong woman was harder than I had thought. Mom still had more than a month in Charleston; we were about to run out of grocery money; and my babysitting income wasn't making up the difference.

I had seen a help-wanted sign in the window of a jewelry store on McDowell Street called Becker's Jewel Box. I put on a lot of makeup, my best dress—it was purple, with tiny white dots and a sash that tied in the back—and a pair of Mom's high heels, since we wore the same size. Then I walked around the mountain to apply for the job.

I pushed open the door, jangling the bells hanging overhead. Becker's Jewel Box was a fancy store, the kind of place I never had occasion to go into, with a humming air conditioner and buzzing fluorescent lights. Locked glass display cases held rings and necklaces and brooches, and a few guitars and banjos hung on the pine-board-paneled walls to diversify the merchandise. Mr. Becker was leaning on the counter with his fingers interlocked. He had a stomach so big that his thin black belt reminded me of the equator circling the globe.

I was afraid that Mr. Becker wouldn't give me the job if he knew I was only thirteen, so I told him I was seventeen. He hired me on the spot for forty dollars a week, in cash. I was thrilled. It was my first real job. Babysitting and tutoring and doing other kids' homework and mowing lawns and redeeming bottles and selling scrap metal didn't count. Forty dollars a week was serious money.

I liked the work. People buying jewelry were always happy, and even though Welch was a poor town, Becker's Jewel Box had plenty of customers: older miners buying their wives a mother's pin, a brooch with a birthstone for each of her children; teenage couples shopping for engagement rings, the girl giggling with excitement, the boy acting proud and manly.

During the slow spells, Mr. Becker and I watched the Watergate hearings on a little black-and-white TV. Mr. Becker was captivated by John Dean's wife, Maureen, who sat behind her husband when he was testifying and wore elegant clothes and pulled her blond hair back in a tight bun. "Hot damn, that's one classy broad," Mr. Becker would say. Sometimes, after watching Maureen Dean, Mr. Becker got so randy that he came behind me while I was cleaning the display case and rubbed up against my backside. I'd pull his hands off and walk away without saying a word, and that horndog would return to the television as if nothing had happened.

When Mr. Becker went across the street to the Mountaineer Diner for lunch, he always took the key to the display case that held the diamond rings. If customers came in wanting to look at the rings, I had to run across the street to get him. Once he forgot to take the key, and when he returned, he made a big point of counting the rings in front of me. It was his way of letting me know he didn't trust me in the slightest. One day after Mr. Becker had come back from lunch and ostentatiously checked the display cases, I was so furious that I looked around to see if there was anything in the entire darn store worth stealing. Necklaces, brooches, banjos—none of them did anything for me. And then the watch display caught my eye.

I had always wanted a watch. Unlike diamonds, watches were practical. They were for people on the run, people with appointments to keep and schedules to meet. That was the kind of person I wanted to be. Dozens of watches ticked away in the counter behind the cash register. There was one in particular that made me ache. It had four different-colored bands—black, brown, blue, and white—so you could change your watchband to match your outfit. It had a price tag of $29.95, ten dollars short of a week's salary. But if I wanted, it could be mine in an instant, and for free. The more I thought about that watch, the more it called to me.

One day the woman who worked at the store Mr. Becker owned in War stopped by. Mr. Becker wanted her to give me some beauty tips. While she was showing me her different makeup applicators, the woman, who had stiff platinum hair and eyelashes tarred in mascara, told me I must be earning a truckload in commissions. When I asked her what she meant, she said that in addition to her forty-dollar-a-week salary, she made 10 percent on every sale. Her commissions were sometimes double her salary. "Hell, welfare'll get you more than forty bucks a week," she said. "If you're not getting commissions, Becker's stiffing you."

When I asked Mr. Becker about commissions, he said they were for salespeople and I was just an assistant. The next day, when Mr. Becker went off to the Mountaineer, I opened the display case and took out the four-band watch. I slipped it into my handbag and rearranged the remaining watches to cover the gap. I had made plenty of sales on my own when Mr. Becker was busy. Since he hadn't paid me any commissions, I was only taking what I was owed.

When Mr. Becker came back from lunch, he studied the diamond-ring display like he always did, but he didn't even glance at the watches. Walking home that evening with the watch hidden in my purse, I felt light and giddy. After dinner, I climbed into my bunk bed, where no one could see me, and tried on the watch with each of the bands, gesturing the way I figured rich people did.

Wearing the watch to work was out of the question, of course. I also realized that I could run into Mr. Becker in town at any time, so I decided that until school started, I'd put the watch on only at home. Then I began to wonder how I'd explain the watch to Brian and Lori and Mom and Dad. I also worried that Mr. Becker might see something thieflike in my expression. Sooner or later, he'd discover the missing watch and would question me, and I'd have to lie convincingly, which I wasn't very good at. If I wasn't convincing, I'd be sent off to a reform school with people like Billy Deel, and Mr. Becker would have the satisfaction of knowing he'd been right all along not to trust me.

I wasn't about to give him that satisfaction. The next morning I took the watch out of the wooden box where I kept my geode, put it in my purse, and brought it back to the store. All morning I nervously waited for Mr. Becker to leave for lunch. When he was finally gone, I opened the display case, slipped the watch inside, and rearranged the other watches around it. I moved fast. The week before, I had stolen the watch without breaking a sweat. But now I was terrified that someone would catch me putting it back.

IN LATE AUGUST, I was washing clothes in the tin pan in the living room when I heard someone coming up the stairs singing. It was Lori. She burst into the living room, duffel bag over her shoulder, laughing and belting out one of those goofy summer-camp songs kids sing at night around the fire. I'd never heard Lori cut loose like this before. She positively glowed as she told me about the hot meals and the hot showers and all the friends she'd made. She'd even had a boyfriend who kissed her. "Everyone assumed I was a normal person," she said. "It was weird." Then she told me that it had occurred to her that if she got out of Welch, and away from the family, she might have a shot at a happy life. From then on, she began looking forward to the day she'd leave Little Hobart Street and be on her own.

A few days later, Mom came home. She seemed different, too. She had lived in a dorm on the university campus, without four kids to take care of, and she had loved it. She'd attended lectures and she'd painted. She'd read stacks of self-help books, and they had made her realize that she'd been living her life for other people. She intended to quit her teaching job and devote herself to her art. "It's time I did something for myself," she said. "It's time I started living my life for me."

"Mom, you spent the whole summer renewing your certificate."

"If I hadn't done that, I never would have had this breakthrough."

"You can't quit your job," I said. "We need the money."

"Why do I always have to be the one who earns the money?" Mom asked. "You have a job. You can earn money. Lori can earn money, too. I've got more important things to do."

I thought Mom was having another tantrum. I assumed that come opening day, she'd be off in Lucy Jo's Dart to Davy Elementary, even if we had to cajole her. But on that first day of school, Mom refused to get out of bed. Lori, Brian, and I pulled back the covers and tried to drag her out, but she wouldn't budge.

I told her she had responsibilities. I told her child welfare might come down on us again if she wasn't working. She folded her arms across her chest and stared us down. "I'm not going to school," she said.

"Why not?" I asked.

"I'm sick."

"What's wrong?" I asked.

"My mucus is yellow," Mom said.

"If everyone who had yellow mucus stayed home, the schools would be pretty empty," I told her.

Mom's head snapped up. "You can't talk to me like that," she said. "I'm your mother."

"If you want to be treated like a mother," I said, "you should act like one."

Mom rarely got angry. She was usually either singing or crying, but now her face twisted up with fury. We both knew I had crossed a line, but I didn't care. I'd also changed over the summer.

"How dare you?" she shouted. "You're in trouble now—big trouble. I'm telling your dad. Just you wait until he comes home."

Mom's threat didn't worry me. The way I saw it, Dad owed me. I'd looked after his kids all summer, I'd kept him in beer and cigarette money, and I'd helped him fleece that miner Robbie. I figured I had Dad in my back pocket.

When I got home from school that afternoon, Mom was still curled up on the sofa bed, a small pile of paperbacks next to her. Dad was sitting at the drafting table, rolling a cigarette. He beckoned to me to follow him into the kitchen. Mom watched us go.

Dad closed the door and looked at me gravely. "Your mother claims you back-talked her."

"Yes," I said. "It's true."

"Yes, sir," he corrected me, but I didn't say anything.

"I'm disappointed in you," he went on. "You know damn good and well that you are to respect your parents."

"Dad, Mom's not sick, she's playing hooky," I said. "She has to take her obligations more seriously. She has to grow up a little."

"Who do you think you are?" he asked. "She's your mother."

"Then why doesn't she act like one?" I looked at Dad for what felt like a very long moment. Then I blurted out, "And why don't you act like a dad?"

I could see the blood surge into his face. He grabbed me by the arm. "You apologize for that comment!"

"Or what?" I asked.

Dad shoved me up against the wall. "Or by God I'll show you who's boss around here."

His face was inches from mine. "What are you going to do to punish me?" I asked. "Stop taking me to bars?"

Dad drew back his hand as if to smack me. "You watch your mouth, young lady. I can still whip your butt, and don't think I won't."

"You can't be serious," I said.

Dad dropped his hand. He pulled his belt out of the loops on his work pants and wrapped it a couple of times around his knuckles.

"Apologize to me and to your mother," he said.

"No."

Dad raised the belt. "Apologize."

"No."

"Then bend over."

Dad was standing between me and the door. There was no way out except through him. But it never occurred to me to either run or fight. The way I saw it, he was in a tighter spot than I was. He had to back down, because if he sided with Mom and gave me a whipping, he would lose me forever.

We stared at each other. Dad seemed to be waiting for me to drop my eyes, to apologize and tell him I was wrong so we could go back to being like we were, but I kept holding his gaze. Finally, to call his bluff, I turned around, bent over slightly, and rested my hands on my knees.

I expected him to turn and walk away, but there were six stinging blows on the backs of my thighs, each accompanied by a whistle of air. I could feel the welts rising even before I straightened up.

I walked out of the kitchen without looking at Dad. Mom was outside the door. She'd been standing there, listening to everything. I didn't look at her, but I could see from the corner of my eye her triumphant expression. I bit my lip so I wouldn't cry.

As soon as I got outside, I ran up into the woods, pushing tree branches and wild grape vines out of my face. I thought I'd start crying now that I was away from the house, but instead, I threw up. I ate some wild mint to get rid of the taste of bile, and I walked for what felt like hours through the silent hills. The air was clear and cool, and the forest floor was thick with leaves that had fallen from the buckeyes and poplars. Late in the afternoon, I sat down on a tree trunk, leaning forward because the backs of my thighs still stung. All through the long walk, the pain had kept me thinking, and by the time I reached the tree trunk, I had made two decisions.

The first was that I'd had my last whipping. No one was ever going to do that to me again. The second was that, like Lori, I was going to get out of Welch. The sooner, the better. Before I finished high school, if I could. I had no idea where I would go, but I did know I was going. I also knew it would not be easy. People got stuck in Welch. I had been counting on Mom and Dad to get us out, but I now knew I had to do it on my own. It would take saving and planning. I decided the next day I'd go to G. C. Murphy and buy a pink plastic piggy bank I'd seen there. I'd put in the seventy-five dollars I had managed to save while working at Becker's Jewel Box. It would be the beginning of my escape fund.

THAT FALL, TWO GUYS showed up in Welch who were different from anyone I'd ever met. They were filmmakers from New York City, and they'd been sent to Welch as part of a government program to bring cultural uplift to rural Appalachia. Their names were Ken Fink and Bob Gross.

At first, I thought they were joking. Ken Fink and Bob Gross? As far as I was concerned, they might as well have said their names were Ken Stupid and Bob Ugly. But Ken and Bob weren't joking. They didn't think their names were funny at all, and they didn't smile when I asked if they were putting me on.

Ken and Bob both talked so fast—their conversation filled with references to people I'd never heard of, like Stanley Kubrick and Woody Allen—that it was sometimes hard to follow them. Although they had no sense of humor about their names, Ken and Bob did like to joke a lot. It wasn't the sort of Welch High humor I was used to—Polack jokes and guys cupping their hand under their armpit to make fart noises. Ken and Bob had this smart, competitive way of joking where one would make a wisecrack and the other would have a comeback and the first would have a retort to the comeback. They could keep it up until my head spun.

One weekend Ken and Bob showed a Swedish film in the school auditorium. It was shot in black and white, and had subtitles and a plot heavy on symbolism, so fewer than a dozen people came, even though it was free. Afterward, Lori showed Ken and Bob some of her illustrations. They told her she had talent and said if she was serious about becoming an artist, she needed to go to New York City. It was a place of energy and creativity and intellectual stimulation the likes of which we'd never seen. It was filled with people who, because they were such unique individuals, didn't fit in anywhere else.

That night Lori and I lay in our rope beds and discussed New York City. The things I had heard always made it sound like a big, noisy place with a lot of pollution and mobs of people in suits elbowing one another on the sidewalks. But Lori began to see New York as a sort of Emerald City—this glowing, bustling place at the end of a long road where she could become the person she was meant to be.

What Lori liked most about Ken and Bob's description was that the city attracted people who were different. Lori was about as different as it was possible to be in Welch. While almost all the other kids wore jeans, Converse sneakers, and T-shirts, she showed up at school in army boots, a white dress with red polka dots, and a jean jacket with dark poetry she'd painted on the back. The other kids threw bars of soap at her, pushed one another into her path, and wrote graffiti about her on the bathroom walls. In return, she cursed them out in Latin.

At home she read and painted late into the night, by candlelight or kerosene lamp if the electricity was turned off. She liked Gothic details: mist hanging over a silent lake, gnarled roots heaving up from the earth, a solitary crow in the branches of a bare tree on the shoreline. I thought Lori was amazing, and I had no doubt she would become a successful artist, but only if she could get to New York. I decided I wanted to go there, too, and that winter we came up with a plan. Lori would leave by herself for New York in June, after she graduated. She'd settle in, find a place for us, and I'd follow her as soon as I could.

I told Lori about my escape fund, the seventy-five dollars I'd saved. From now on, I said, it would be our joint fund. We'd take on extra work after school and put everything we earned into the piggy bank. Lori could take it to New York and use it to get established, so that by the time I arrived, everything would be set.

Lori had always made very good posters, for football rallies, for the plays the drama club put on, and for candidates running for student council. Now she started doing commissioned posters for a dollar-fifty apiece. She was too shy to solicit orders, so I did it for her. Lots of kids at Welch High wanted customized posters to hang on their bedroom walls—of their boyfriend's or girlfriend's name, of their car or their astrological sign or their favorite band. Lori designed the names in big fat overlapping three-dimensional letters like the kind on rock albums, then painted them in Day-Glo colors, outlined in india ink so the letters popped, and surrounded them with stars and dots and squiggly lines that made the letters seem like they were moving. The posters were so good that word of mouth spread, and soon Lori had such a backlog of orders that she was up working until one or two every morning.

I made money babysitting and doing other kids' homework. I did book reports, science essays, and math. I charged a dollar per assignment and guaranteed at least an A– or the customer was entitled to a full refund. After school, I babysat for a dollar an hour and could usually do the homework then. I also tutored kids for two dollars an hour.

We told Brian about the escape fund, and he pitched in, even though we hadn't included him in our plans because he was only in the seventh grade. He mowed lawns or chopped wood or cut hillside weeds with a scythe. He worked after school until the sun went down and all day Saturday and Sunday and came home with his arms and face scratched from the brush he'd cleared. Without looking for thanks or praise, he quietly added his earnings to the pig, which we named Oz.

We kept Oz on the old sewing machine in the bedroom. Oz had no plugged hole on the bottom, and the slot on the top was too narrow to work bills out, even if you used a knife, so once you'd put money into Oz, it stayed there. We tested it to make sure. We couldn't count the money, but because Oz was translucent, we could see our cash accumulating inside when we held him up to the light.

One day that winter, when I came home from school, a gold Cadillac Coupe DeVille was parked in front of the house. I wondered if the welfare agency had found some millionaires to be our foster parents and they had arrived to take us away, but Dad was inside the house, twirling a set of keys on his finger. He explained that the Cadillac was the new official Walls family vehicle. Mom was carrying on about how it was one thing to live in a three-room shack with no electricity, since there was a certain dignity in poverty, but to live in a three-room shack and own a gold Cadillac meant you were bona fide poor white trash.

"How'd you get it?" I asked Dad.

"One helluva good poker hand," he said, "and an even better bluff."

We'd owned a couple of cars since we'd been in Welch, but they were true buckets of bolts, with shuddering engines and cracked windshields, and as we drove along, we could see the blur of the asphalt through the rusted-out floor panels. Those cars never lasted more than a couple of months, and like the Oldsmobile we'd driven from Phoenix, we never named them, much less got them registered and inspected. The Coupe DeVille actually had an unexpired inspection sticker. It was such a beauty that Dad declared the time had come to revive the tradition of naming our cars. "That there Caddy," he said, "strikes me as Elvis."

It crossed my mind that Dad ought to sell Elvis and use the money to install an indoor toilet and buy us all new clothes. The black leather shoes I had bought for fifty cents at the Dollar General Store were held together with safety pins, which I'd tried to blacken with a Magic Marker so you wouldn't notice them. I'd also used Magic Markers to make colored blotches on my legs that I hoped would camouflage the holes in my pants. I figured that was less noticeable than if I sewed on patches. I had one blue pair and one green pair, so my legs, when I took my pants off, were covered with blue and green spots.

But Dad loved Elvis too dearly to consider selling it. And the truth was, I loved Elvis almost as much. Elvis was as long and sleek as a racing yacht. It had air-conditioning, gold shag upholstery, windows that went up and down with the push of a button, and a working turn signal, so Dad didn't have to stick his arm out. Every time we drove through town in Elvis, I'd nod graciously and smile at the people on the sidewalk, feeling like an heiress. "You've got true noblesse oblige, Mountain Goat," Dad would say.

Mom grew to love Elvis, too. She hadn't gone back to teaching and instead spent her time painting, and on the weekends we began to drive to craft fairs all throughout West Virginia: shows where bearded men in overalls played dulcimers and women in granny dresses sold corncob back scratchers and coal sculptures of black bears and miners. We filled Elvis's trunk with Mom's paintings and tried to sell them at the fairs. Mom also drew pastel portraits on the spot for anyone willing to pay eighteen dollars, and every now and then she got a commission.

We all slept in Elvis on those trips, because a lot of times we made only enough to pay for the gas, or not even that. Still, it felt good to be on the move again. Our trips in Elvis reminded me how easy it was to pick up and move on when the urge struck. Once you'd resolved to go, there was nothing to it at all.

As SPRING APPROACHED and the day of Lori's graduation drew closer, I lay awake at night, thinking about her life in New York City. "In exactly three months," I said to her, "you'll be living in New York." The following week, I said, "In exactly two months and three weeks, you'll be living in New York."

"Would you please shut up," she said.

"You're not nervous, are you?" I asked.

"What do you think?"

Lori was terrified. She was not sure what she was supposed to do once she got to New York. That had always been the vaguest part of our escape plan. Back in the fall, I'd had no doubt that she could get a scholarship to one of the city's universities. She'd been a finalist for a National Merit Scholarship, but she'd had to hitchhike into Bluefield to take the test, and she got rattled when the trucker who picked her up put the moves on her; she arrived nearly an hour late and botched the test.

Mom, who supported Lori's New York plans and kept saying she wished she were going to the big city herself, suggested that Lori apply to the Cooper Union art school. Lori put together a portfolio of her drawings and paintings, but just before the submissions deadline, she spilled a pot of coffee on them, which made Mom wonder aloud if Lori had a fear of success.

Then Lori heard about a scholarship sponsored by a literary society for the student who created the best work of art inspired by one of the geniuses of the English language. She decided to make a clay bust of Shakespeare. She worked on it for a week, using a sharpened Popsicle stick to shape the slightly bulging eyes and the goatee and earring and longish hair. When it was finished, it looked exactly like Shakespeare.

That night we were all sitting at the drafting table watching Lori put the final touches on Shakespeare's hair when Dad came home drunk. "That does indeed resemble old Billy," Dad said. "Only thing is, as I been telling you, he was a goddamn fake."

For years, every time Mom brought out Shakespeare's plays, Dad would carry on about how they'd been written not by William Shakespeare of Avon but by a bunch of people, including someone named the Earl of Oxford, because no single person in Elizabethan England could have had Shakespeare's thirty-thousand-word vocabulary. All this bunk about little Billy Shakespeare, Dad would say, the great genius despite his grammar-school education, his small Latin and less Greek, was a lot of sentimental mythology.

"You're helping perpetuate this fraud," he told Lori.

"Dad, it's just a bust," Lori said.

"That's the problem," Dad said.

He studied the sculpture, then suddenly reached over and smeared off Shakespeare's mouth with his thumb.

"What the hell are you doing?" Lori cried out.

"It's no longer *just* a bust," Dad said. "Now it has symbolic value. You can call it *Mute Bard*."

"I spent days on that," Lori shouted. "And you've ruined it!"

"I elevated it," Dad said. He told Lori he would help her write a paper that would demonstrate that Shakespeare's plays had multiple authors, like Rembrandt's paintings. "By God, you'll set the literary world on edge," he said.

"I don't want to set the world on edge!" Lori screamed. "I just want to win a stupid little scholarship!"

"Goddammit, you're in a horse race, but you're thinking like a sheep," Dad said. "Sheep don't win horse races."

Lori didn't have the spirit to rework the bust. The next day she smushed the clay into a big glob and left it on the drafting table. I told Lori that if she hadn't been accepted into an art school by the time she graduated, she should go to New York anyway. She could support herself with the money we'd saved up until she found a job, and then she could apply to a school. That became our new plan.

Everyone was mad at Dad, which gave him a case of the sulks. He said he didn't know why he even bothered to come home anymore, since he no longer got the slightest bit of appreciation for his ideas. He insisted he wasn't trying to keep Lori from leaving for New York, but if she had the sense that God gave a goose, she would stay put. "New York is a sorry-ass sinkhole," he said more than once, "filled with faggots and rapists." She'd get mugged and find herself on the streets, he warned, forced into prostitution and winding up a drug addict like all those runaway teenagers. "I'm only telling you this because I love you," he said. "And I don't want to see you hurt."

One evening in May, when we'd been saving our money for almost nine months, I came home with a couple of dollars I'd made babysitting and went into the bedroom to stash them in Oz. The pig was not on the old sewing machine. I began looking through all the junk in the bedroom and finally found Oz on the floor. Someone had slashed him apart with a knife and stolen all the money.

I knew it was Dad, but at the same time, I couldn't believe he'd stoop this low. Lori obviously didn't know yet. She was in the living room humming away as she worked on a poster. My first impulse was to hide Oz. I had this wild thought that I could somehow replace the money before Lori discovered it was missing. But I knew how ridiculous that was; three of us had spent the better part of a year accumulating the money. It would be impossible for me to replace it in the month before Lori graduated.

I went into the living room and stood beside her, trying to think of what to say. She was working on a poster that said TAMMY! in Day-Glo colors. After a moment, she looked up. "What?" she said.

Lori could tell by my face that something was wrong. She stood up so abruptly she knocked over a bottle of india ink, and ran into the bedroom. I braced myself, expecting to hear a scream, but there was only silence and then a small, broken whimpering.

Lori stayed up all night to confront Dad, but he didn't come home. She skipped school the following day in case he returned, but Dad was AWOL for three days before we heard him climbing the rickety staircase to the porch.

"You bastard!" Lori shouted. "You stole our money!"

"What the goddamn hell are you talking about?" Dad asked. "And watch your language." He leaned against the door and lit a cigarette.

Lori held up the slashed pig and threw it as hard as she could at Dad, but it was empty and nearly weightless. It struck his shoulder lightly, then bounced to the floor. He bent down carefully, as if the floor beneath him could shift at any moment, picked up our ravaged piggy bank, and turned it over in his hands. "Someone sure as hell gutted old Oz, didn't they?" He turned to me. "Jeannette, do you know what happened?"

He was actually half grinning at me. After the whipping, Dad had jacked up the charm with me, and even though I was planning to leave, he could make me laugh when he tried, and he still considered me an ally. But now I wanted to knock him over the head. "You took our money," I said. "That's what happened."

"Well, don't that beat all," Dad said. He started going on about how a man comes home from slaying dragons, trying to keep his family safe, and all he wants in return for his toil and sacrifice is a little love and respect, but it seemed these days that was just too damn much to ask for. He said he didn't take our New York money, but if Lori was hell-bent on living in that cesspool, he'd finance her trip himself.

He reached into his pocket and pulled out a few wadded dollar bills. We just stared at him, so he let the crumpled money fall to the floor. "Suit yourself," he said.

"Why are you doing this to us, Dad?" I asked. "Why?"

His face tightened with anger, then he staggered to the sofa bed and passed out.

"I'll never get out of here," Lori kept saying. "I'll never get out of here."

"You will," I said. "I swear it." I believed she would. Because I knew that if Lori never got out of Welch, neither would I.

I went back to G. C. Murphy the next day and stared at the shelf of piggy banks. They were all either plastic or porcelain or glass, easily broken. I studied a collection of metal boxes with locks and keys. The hinges were too flimsy. Dad could pry them apart. I bought a blue change purse. I wore it on a belt under my clothes at all times. When it got too full, I put the money in a sock that I hid in a hole in the wall below my bunk.

We started saving again, but Lori felt too defeated to paint much, and the money didn't come as quickly. A week before school was out, we had only $37.20 in the sock. Then one of the women I'd been babysitting for, a teacher named Mrs. Sanders, told me she and her family were moving back to their hometown in Iowa and asked if I wanted to spend the summer with them there. If I came along and helped look after her two toddlers, she said she'd pay me two hundred dollars at the end of the summer and buy me a bus ticket back to Welch.

I thought about her offer. "Take Lori instead of me," I said. "And at the end of the summer, buy her a bus ticket to New York City."

Mrs. Sanders agreed.

Low-lying pewter-colored clouds rested on the mountaintops around Welch on the morning of Lori's departure. They were there most mornings, and when I noticed them, they reminded me of how isolated and forgotten the town was, a sad, lost place adrift in the clouds. The clouds usually burned away by midmorning, when the sun climbed above the steep hills, but some days, like the one Lori left, they clung to the mountains, and a fine mist formed in the valley that turned your hair and face damp.

When the Sanders family pulled up in their station wagon, Lori was ready. She had packed her clothes, her favorite books, and her art supplies in a single cardboard box. She hugged all of us except Dad—she had refused to speak a word to him since he plundered Oz—promised to write, and climbed into the station wagon.

We all stood watching as the car disappeared down Little Hobart Street. Lori never once looked back. I took that as a good sign. When I climbed the staircase to the house, Dad was standing on the porch, smoking a cigarette.

"This family is falling apart," he said.

"It sure is," I told him.

THAT FALL, WHEN I was going into the tenth grade, Miss Bivens made me news editor of *The Maroon Wave*. After working as a proofreader in the seventh grade, I'd started laying out pages in the eighth grade, and in the ninth grade I began reporting and writing articles and taking photographs. Mom had bought a Minolta camera to take pictures of her pictures, so she could send them to Lori, who could show them around art galleries in New York. When Mom wasn't using it, I wore the Minolta everywhere, because you never knew when you'd see something newsworthy. What I loved most about calling myself a reporter was that it gave me an excuse to show up anyplace. Since I'd never made a lot of friends in Welch, I hardly ever went to the school's football games or dances or rallies. I felt awkward sitting by myself when everyone else was with friends. But when I was working for the *Wave*, I had a reason to be there. I was on assignment, a member of the working press, with my notepad in hand and the Minolta around my neck.

I began going to just about every extracurricular event at the school, and the kids who shunned me before now accepted me and even sought me out, posing and clowning in hopes of getting their picture in the paper. As someone who could make them famous among their peers, I was no longer a person to be trifled with.

Even though the *Wave* came out only once a month, I worked on it every day. Instead of hiding in the bathroom during lunch hour, I spent it in Miss Bivens's classroom, where I wrote my articles, edited the stories written by other students, and counted the letters in headlines to make sure they fit the columns. I finally had a good excuse for why I never ate lunch. "I'm on deadline," I'd say. I also stayed after school to develop my photographs in the darkroom, and that had a hidden benefit. I could sneak into the cafeteria once everyone had left and dig through the garbage pails. I'd find industrial-sized cans of corn that were nearly full and huge containers of cole slaw and tapioca pudding. I no longer had to root through the bathroom wastebaskets for food, and I hardly ever went hungry again.

When I was a junior, Miss Bivens made me the editor in chief, though the job was supposed to go to a senior. Only a handful of students wanted to work for the *Wave,* and I ended up writing so many of the articles that I abolished bylines; it looked a little ridiculous having my name appear four times on the front page.

The paper cost fifteen cents, and I sold it myself, going from class to class and standing in the hallways, hawking it like a newsboy. Welch High had about twelve hundred students, but we sold only a couple hundred copies of the paper. I tried various schemes to boost the circulation: I held poetry competitions, added a fashion column, and wrote controversial editorials, including one questioning the validity of standardized tests, which provoked an irate letter from the head of the state Department of Education. Nothing worked.

One day a student I was trying to get to buy the *Wave* told me he had no use for it because the same names appeared in the paper again and again: the school's athletes and cheerleaders and the handful of kids known as slide rules who always won the academic prizes. So I started a column called "Birthday Corner," listing the names of the eighty or so people who had their birthday in the coming month. Most of these people had never appeared in the paper, and they were so excited to see their names in print, they bought several copies. Circulation doubled. Miss Bivens wondered aloud if "Birthday Corner" represented serious journalism. I told her I didn't care—it sold papers.

Chuck Yeager visited Welch High that year. I'd been hearing about Chuck Yeager all my life from Dad, about how he'd been born in West Virginia, in the town of Myra on the Mud River over in Lincoln County, about how he joined the air force during World War II and had shot down eleven German planes by the time he was twenty-two, about how he became a test pilot at Edwards Air Force Base high up on the Mojave Desert in California, and about how one day in 1947 he became the first man to break the sound barrier in his X-1, even though the night before, he'd been up drinking and had been thrown from a horse and cracked some ribs.

Dad would never admit to having heroes, but the brass-balled, liquor-loving, coolly calculating Chuck Yeager was the one man in the world he admired above all others. When he heard that Chuck Yeager was giving a speech at Welch High and that he'd agreed to let me interview him afterward, Dad could hardly contain his excitement. He was waiting on the porch for me with a pen and paper when I got home from school the day before the big interview. He sat down to help me draw up a list of intelligent questions so I wouldn't embarrass myself in front of this greatest of West Virginia's native sons.

What was going through your head when you first broke Mach I?
What was going through your head when A. Scott Crossfield
  broke Mach II?
What is your favorite aircraft?
What are your thoughts on the feasibility of flying at the speed of
  light?

Dad wrote up about twenty-five or thirty questions like that and then insisted we rehearse the interview. He pretended to be Chuck Yeager and gave me detailed answers to the questions he'd written out. His eyes got misty as he described what it was like to break the sound barrier. Then he decided I needed some solid grounding in aviation history, and he stayed up half the night briefing me, by the light of a kerosene lamp, on the test-flight program, basic aerodynamics, and the Austrian physicist Ernst Mach.

The next day Mr. Jack, the principal, introduced Chuck Yeager during assembly in the auditorium. He looked more like a cowboy than a West Virginian, with his horseman's gait and his lean leathery face, but as soon as he started speaking, his voice was pure up-hollow. As he talked, the fidgety students settled into their folding chairs and became enraptured by the legendary, world-traveled man who told us how proud he was of his West Virginia roots, and how we, too, should be proud of those roots, roots we all shared; and how, regardless of where we came from, each and every one of us could and should follow our dreams, just as he had followed his. When he finished talking, the applause about shattered the glass in the windows.

I climbed up on the stage before the students filed out. "Mr. Yeager," I said, holding out my hand, "I'm Jeannette Walls with *The Maroon Wave*."

Chuck Yeager took my hand and grinned. "Jes' spell my name right, ma'am," he said, "so's my kin'll know who you're writin' about."

We sat down on some folding chairs and talked for nearly an hour. Mr. Yeager took every question seriously and acted like he had all the time in the world for me. When I mentioned various aircraft he'd flown, the aircraft Dad had briefed me about, he grinned again and said, "Heck, I do believe we got an aviation expert on our hands."

In the hallways afterward, the other kids kept coming up to tell me how lucky I was. "What was he really like?" they asked. "What did he say?" Everyone treated me with the deference accorded only to the school's top athletes. Even the varsity quarterback caught my eye and nodded. I was the girl who had actually talked to Chuck Yeager.

Dad was so eager to hear how the interview went that he was not only home when I got back from school, he was even sober. He insisted on helping me with the article to ensure its technical accuracy.

I already had a lead figured out in my head. I sat down in front of Mom's Remington and typed it out:

The pages of the history books came alive this month when Chuck Yeager, the man who first broke the sound barrier, visited Welch High.

Dad looked over my shoulder. "Great," he said. "But let's juice it up a little."

Lori had been writing to us regularly from New York. She loved it there. She was living in a hotel for women in Greenwich Village, working as a waitress in a German restaurant, and taking art classes and even fencing lessons. She'd met the most fascinating group of people, every one of them a weird genius. People in New York loved art and music so much, she said, that artists sold paintings right on the sidewalk next to string quartets playing Mozart. Even Central Park wasn't as dangerous as people in West Virginia thought. On the weekends, it was filled with roller skaters and Frisbee players and jugglers and mimes with their faces painted white. She knew I'd love it once I got there. I knew it, too.

Ever since I'd started eleventh grade, I'd been counting off the months—twenty-two of them—until I would join Lori. I had my plan worked out. Once I had graduated from high school, I'd move to New York, enroll at a city college, and then get a job with AP or UPI, the wire services whose stories unspooled from the *Welch Daily News* Teletype machines, or with one of the famous New York papers. I'd overhear the reporters at *The Welch Daily News* make jokes to one another about the highfalutin writers who worked at those papers. I was determined to become one.

In the middle of my junior year, I went to Miss Katona, the high school guidance counselor, to ask for the names of colleges in New York. Miss Katona lifted the glasses that dangled from a cord around her neck and peered at me through them. Bluefield State was only thirty-six miles away, she said, and with my grades, I could probably get a full scholarship.

"I want to go to college in New York," I said.

Miss Katona gave me a puzzled frown. "Whatever for?"

"That's where I want to live."

Miss Katona said that in her view, this was a bad idea. It was easier to go to college in the state where you had attended high school. You were considered in-state, which meant acceptance was more likely and tuition was cheaper.

I thought about this for a minute. "Maybe I should move to New York City right now and graduate from high school there. Then I'd be considered in-state."

Miss Katona squinted at me. "But you live here," she said. "This is your home."

Miss Katona was a fine-boned woman who always wore button-up sweaters and stout shoes. She had gone to Welch High School, and it seemed not to have occurred to her to live anywhere else. To leave West Virginia, even to leave Welch, would have been unthinkably disloyal, like deserting your family.

"Just because I live here now," I said, "doesn't mean I couldn't move."

"That would be a terrible mistake. You live here. Think of what you'd miss. Your family and friends. And senior year is the highlight of your entire high school experience. You'd miss Senior Day. You'd miss the senior prom."

I walked home slowly that evening, thinking over what Miss Katona had said. It was true that many grown-ups in Welch talked about how senior year in high school was the highlight of their lives. On Senior Day, something the school had set up to keep juniors from dropping out, the seniors wore funny clothes and got to skip classes. It was not exactly a compelling reason to stay on in Welch for one more year. As for the senior prom, I had about as much chance of getting a date as Dad did of ending corruption in the unions.

I'd been speaking hypothetically about moving to New York a year early. But as I walked, I realized that if I wanted to, I could up and go. I could really do it. Maybe not right now, not this minute—it was the middle of the school year—but I could wait until I finished eleventh grade. By then I'd be seventeen. I had almost a hundred dollars saved, enough to get me started in New York. I could leave Welch in under five months.

I got so excited that I started running. I ran, faster and faster, along the Old Road overhung with bare-branched trees, then on to Grand View and up Little Hobart Street, past the barking yard-dogs and the frost-covered coal piles, past the Noes' house and the Parishes' house, the Halls' house and the Renkos' house until, gasping for air, I came to a stop in front of our house. For the first time in years, I noticed my half-finished yellow paint job. I'd spent so much time in Welch trying to make things a little bit better, but nothing had worked.

In fact, the house was getting worse. One of the supporting pillars was starting to buckle. The leak in the roof over Brian's bed had gotten so bad that when it rained, he slept under an inflatable raft Mom had won in a sweepstakes by sending in Benson & Hedges 100s packages we'd dug out of trash cans. If I left, Brian could have my old bed. My mind was made up. I was going to New York City as soon as the school year was out.

I clambered up the mountainside to the rear of the house—the stairs had completely rotted through—and climbed through the back window we now used as a door. Dad was at the drafting table, working on some calculations, and Mom was going through her stacks of paintings. When I told them about my plan, Dad stubbed out his cigarette, stood up, and climbed out the back window without saying a word. Mom nodded and looked down, dusting off one of her paintings, murmuring something to herself.

"So, what do you think?" I asked.

"Fine. Go."

"What's wrong?"

"Nothing. You should go. It's a good plan." She seemed on the verge of tears.

"Don't be sad, Mom. I'll write."

"I'm not upset because I'll miss you," Mom said. "I'm upset because you get to go to New York and I'm stuck here. It's not fair."

Lori, when I called her, approved of my plan. I could live with her, she said, if I got a job and chipped in on the rent. Brian liked my idea, too, especially when I pointed out that he could have my bed. He began making wisecracks in a lockjaw accent about how I was going to become one of those fur-wearing, pinkie-extending, nose-in-the-air New Yorkers. He began counting down the weeks until I left, just as I had counted them down for Lori. "In sixteen weeks, you'll be in New York," he'd say. The next week, "In three months and three weeks, you'll be in New York."

Dad had barely spoken to me since I announced my decision. One night that spring, he came into the bedroom where I was up on my bunk studying. He had some papers rolled up under his arm.

"Got a minute to look at something?" he asked.

"Sure."

I followed him into the living room, where he spread the papers on the drafting table. They were his old blueprints for the Glass Castle, all stained and dog-eared. I couldn't remember the last time I'd seen them. We'd stopped talking about the Glass Castle once the foundation we'd dug was filled up with garbage.

"I think I finally worked out how to deal with the lack of sunlight on the hillside," Dad said. It involved installing specially curved mirrors in the solar cells. But what he wanted to talk to me about was the plans for my room. "Now that Lori's gone," he said, "I'm reconfiguring the layout, and your room will be a lot bigger."

Dad's hands trembled slightly as he unrolled different blueprints. He had drawn frontal views, side views, and aerial views of the Glass Castle. He had diagrammed the wiring and the plumbing. He had drawn the interiors of rooms and labeled them and specified their dimensions, down to the inches, in his precise, blocky handwriting.

I stared at the plans. "Dad," I said, "you'll never build the Glass Castle."

"Are you saying you don't have faith in your old man?"

"Even if you do, I'll be gone. In less than three months, I'm leaving for New York City."

"What I was thinking was you don't have to go right away," Dad said. I could stay and graduate from Welch High and go to Bluefield State, as Miss Katona had suggested, then get a job at *The Welch Daily News*. He'd help me with the articles, like he'd helped me with my piece on Chuck Yeager. "And I'll build the Glass Castle, I swear it. We'll all live in it together. It'll be a hell of a lot better than any apartment you'll ever find in New York City, I can guaran-goddamn-tee that."

"Dad," I said, "as soon as I finish classes, I'm getting on the next bus out of here. If the buses stop running, I'll hitchhike. I'll walk if I have to. Go ahead and build the Glass Castle, but don't do it for me."

Dad rolled up the blueprints and walked out of the room. A minute later, I heard him scrambling down the mountainside.

IT HAD BEEN A mild winter, and summer came early to the mountains. By late May, the wild bleeding hearts and the rhododendrons had bloomed, and the fragrance of honeysuckle drifted down the hillside and into the house. We had our first hot days before school was out.

Those last couple of weeks, I'd go from feeling excited to nervous to just plain scared back to excited in a matter of minutes. On the last day of school, I cleaned out my locker and went to say goodbye to Miss Bivens.

"I've got a feeling about you," she said. "I think you'll do all right up there. But you've left me with a problem. Who's going to edit the *Wave* next year?"

"You'll find someone, I'm sure."

"I've thought of trying to entice your brother into it."

"People might start thinking that the Wallses are building a dynasty."

Miss Bivens smiled. "Maybe you are."

At home that night, Mom cleaned out a suitcase she'd used for her collection of dancing shoes, and I filled it with my clothes and my bound copies of *The Maroon Wave*. I wanted to leave everything from the past behind, even the good things, so I gave Maureen my geode. It was dusty and dull, but I told her that if she scrubbed it hard, it would sparkle like a diamond. As I cleared out the box on the wall next to my bed, Brian said, "Guess what? In one more day you'll be in New York City." Then he started impersonating Frank Sinatra, singing "New York, New York" off-key and doing his lounge-lizard dance.

"Shut up, you big dummy!" I said and hit him hard on the shoulder.

"You're the dummy!" he said and hit me hard back. We tossed a few more punches and then looked at each other awkwardly.

The one bus out of Welch left at seven-ten in the morning. I needed to be at the station before seven. Mom announced that since she was not by nature an early riser, she would not be getting up to see me off. "I know what you look like, and I know what the bus station looks like," she said. "And those big farewells are so sentimental."

I could hardly sleep that night. Neither could Brian. From time to time, he'd break the silence by announcing that in seven hours I'd be leaving Welch, in six hours I'd be leaving Welch, and we'd both start cracking up. I fell asleep only to be woken at first light by Brian, who, like Mom, wasn't an early riser. He was tugging at my arm. "No more joking about it," he said. "In two hours, you'll be gone."

Dad hadn't come home that night, but when I climbed through the back window with my suitcase, I saw him sitting at the bottom of the stone steps, smoking a cigarette. He insisted on carrying the suitcase for me, and we set off down Little Hobart Street and around the Old Road.

The empty streets were damp. Every now and then Dad would look over at me and wink, or make a tocking sound with his tongue as if I were a horse and he was urging me on. It seemed to make him feel like he was doing what a father should, plucking up his daughter's courage, helping her face the terrors of the unknown.

When we got to the station, Dad turned to me. "Honey, life in New York may not be as easy as you think it's going to be."

"I can handle it," I told him.

Dad reached into his pocket and pulled out his favorite jackknife, the one with the horn handle and the blade of blue German steel that we'd used for Demon Hunting.

"I'll feel better knowing you have this." He pressed the knife into my hand.

The bus turned down the street and stopped with a hiss of compressed air in front of the Trailways station. The driver opened up the luggage compartment and slid my suitcase in next to the others. I hugged Dad. When our cheeks touched, and I breathed in his smell of tobacco, Vitalis, and whiskey, I realized he'd shaved for me.

"If things don't work out, you can always come home," he said. "I'll be here for you. You know that, don't you?"

"I know." I knew that in his way, he would be. I also knew I'd never be coming back.

Only a few passengers were on the bus, so I got a good seat next to a window. The driver closed the door, and we pulled out. At first I resolved not to turn around. I wanted to look ahead to where I was going, not back at what I was leaving, but then I turned anyway.

Dad was lighting a cigarette. I waved, and he waved back. Then he shoved his hands in his pockets, the cigarette dangling from his mouth, and stood there, slightly stoop-shouldered and distracted-looking. I wondered if he was remembering how he, too, had left Welch full of vinegar at age seventeen and just as convinced as I was now that he'd never return. I wondered if he was hoping that his favorite girl would come back, or if he was hoping that, unlike him, she would make it out for good.

I reached into my pocket and touched the horn-handled jackknife, then waved again. Dad just stood there. He grew smaller and smaller, and then we turned a corner and he was gone.

IV

NEW YORK CITY

IT WAS DUSK WHEN I got my first glimpse of it off in the distance, beyond a ridge. All I could see were the spires and blocky tops of buildings. And then we reached the crest of the ridge, and there, across a wide river, was a huge island jammed tip to tip with skyscrapers, their glass glowing like fire in the setting sun.

My heart started to race, and my palms grew damp. I walked down the bus aisle to the tiny restroom in the rear and washed up in the metal basin. I studied my face in the mirror and wondered what New Yorkers would think when they looked at me. Would they see an Appalachian hick, a tall, gawky girl, still all elbows and knees and jutting teeth? For years Dad had been telling me I had an inner beauty. Most people didn't see it. I had trouble seeing it myself, but Dad was always saying he could damn well see it and that was what mattered. I hoped when New Yorkers looked at me, they would see whatever it was that Dad saw.

When the bus pulled into the terminal, I collected my suitcase and walked to the middle of the station. A blur of hurrying bodies streamed past me, leaving me feeling like a stone in a creek, and then I heard someone calling my name. He was a pale guy with thick, black-framed glasses that made his eyes look tiny. His name was Evan, and he was a friend of Lori's. She was at work and had asked him to come meet me. Evan offered to carry my suitcase and led me out to the street, a noisy place with crowds backed up waiting to cross the intersection, cars jammed together, and papers blowing every which way. I followed him right into the thick of it.

After one block, Evan put down my suitcase. "This is heavy," he said. "What do you have in here?"

"My coal collection."

He looked at me blankly.

"Just funning with you," I said and punched him in the shoulder.

Evan wasn't too quick on the uptake, but I took that as a good sign. There was no reason for me to be automatically in awe of the wit and intellect of these New Yorkers.

I picked up the suitcase. Evan did not insist I give it back to him. In fact, he seemed sort of relieved that I was carrying it. We continued on down the block, and he kept glancing at me sideways.

"You West Virginia girls are one tough breed," he said.

"You got that right," I told him.

Evan dropped me off at a German restaurant called Zum Zum. Lori was behind the counter, carrying four beer steins in each hand, her hair in twin buns and speaking in a thick German accent because, she explained later, it increased tips. "*Dees ees mein seester!*" she called out to the men at one of her tables. They raised their beer steins and shouted, "*Velkomen to New Yorken!*"

I didn't know any German, so I said, "*Grazi!*"

They all got a chuckle out of that. Lori was in the middle of her shift, so I went out to wander the streets. I got lost a couple of times and had to ask directions. People had been warning me for months about how rude New Yorkers were. It was true, I learned that night, that if you tried to stop them on the street, a lot of them kept on walking, shaking their heads; those who did stop didn't look at you at first. They gazed off down the block, their faces closed. But as soon as they realized you weren't trying to hustle them or panhandle money, they warmed right up. They looked you in the eye and gave you detailed instructions about how, to get to the Empire State Building, you went up nine blocks and made a right and cut across two blocks and so on. They even drew you maps. New Yorkers, I figured, just pretended to be unfriendly.

Later, Lori and I took a subway down to Greenwich Village and walked over to the Evangeline, a women's hostel where she had been living. That first night I woke up at three a.m. and saw the sky all lit up a bright orange. I wondered if there was a big fire somewhere, but in the morning Lori told me that the orange glow came from the air pollution refracting the light off the streets and buildings. The night sky here, she said, always had that color. What it meant was that in New York, you could never see the stars. But Venus wasn't a star. I wondered if I'd be able to see it.

The very next day, I landed a job at a hamburger joint on Fourteenth Street. After taxes and social security, I'd be taking home over eighty dollars a week. I had spent a lot of time imagining what New York would be like, but the one thing that had never occurred to me was that the opportunities would come so easily. Aside from having to wear those embarrassing red-and-yellow uniforms with matching floppy hats, I loved the job. The lunch and dinner rushes were always exciting, with the lines backing up at the counter, the cashiers shouting orders over the microphones, the grill guys shoveling hamburgers through the flame-broiling conveyer belt, everyone running from the fixings counter to the drinks station to the infrared fries warmer, staying on top of the orders, the manager jumping in to help whenever a crisis cropped up. We got 20 percent off on our meals, and for the first few weeks there, I had a cheeseburger and a chocolate milk shake every day for lunch.

In the middle of the summer, Lori found us an apartment in a neighborhood we could afford—the South Bronx. The yellow art deco building must have been pretty fancy when it opened, but now graffiti covered the outside walls, and the cracked mirrors in the lobby were held together with duct tape. Still, it had what Mom called good bones.

Our apartment was bigger than the entire house on Little Hobart Street, and way fancier. It had shiny oak parquet floors, a foyer with two steps leading down into the living room—where I slept—and, off to the side, a bedroom that became Lori's. We also had a kitchen with a working refrigerator and a gas stove that had a pilot light, so you didn't need matches to get it going, you just turned the dial, listened to the clicking, then watched the circle of blue flame flare up through the tiny holes in the burner. My favorite room was the bathroom. It had a black-and-white tile floor, a toilet that flushed with a powerful whoosh, a tub so deep you could submerge yourself completely in it, and hot water that never ran out.

It didn't bother me that the apartment was in a rough neighborhood; we'd always lived in rough neighborhoods. Puerto Rican kids hung out on the block at all hours, playing music, dancing, sitting on abandoned cars, clustering at the entrance to the elevated subway station and in front of the bodega that sold single cigarettes called loosies. I got jumped a number of times. People were always telling me that if I was robbed, I should hand over my money rather than risk being killed. But I was darned if I was going to give some stranger my hard-earned cash, and I didn't want to become known in the neighborhood as an easy target, so I always fought back. Sometimes I won, sometimes I lost. What worked best was to keep my wits about me. Once, as I was getting on the train, some guy tried to grab my purse, but I jerked it back and the strap broke. He fell empty-handed to the platform floor, and as the train pulled out, I looked through the window and gave him a big sarcastic wave.

That fall, Lori helped me find a public school where, instead of going to classes, the students signed up for internships all over the city. One of my internships was at *The Phoenix*, a weekly newspaper run out of a dingy storefront on Atlantic Avenue in downtown Brooklyn, near the old Ex-Lax factory. The owner, publisher, and editor in chief was Mike Armstrong. He saw himself as a muckraking gadfly and had mortgaged his brownstone five times to keep *The Phoenix* going. The staff all used Underwood manual typewriters with threadbare ribbons and yellowed keys. The E on mine was broken, so I used the @ in its place. We never had copy paper and instead wrote on discarded press releases we dug out of the trash. At least once a month, someone's paycheck bounced. Reporters were always quitting in disgust. In the spring, when Mr. Armstrong was interviewing a journalism school graduate for a job opening, a mouse ran over her foot, and she screamed. After she'd left, Mr. Armstrong looked at me. The Brooklyn zoning board was meeting that afternoon and he had no one to cover it. "If you start calling me Mike instead of Mr. Armstrong," he said, "you can have the job."

I had just turned eighteen. I quit my job at the hamburger joint the next day and became a full-time reporter for *The Phoenix*. I'd never been happier in my life. I worked ninety-hour weeks, my telephone rang constantly, I was always hurrying off to interviews and checking the ten-dollar Rolex I'd bought on the street to make sure I wasn't running late, rushing back to file my copy, and staying up until four a.m. to set type when the typesetter quit. And I was bringing home $125 a week. If the check cleared.

I wrote Brian long letters describing the sweet life in New York City. He wrote back saying things in Welch were still going downhill. Dad was drunk all the time except when he was in jail; Mom had completely withdrawn into her own world; and Maureen was more or less living with neighbors. The ceiling in the bedroom had collapsed, and Brian had moved his bed onto the porch. He made walls by nailing boards along the railings, but it leaked pretty badly out there, too, so he still slept under the inflatable raft.

I told Lori that Brian should come live with us in New York, and she agreed. But I was afraid Brian would want to stay in Welch. He seemed more of a country boy than a city kid. He was always wandering through the woods, tinkering with a discarded two-stroke engine, chopping wood, or carving a block of wood into an animal head. He never complained about Welch, and unlike Lori and me, he'd made a lot of friends there. But I thought it was in Brian's long-term interest to get out of the town. I made a list of reasons he should move to New York, so I could argue him into it.

I called him at Grandpa's and presented my case. He'd need to get a job to pay his share of the rent and groceries, I said, but jobs were going begging in the city. He could share the living room with me—there was plenty of space for a second bed—the toilet flushed, and the ceiling never leaked.

When I finished, Brian was silent for a moment. Then he said, "When's the soonest I can come?"

Just like me, Brian hopped the Trailways bus the morning after completing his junior year. The day after he got to New York, he found a job at an ice-cream parlor in Brooklyn, not far from *The Phoenix*. He said he liked Brooklyn better than Manhattan or the Bronx, but he also developed a habit of dropping by *The Phoenix* when he got off work and waiting for me until three or four in the morning so we could take the subway together up to the South Bronx. He never said anything, but I think he figured that, as when we were kids, we both stood a better chance if we took on the world together.

I now saw no point in going to college. It was expensive, and my aim in going would have been to get a degree to qualify me for a job as a journalist. But I now had my job at *The Phoenix*. As for the learning itself, I figured you didn't need a college degree to become one of the people who knew what was really going on. If you paid attention, you could pick things up on your own. And so, if I overheard mention of something I was ignorant about—keeping Kosher, Tammany Hall, haute couture—I researched it later on. One day I interviewed a community activist who described a particular job program as a throwback to the Progressive Era. I had no idea what the Progressive Era was, and back in the office, I got out the *World Book Encyclopedia*. Mike Armstrong wanted to know what I was doing, and when I explained, he asked me if I had ever thought of going to college.

"Why should I give up this job to go to college?" I asked. "You've got college graduates working here who are doing what I'm doing."

"You may not believe this," he said, "but there are better jobs out there than the one you've got now. You might get one of them one of these days. But not without a college degree." Mike promised me that if I went to college, I could come back to *The Phoenix* anytime I wanted. But, he added, he didn't think I would.

Lori's friends told me that Columbia University was the best in New York City. Since it took only men at the time, I applied to its sister college, Barnard, and was accepted. I received grants and loans to cover most of the tuition, which was steep, and I'd saved a little money while working at *The Phoenix*. But to pay for the rest, I had to spend a year answering phones at a Wall Street firm.

Once school started, I could no longer pay my share of the rent, but a psychologist let me have a room in her Upper West Side apartment in exchange for looking after her two small sons. I found a weekend job in an art gallery, crowded all my classes into two days, and became the news editor of the *Barnard Bulletin*. But I gave that up when I was hired as an editorial assistant three days a week at one of the biggest magazines in the city. Writers there had published books and covered wars and interviewed presidents. I got to forward their mail, check their expense accounts, and do word counts on their manuscripts. I felt I'd arrived.

Mom and Dad called us now and then from Grandpa's to bring us up to date on life in Welch. I began to dread those calls, since every time we heard from them, there was a new problem: a mudslide had washed away what was left of the stairs; our neighbors the Freemans were trying to get the house condemned; Maureen had fallen off the porch and gashed her head.

When Lori heard that, she declared it was time for Maureen to move to New York, too. But Maureen was only twelve, and I worried that she might be too young to leave home. She'd been four when we moved to West Virginia, and it was all she really knew.

"Who's going to look after her?" I asked.

"I will," Lori said. "She can stay with me."

Lori called Maureen, who got squeally with excitement about the idea, and then Lori talked to Mom and Dad. Mom thought it was a great plan, but Dad accused Lori of stealing his children and declared he was disowning her. Maureen arrived in early winter. By then Brian had moved into a walk-up near the Port Authority bus terminal, and using his address, we enrolled Maureen in a good public school in Manhattan. On weekends, we all met at Lori's apartment. We made fried pork chops or heaping plates of spaghetti and meatballs and sat around talking about Welch, laughing so hard at the idea of all that craziness that our eyes watered.

ONE MORNING THREE years after I'd moved to New York, I was getting ready for class and listening to the radio. The announcer reported a terrible traffic jam on the New Jersey Turnpike. A van had broken down, spilling clothes and furniture all over the road and creating a big backup. The police were trying to clear the highway, but a dog had jumped out of the van and was running up and down the turnpike as a couple of officers chased after him. The announcer got a lot of mileage out of the story, going on about the rubes with their clunker of a vehicle and yapping dog who were making thousands of New York commuters late for work.

That night the psychologist told me I had a phone call.

"Jeannettie-kins!" It was Mom. "Guess what?" she asked in a voice brimming with excitement. "Your daddy and I have moved to New York!"

The first thing I thought about was the van that had broken down on the turnpike that morning. When I asked Mom about it, she admitted that yes, she and Dad had a teensy bit of technical difficulty with the van. It had popped a belt on some big, crowded highway, and Tinkle, who was sick and tired of being cooped up, you know how that goes, had gotten loose. The police had shown up, and Dad got into an argument with them, and they threatened to arrest him, and gosh it was quite the drama. "How did you know?" she asked.

"It was on the radio."

"On the radio?" Mom asked. She couldn't believe it. "With everything going on in the world these days, an old van popping a belt is news?" But there was genuine glee in her voice. "We only just got here, and we're already famous!"

After talking to Mom, I looked around my room. It was the maid's room off the kitchen, and it was tiny, with one narrow window and a bathroom that doubled as a closet. But it was mine. I had a room now, and I had a life, too, and there was no place in either one for Mom and Dad.

Still, the next day I went up to Lori's apartment to see them. Everyone was there. Mom and Dad hugged me. Dad pulled a pint of whiskey out of a paper bag while Mom described their various adventures on the trip. They had gone sightseeing earlier that day, and taken their first ride on the subway, which Dad called a goddamn hole in the ground. Mom said the art deco murals at Rockefeller Center were disappointing, not nearly as good as some of her own paintings. None of us kids was doing much to help carry the conversation.

"So, what's the plan?" Brian finally asked. "You're moving here?"

"We have moved," Mom said.

"For good?" I asked.

"That's right," Dad said.

"Why?" I asked. The question came out sharply.

Dad looked puzzled, as if the answer should have been obvious. "So we could be a family again." He raised his pint. "To the family," he said.

Mom and Dad found a room in a boardinghouse a few blocks from Lori's apartment. The steely-haired landlady helped them move in, and a couple of months later, when they fell behind on their rent, she put their belongings on the street and padlocked their room. Mom and Dad moved into a six-story flophouse in a more dilapidated neighborhood. They lasted there a few months, but when Dad set their room on fire by falling asleep with a burning cigarette in his hand, they got kicked out. Brian believed that Mom and Dad needed to be forced to be self-sufficient or they'd be dependent on us forever, so he refused to take them in. But Lori had moved out of the South Bronx and into an apartment in the same building as Brian, and she let them come stay with her and Maureen. It would be for just a week or two, Mom and Dad assured her, a month at the most, while they got a kitty together and looked for a new place.

One month at Lori's became two months and then three and four. Each time I visited, the apartment was more jam-packed. Mom hung paintings on the walls and stacked street finds in the living room and put colored bottles in the windows for that stained-glass effect. The stacks reached the ceiling, and then the living room filled up, and Mom's collectibles and found art overflowed into the kitchen.

But it was Dad who was really getting to Lori. While he hadn't found steady work, he always had mysterious ways of hustling up pocket money, and he'd come home at night drunk and gunning for an argument. Brian saw that Lori was on the verge of snapping, so he invited Dad to come live with him. He put a lock on the booze cabinet, but Dad had been there under a week when Brian came home and found that Dad had used a screwdriver to take the door off its hinges and then guzzled down every single bottle.

Brian didn't lose his temper. He told Dad he had made a mistake by leaving liquor in the apartment. He said he'd allow Dad to stay, but Dad had to follow some rules, the first being that he stop drinking as long as he was there. "You're the king of your own castle, and that's the way it should be," Dad replied. "But it'll be a chilly day in hell before I bow to my own son." He and Mom still had the white van they'd driven up from West Virginia, and he started sleeping in that.

Lori, meanwhile, had given Mom a deadline to clean out the apartment. But the deadline came and went, and so did a second and a third. Also, Dad was always dropping by to visit Mom, but then they got into such screeching arguments that the neighbors banged on the walls. Dad starting fighting with them, too.

"I can't take it anymore," Lori told me one day.

"Maybe you're just going to have to kick Mom out," I said.

"But she's my mother."

"It doesn't matter. She's driving you crazy."

Lori finally agreed. It almost killed her to tell Mom she would have to leave, and she offered to do whatever it took to help her get reestablished, but Mom insisted she'd be fine.

"Lori's doing the right thing," she said to me. "Sometimes you need a little crisis to get your adrenaline flowing and help you realize your potential."

Mom and Tinkle moved into the van with Dad. They lived there for a few months, but one day they left it in a no-parking zone and it was towed. Because the van was unregistered, they couldn't get it back. That night, they slept on a park bench. They were homeless.

MOM AND DAD CALLED regularly from pay phones to check up on us, and once or twice a month, we'd all get together at Lori's.

"It's not such a bad life," Mom told us after they'd been homeless for a couple of months.

"Don't you worry a lick about us," Dad added. "We've always been able to fend for ourselves."

Mom explained that they'd been busy learning the ropes. They'd visited the various soup kitchens, sampling the cuisines, and had their favorites. They knew which churches passed out sandwiches and when. They'd found the public libraries with good bathrooms where you could wash thoroughly—"We wash as far down as possible and as far up as possible, but we don't wash possible," was how Mom put it—and brush your teeth and shave. They fished newspapers from the trash cans and looked up free events. They went to plays and operas and concerts in the parks, listened to string quartets and piano recitals in office-building lobbies, attended movie screenings, and visited museums. When they first became homeless, it was early summer, and they slept on park benches or in the bushes that lined park paths. Sometimes a cop would wake them up and tell them to move, but they'd just find some other place to sleep. During the day, they'd stash their bedrolls in the underbrush.

"You can't just live like this," I said.

"Why not?" Mom said. "Being homeless is an adventure."

As fall came and the days shortened and the weather cooled, Mom and Dad began spending more time in the libraries, which were warm and comfortable, and some of which remained open well into the evening. Mom was working her way through Balzac. Dad had become interested in chaos theory and was reading *Los Alamos Science* and the *Journal of Statistical Physics*. He said it had already helped his pool game.

"What are you going to do when winter comes?" I asked Mom.

She smiled. "Winter is one of my favorite seasons," she said.

I didn't know what to do. Part of me wanted to do whatever I could to take care of Mom and Dad, and part of me just wanted to wash my hands of them. The cold came early that year, and every time I left the psychologist's apartment, I found myself looking into the faces of the homeless people I passed on the street, wondering each time if one of them would turn out to be Mom or Dad. I usually gave homeless people whatever spare change I had, but I couldn't help feeling like I was trying to ease my conscience about Mom and Dad wandering the streets while I had a steady job and a warm room to come home to.

One day I was walking down Broadway with another student named Carol when I gave some change to a young homeless guy. "You shouldn't do that," Carol said.

"Why?"

"It only encourages them. They're all scam artists."

What do you know? I wanted to ask. I felt like telling Carol that my parents were out there, too, that she had no idea what it was like to be down on your luck, with nowhere to go and nothing to eat. But that would have meant explaining who I really was, and I wasn't about to do that. So at the next street corner, I went my way without saying a thing.

I knew I should have stood up for Mom and Dad. I'd been pretty scrappy as a kid, and our family had always fought for one another, but back then we'd had no choice. The truth was, I was tired of taking on people who ridiculed us for the way we lived. I just didn't have it in me to argue Mom and Dad's case to the world.

That was why I didn't own up to my parents in front of Professor Fuchs. She was one of my favorite teachers, a tiny dark passionate woman with circles under her eyes who taught political science. One day Professor Fuchs asked if homelessness was the result of drug abuse and misguided entitlement programs, as the conservatives claimed, or did it occur, as the liberals argued, because of cuts in social-service programs and the failure to create economic opportunity for the poor? Professor Fuchs called on me.

I hesitated. "Sometimes, I think, it's neither."

"Can you explain yourself?"

"I think that maybe sometimes people get the lives they want."

"Are you saying homeless people want to live on the street?" Professor Fuchs asked. "Are you saying they don't want warm beds and roofs over their heads?"

"Not exactly," I said. I was fumbling for words. "They do. But if some of them were willing to work hard and make compromises, they might not have ideal lives, but they could make ends meet."

Professor Fuchs walked around from behind her lectern. "What do you know about the lives of the underprivileged?" she asked. She was practically trembling with agitation. "What do you know about the hardships and obstacles that the underclass faces?"

The other students were staring at me.

"You have a point," I said.

THAT JANUARY IT GOT so cold you could see chunks of ice the size of cars floating down the Hudson River. On those midwinter nights, the homeless shelters filled up quickly. Mom and Dad hated the shelters. Human cesspools, Dad called them, goddamn vermin pits. Mom and Dad preferred to sleep on the pews of the churches that opened their doors to the homeless, but on some nights every pew in every church was taken. On those nights Dad would end up in a shelter, while Mom would show up at Lori's, Tinkle in tow. At times like that, her cheerful facade would crack, and she'd start crying and confess to Lori that life in the streets could be hard, just really hard.

For a while I considered dropping out of Barnard to help. It felt unbearably selfish, just downright wrong, to be indulging myself with an education in the liberal arts at a fancy private college while Mom and Dad were on the streets. But Lori convinced me that dropping out was a lame-brained idea. It wouldn't do any good, she said, and besides, dropping out would break Dad's heart. He was immensely proud that he had a daughter in college, and an Ivy League college at that. Every time he met someone new, he managed to work it into the first few minutes of conversation.

Mom and Dad, Brian pointed out, had options. They could move back to West Virginia or Phoenix. Mom could work. And she was not destitute. She had her collection of antique Indian jewelry, which she kept in a self-storage locker. There was the two-carat diamond ring that Brian and I had found under the rotten lumber back in Welch; she wore it even when sleeping on the street. She still owned property in Phoenix. And she had the land in Texas, the source of her oil-lease royalties.

Brian was right. Mom did have options. I met her at a coffee shop to discuss them. First off, I suggested that she might think of finding an arrangement like mine: a room in someone's nice apartment in exchange for taking care of children or the elderly.

"I've spent my life taking care of other people," Mom said. "Now it's time to take care of me."

"But you're not taking care of you."

"Do we have to have this conversation?" Mom asked. "I've seen some good movies lately. Can't we talk about the movies?"

I suggested to Mom that she sell her Indian jewelry. She wouldn't consider it. She loved that jewelry. Besides, they were heirlooms and had sentimental value.

I mentioned the land in Texas.

"That land's been in the family for generations," Mom said, "and it's staying in the family. You never sell land like that."

I asked about the property in Phoenix.

"I'm saving that for a rainy day."

"Mom, it's pouring."

"This is just a drizzle," she said. "Monsoons could be ahead!" She sipped her tea. "Things usually work out in the end."

"What if they don't?"

"That just means you haven't come to the end yet."

She looked across the table and smiled at me with the smile you give people when you know you have the answers to all their questions. And so we talked about movies.

MOM AND DAD SURVIVED the winter, but every time I saw them, they looked a little worse for wear: dirtier, more bruised, their hair more matted.

"Don't you fret a bit," Dad said. "Have you ever known your old man to get himself in a situation he couldn't handle?"

I kept telling myself Dad was right, that they knew how to look after themselves and each other, but in the spring, Mom called me to say Dad had come down with tuberculosis.

Dad almost never got sick. He was always getting banged up and then recovering almost immediately, as if nothing could truly hurt him. A part of me still believed all those childhood stories he'd told us about how invincible he was. Dad had asked that no one visit him, but Mom said she thought he'd be pretty pleased if I dropped by the hospital.

I waited at the nurse's station while an orderly went to tell him he had a visitor. I thought Dad might be under an oxygen tent or lying in a bed coughing up blood into a white handkerchief, but after a minute, he came hurrying down the hall. He was paler and more gaunt than usual, but despite all his years of hard living, he had aged very little. He still had all his hair, and it was still coal black, and his dark eyes twinkled above the paper surgical mask he was wearing.

He wouldn't let me hug him. "Whoa, Nelly, stay back," he said. "You're sure a sight for sore eyes, honey, but I don't want you catching this sonofabitch of a bug."

Dad escorted me back to the TB ward and introduced me to all of his friends. "Believe it or not, ol' Rex Walls did produce something worth bragging about, and here she is," he told them. Then he started coughing.

"Dad, are you going to be okay?" I asked.

"Ain't none of us getting out of this alive, honey," Dad said. It was an expression he used a lot, and now he seemed to find a special satisfaction in it.

Dad led me over to his cot. A neat pile of books was stacked next to it. He said his bout with TB had set him to pondering about mortality and the nature of the cosmos. He'd been stone-cold sober since entering the hospital, and reading a lot more about chaos theory, particularly about the work of Mitchell Feigenbaum, a physicist at Los Alamos who had made a study of the transition between order and turbulence. Dad said he was damned if Feigenbaum didn't make a persuasive case that turbulence was not in fact random but followed a sequential spectrum of varying frequencies. If every action in the universe that we thought was random actually conformed to a rational pattern, Dad said, that implied the existence of a divine creator, and he was beginning to rethink his atheistic creed. "I'm not saying there's a bearded old geezer named Yahweh up in the clouds deciding which football team is going to win the Super Bowl," Dad said. "But if the physics—the quantum physics— suggests that God exists, I'm more than willing to entertain the notion."

Dad showed me some of the calculations he'd been working on. He saw me looking at his trembling fingers and held them up. "Lack of liquor or fear of God—don't know which is causing it," he said. "Maybe both."

"Promise you'll stay here until you get better," I said. "I don't want you doing the skedaddle."

Dad burst into laughter that ended in another fit of coughing.

DAD STAYED IN THE hospital for six weeks. By then he'd not only beaten back the TB, he'd been sober longer than any time since the Phoenix detox. He knew that if he went back to the streets, he'd start drinking again. One of the hospital administrators got him a job as a maintenance man at an upstate resort, room and board included. He tried to talk Mom into going with him, but she flatly refused. "Upstate's the sticks," she said.

So Dad went alone. He called me from time to time, and it sounded like he'd put together a life that worked for him. He had a one-room apartment over a garage, enjoyed doing the repairs and upkeep on the old lodge, loved being back within walking distance of untamed country, and was staying sober. Dad worked at the resort through the summer and into the fall. As it began to turn cold again, Mom called him and mentioned how much easier it was for two people to stay warm during the winter, and how much Tinkle the dog missed him. In November, after the first hard frost, I got a call from Brian, who said that Mom had succeeded in persuading Dad to quit his job and return to the city.

"Do you think he'll stay sober?" I asked.

"He's already back on the booze," Brian said.

A few weeks after Dad got back, I saw him at Lori's. He was sitting on the sofa with an arm around Mom and a pint bottle in his hand. He laughed. "This crazy-ass mother of yours, can't live with her, can't live without her. And damned if she doesn't feel the same about me."

All of us kids had our own lives by then. I was in college, Lori had become an illustrator at a comic-book company, Maureen lived with Lori and went to high school, and Brian, who had wanted to be a cop ever since he'd had to call a policeman to our house in Phoenix to break up a fight between Mom and Dad, had become a warehouse foreman and was serving on the auxiliary force until he was old enough to take the police department's entrance exam. Mom suggested we all celebrate Christmas at Lori's apartment. I bought Mom an antique silver cross, but finding a gift for Dad was harder; he always said he never needed anything. Since it looked like it was going to be another hard winter, and since Dad wore nothing but his bomber jacket in even the coldest weather, I decided to get him some warm clothes. At an army-surplus store, I bought flannel shirts, thermal underwear, thick wool socks, the kind of blue work pants that auto mechanics wear, and a new pair of steel-toed boots.

Lori decorated her apartment with colored lights and pine boughs and paper angels; Brian made eggnog; and to demonstrate that he was on his best behavior, Dad went to great lengths to make sure there was no alcohol in it before he accepted a glass. Mom passed around their presents, each wrapped in newspaper and tied with butcher's twine. Lori got a cracked lamp that might have been a Tiffany; Maureen, an antique porcelain doll that had lost most of her hair; Brian, a nineteenth-century book of poetry, missing the cover and the first few pages. My present was an orange crewneck sweater, slightly stained but made, Mom pointed out, of genuine Shetland wool.

When I passed Dad my stack of carefully wrapped boxes, he protested that he needed and wanted nothing. "Go ahead," I said. "Open them."

I watched as he carefully removed the wrapping. He lifted the lids and stared at the folded clothes. His face took on that wounded expression he got whenever the world called his bluff. "You must be mighty ashamed of your old man," he said.

"What do you mean?" I asked.

"You think I'm some sort of goddamn charity case."

Dad stood up and put on his bomber jacket. He was avoiding all our eyes.

"Where are you going?" I asked.

Dad just turned up his collar and walked out of the apartment. I listened to the sound of his boots going down the stairs.

"What did I do?" I asked.

"Look at it from his perspective," Mom said. "You buy him all these nice new things, and all he has for you is junk from the street. He's the father. He's the one who's supposed to be taking care of you."

The room was quiet for a while. "I guess you don't want your presents, either," I said to Mom.

"Oh, no," she said. "I love getting presents."

By the following summer, Mom and Dad were heading into their third year on the streets. They'd figured out how to make it work for them, and I gradually came around to accepting the notion that whether I liked it or not, this was how it was going to be. "It's sort of the city's fault," Mom told me. "They make it too easy to be homeless. If it was really unbearable, we'd do something different."

In August, Dad called to go over my course selection for the fall semester. He also wanted to discuss some of the books on the reading lists. Since he'd come to New York, he'd been borrowing my assigned books from the public library. He read every single one, he said, so he could answer any questions I might have. Mom said it was his way of getting a college education along with me.

When he asked me what courses I had signed up for, I said, "I'm thinking of dropping out."

"The hell you are," Dad said.

I told him that while most of my tuition was covered by grants and loans and scholarships, the school expected me to contribute two thousand dollars a year. But over the summer, I had been able to save only a thousand dollars. I needed another thousand and had no way to come up with it.

"Why didn't you tell me sooner?" Dad asked.

Dad called a week later and told me to meet him at Lori's. When he arrived with Mom, he was carrying a large plastic garbage bag and had a small brown paper bag tucked under his arm. I assumed it was a bottle of booze, but then he opened the paper bag and turned it upside down. Hundreds of dollar bills—ones, fives, tens, twenties, all wrinkled and worn—spilled into my lap.

"There's nine hundred and fifty bucks," Dad said. He opened the plastic bag, and a fur coat tumbled out. "That there's mink. You should be able to pawn it for fifty, at least."

I stared at the loot. "Where did you get all this?" I finally asked.

"New York City is full of poker players who wouldn't know their ass from a hole in the ground."

"Dad," I said, "you guys need this money more than I do."

"It's yours," Dad said. "Since when is it wrong for a father to take care of his little girl?"

"But I can't." I looked at Mom.

She sat down next to me and patted my leg. "I've always believed in the value of a good education," she said.

So, when I enrolled for my final year at Barnard, I paid what I owed on my tuition with Dad's wadded, crumpled bills.

A MONTH LATER, I got a call from Mom. She was so excited she was tripping over her own words. She and Dad had found a place to live. Their new home, Mom said, was in an abandoned building on the Lower East Side. "It's a tad run-down," she admitted. "But all it really needs is a little TLC. And best of all, it's free."

Other folks were also moving into abandoned buildings, she said. They were called squatters, and the buildings were called squats. "Your father and I are pioneers," Mom said. "Just like my great-great-grandfather, who helped tame the Wild West."

Mom called in a few weeks and said that although the squat still needed a few finishing touches—a front door, for example—she and Dad were officially accepting visitors. I took the subway to Astor Place on a late spring day and headed east. Mom and Dad's apartment was in a six-story walk-up. The mortar was crumbling and bricks had come loose. All the windows on the first floor had been boarded up. I reached to open the building's front door, but where the lock and handle should have been, there was only a hole. Inside, a single naked lightbulb hung from a wire in the hallway. On one wall, chunks of plaster had crumbled away, revealing the wooden ribs and pipes and wiring. On the third floor, I knocked on the door to Mom and Dad's apartment and heard Dad's muffled voice. Instead of the door swinging inward, fingers appeared on both sides, and it was lifted out of the frame altogether. There was Dad, beaming and hugging me while he went on about how he'd yet to install door hinges. As a matter of fact, they'd only just gotten the door itself, which he'd found in the basement of another abandoned building.

Mom came running up behind him, grinning so widely you could see her molars, and gave me a big hug. Dad knocked a cat off a chair—they had already taken in a few strays—and offered me a seat. The room was crammed with broken furniture, bundles of clothes, stacks of books, and Mom's art supplies. Four or five electric space heaters blasted away. Mom explained that Dad had hooked up every squat in the building to an insulated cable he'd hot-wired off a utility pole down the block. "We're all getting free juice, thanks to your father," Mom said. "No one in the building could survive without him."

Dad chuckled modestly. He told me how complicated the process had been, because the wiring in the building was so ancient. "Damnedest electrical system I've ever seen," he said. "The manual must have been written in hieroglyphics."

I looked around, and it hit me that if you replaced the electric heaters with a coal stove, this squat on the Lower East Side looked pretty much like the house on Little Hobart Street. I had escaped from Welch once, and now, breathing in those same old smells of turpentine, dog hair, and dirty clothes, of stale beer and cigarette smoke and unrefrigerated food slowly going bad, I had the urge to bolt. But Mom and Dad were clearly proud, and as I listened to them talk—interrupting each other in their excitement to correct points of fact and fill in gaps in the story—about their fellow squatters and the friends they'd made in the neighborhood and the common fight against the city's housing agency, it became clear they'd stumbled on an entire community of people like themselves, people who lived unruly lives battling authority and who liked it that way. After all those years of roaming, they'd found home.

I graduated from Barnard that spring. Brian came to the ceremony, but Lori and Maureen had to work, and Mom said it would just be a lot of boring speeches about the long and winding road of life. I wanted Dad to come, but chances were he'd show up drunk and try to debate the commencement speaker.

"I can't risk it, Dad," I told him.

"Hell," he said. "I don't have to see my Mountain Goat grabbing a sheepskin to know she's got her college degree."

The magazine where I'd been working two days a week had offered me a full-time job. What I needed was a place to live. For several years, I had been dating a man named Eric, a friend of one of Lori's eccentric-genius friends, who came from a wealthy family, ran a small company, and lived alone in the apartment on Park Avenue in which he'd been raised. He was a detached, almost fanatically organized guy who maintained detailed time-management logs and could recite endless baseball statistics. But he was decent and responsible, never gambled or lost his temper, and always paid his bills on time. When he heard that I was looking for a roommate to share an apartment, he suggested I move in with him. I couldn't afford half the rent, I told him, and I wouldn't live there unless I could pay my own way. He suggested that I begin by paying what I could afford, and as my salary went up, I could increase the payment. He made it sound like a business proposition, but a solid one, and after thinking it over, I agreed.

When I told Dad about my plans, he asked if Eric made me happy and treated me well. "Because if he doesn't," Dad said, "I will by God kick his butt so hard, his asshole will be up between his shoulder blades."

"He treats me fine, Dad," I said. What I wanted to say was that I knew Eric would never try to steal my paycheck or throw me out the window, that I'd always been terrified I'd fall for a hard-drinking, hell-raising, charismatic scoundrel like you, Dad, but I'd wound up with a man who was exactly the opposite.

All my belongings fit into two plastic milk crates and a garbage bag. I hauled them to the street, hailed a taxi, and took it across town to Eric's building. The doorman, in a blue uniform with gold piping, hurried out from under the awning and insisted on carrying the milk crates into the lobby.

Eric's apartment had crossbeamed ceilings and a fireplace with an art deco mantel. I actually live on Park Avenue, I kept telling myself as I hung my clothes in the closet Eric had cleared out for me. Then I started thinking about Mom and Dad. When they had moved into their squat—a fifteen-minute subway ride south and about half a dozen worlds away—it seemed as if they had finally found the place where they belonged, and I wondered if I had done the same.

I INVITED MOM and Dad up to the apartment. Dad said he'd feel out of place, and never did come, but Mom visited almost immediately. She turned over dishes to read the manufacturer's name and lifted the corner of the Persian rug to count the knots. She held the china to the light and ran her finger along the antique campaign chest. Then she went to the window and looked out at the brick and limestone apartment buildings across the street. "I don't really like Park Avenue," she said. "The architecture is too monotonous. I prefer the architecture on Central Park West."

I told Mom she was the snootiest squatter I'd ever met, and that made her laugh. We sat down on the living room couch. I had something I wanted to discuss with her. I now had a good job, I said, and was in a position to help her and Dad. I wanted to buy them something that would improve their lives. It could be a small car. It could be the security deposit and a few months' rent on an apartment. It could be the down payment on a house in an inexpensive neighborhood.

"We don't need anything," Mom said. "We're fine." She put down her teacup. "It's you I'm worried about."

"*You're* worried about *me*?"

"Yes. Very worried."

"Mom," I said. "I'm doing very well. I'm very, very comfortable."

"That's what I'm worried about," Mom said. "Look at the way you live. You've sold out. Next thing I know, you'll become a Republican." She shook her head. "Where are the values I raised you with?"

Mom became even more concerned about my values when my editor offered me a job writing a weekly column about what he called the behind-the-scenes doings of the movers and shakers. Mom thought I should be writing exposés about oppressive landlords, social injustice, and the class struggle on the Lower East Side. But I leaped at the job, because it meant I would become one of those people who knew what was really going on. Also, most people in Welch had a pretty good idea how bad off the Walls family was, but the truth was, they all had their problems, too—they were just better than we were at covering them up. I wanted to let the world know that no one had a perfect life, that even the people who seemed to have it all had their secrets.

Dad thought it was great that I was writing a weekly column about, as he put it, the skinny dames and the fat cats. He became one of my most faithful readers, and would go to the library to research the people in the column, then call me with tips. "This Astor broad has one helluva past," he told me one time. "Maybe we should do a little digging in that direction." Eventually, even Mom acknowledged that I'd done all right. "No one expected you to amount to much," she told me. "Lori was the smart one, Maureen the pretty one, and Brian the brave one. You never had much going for you except that you always worked hard."

I loved my new job even more than I loved my Park Avenue address. I was invited to dozens of parties a week: art-gallery openings, benefit balls, movie premieres, book parties, and private dinners in marble-floored dining rooms. I met real estate developers, agents, heiresses, fund managers, lawyers, clothing designers, professional basketball players, photographers, movie producers, and television correspondents. I met people who owned entire collections of houses and spent more on one restaurant meal than my family had paid for 93 Little Hobart Street.

True or not, I was convinced that if all these people found out about Mom and Dad and who I really was, it would be impossible for me to keep my job. So I avoided discussing my parents. When that was impossible, I lied.

A year after I started the column, I was in a small, overstuffed restaurant across the table from an aging, elegant woman in a silk turban who oversaw the International Best Dressed List.

"So, where are you from, Jeannette?"

"West Virginia."

"Where?"

"Welch."

"How lovely. What's the main industry in Welch?"

"Coal mining."

As she questioned me, she studied what I wore, assessing the fabric and appraising the cost of each item and making a judgment about my taste in general.

"And does your family own coal mines?"

"No."

"What do your parents do?"

"Mom's an artist."

"And your father?"

"He's an entrepreneur."

"Doing what?"

I took a breath. "He's developing a technology to burn low-grade bituminous coal more efficiently."

"And they're still in West Virginia?" she asked.

I decided I might as well go all out. "They love it there," I said. "They have a great old house on a hill overlooking a beautiful river. They spent years restoring it."

My life with Eric was calm and predictable. I liked it that way, and four years after I moved into his apartment, we got married. Shortly after the wedding, Mom's brother, my uncle Jim, died in Arizona. Mom came to the apartment to give me the news and to ask a favor. "We need to buy Jim's land," she said.

Mom and her brother had each inherited half of the West Texas land that had been owned by their father. The whole time we kids were growing up, Mom had been mysteriously vague about how big and how valuable this land was, but I had the impression that it was a few hundred acres of more or less uninhabitable desert, miles from any road.

"We need to keep that land in the family," Mom told me. "It's important for sentimental reasons."

"Let's see if we can buy it, then," I said. "How much will it cost?"

"You can borrow the money from Eric now that he's your husband," Mom said.

"I've got a little money," I said. "How much will it cost?" I'd read somewhere that off-road land in parched West Texas sold for as little as a hundred dollars an acre.

"You can borrow from Eric," Mom said again.

"Well, how much?"

"A million dollars."

"What?"

"A million dollars."

"But Uncle Jim's land is the same size as your land," I said. I was speaking slowly, because I wanted to make sure I understood the implications of what Mom had just told me. "You each inherited half of Grandpa Smith's land."

"More or less," Mom said.

"So if Uncle Jim's land is worth a million dollars, that means your land is worth a million dollars."

"I don't know."

"What do you mean, you don't know? It's the same size as his."

"I don't know how much it's worth, because I never had it appraised. I was never going to sell it. My father taught me you never sell land. That's why we have to buy Uncle Jim's land. We have to keep it in the family."

"You mean you own land worth a million dollars?" I was thunderstruck. All those years in Welch with no food, no coal, no plumbing, and Mom had been sitting on land worth a million dollars? Had all those years, as well as Mom and Dad's time on the street—not to mention their current life in an abandoned tenement—been a caprice inflicted on us by Mom? Could she have solved our financial problems by selling this land she never even saw? But she avoided my questions, and it became clear that to Mom, holding on to land was not so much an investment strategy as it was an article of faith, a revealed truth as deeply felt and incontestable to her as Catholicism. And for the life of me, I could not get her to tell me how much the land was worth.

"I told you I don't know," she said.

"Then tell me how many acres it is, and where exactly it is, and I'll find out how much an acre of land is going for in that area." I wasn't interested in her money; I just wanted to know—needed to know—the answer to my question: How much was that freaking land worth? Maybe she truly didn't know. Maybe she was afraid to find out. Maybe she was afraid of what we'd all think if we knew. But instead of answering me, she kept repeating that it was important to keep Uncle Jim's land—land that had belonged to her father and his father and his father before that—in the family.

"Mom, I can't ask Eric for a million dollars."

"Jeannette, I haven't asked you for a lot of favors, but I'm asking you for one now. I wouldn't if it wasn't important. But this is important."

I told Mom I didn't think Eric would lend me a million dollars to buy some land in Texas, and even if he would, I wouldn't borrow it from him. "It's too much money," I said. "What would I do with the land?"

"Keep it in the family."

"I can't believe you're asking me this," I said. "I've never even seen that land."

"Jeannette," Mom said when she had accepted the fact that she would not get her way, "I'm deeply disappointed in you."

LORI WAS WORKING as a freelance artist specializing in fantasy, illustrating calendars and game boards and book jackets. Brian had joined the police force as soon as he turned twenty. Dad couldn't figure out what he'd done wrong, raising a son who'd grown up to become a member of the gestapo. But I was so proud of my brother on the day he was sworn in, standing there in the ranks of the new officers, straight-shouldered in his navy blue uniform with its glittering brass buttons.

Meanwhile, Maureen had graduated from high school and enrolled in one of the city colleges, but she never really applied herself and ended up living with Mom and Dad. She worked from time to time as a bartender or waitress, but the jobs never lasted long. Ever since she was a kid, she'd been looking for someone to take care of her. In Welch, the Pentecostal neighbors provided for her, and now in New York, with her long blond hair and wide blue eyes, she found various men who were willing to help out.

The boyfriends never lasted any longer than the jobs. She talked about finishing college and going to law school, but distractions kept cropping up. The longer she stayed with Mom and Dad, the more lost she became, and after a while she was spending most of her days in the apartment, smoking cigarettes, reading novels, and occasionally painting nude self-portraits. That two-room squat was cramped, and Maureen and Dad would get into the worst screaming fights, with Maureen calling Dad a worthless drunk and Dad calling Maureen a sick puppy, the runt of the litter, who should have been drowned at birth.

Maureen even stopped reading and slept all day, leaving the apartment only to buy cigarettes. I called and persuaded her to come up to see me and discuss her future. When she arrived, I scarcely recognized her. She'd bleached her hair and eyebrows platinum and was wearing dark makeup as thick as a Kabuki dancer's. She lit one cigarette after another and kept glancing around the room. When I brought up some career possibilities, she told me that the only thing she wanted to do was help fight the Mormon cults that had kidnapped thousands of people in Utah.

"What cults?" I asked.

"Don't pretend you don't know," she said. "That just means you're one of them."

Afterward, I called Brian. "Do you think Maureen's on drugs?" I asked.

"If she's not, she should be," he said. "She's gone nuts."

I told Mom that Maureen should get professional help, but Mom kept insisting that all Maureen needed was fresh air and sunshine. I talked to several doctors, but they told me that since it sounded like Maureen would refuse to seek help on her own, she could be treated only on the order of a court, if she proved she was a danger to herself or others.

Six months later, Maureen stabbed Mom. It happened after Mom decided it was time for Maureen to develop a little self-sufficiency by moving out and finding a place of her own. God helps those who help themselves, Mom told Maureen, and so for her own good, she would have to leave the nest and make her way in the world. Maureen couldn't bear the idea that her own mom would kick her out onto the street, and she snapped. Mom insisted Maureen had not actually been trying to kill her—she'd just become confused and upset, she said—but the wounds required stitches, and the police arrested Maureen.

She was arraigned a few days later. Mom and Dad and Lori and Brian and I were all there. Brian was fuming. Lori looked grief-stricken. Dad was half potted and kept trying to pick fights with the security guards. But Mom acted like her normal self—nonchalant in the face of adversity. As we sat waiting on the courtroom benches, she hummed tunelessly and sketched the other spectators.

Maureen shuffled into the courtroom, shackled and wearing an orange jumpsuit. Her face was puffy, and she looked dazed, but when she saw us, she smiled and waved. Her lawyer asked the judge to set bail. I had borrowed several thousand dollars from Eric and had the cash in my purse. But after listening to the prosecutor's version of events, the judge shook her head grimly: "Bail is denied."

In the hallway, Lori and Dad got into a loud argument over who was responsible for pushing Maureen over the edge. Lori blamed Dad for creating a sick environment, while Dad maintained that Maureen had faulty wiring. Mom chimed in that all the junk food Maureen ate had led to a chemical imbalance, and Brian started yelling at them all to shut the hell up or he'd arrest them. I just stood there looking from one distorted face to another, listening to this babble of enraged squabbling as the members of the Walls family gave vent to all their years of hurt and anger, each unloading his or her own accumulated grievances and blaming the others for allowing the most fragile one of us to break into pieces.

The judge sent Maureen to an upstate hospital. She was released after a year and immediately bought a one-way bus ticket to California. I told Brian that we had to stop her. She didn't know a single person in California. How would she survive? But Brian thought it was the smartest thing she could do for herself. He said she needed to get as far away from Mom and Dad, and probably the rest of us, as possible.

I decided Brian was right. But I also hoped that Maureen had chosen California because she thought that was her true home, the place where she really belonged, where it was always warm and you could dance in the rain, pick grapes right off the vines, and sleep outside at night under the stars.

Maureen did not want any of us to see her off. I rose just after first light the morning she was scheduled to leave. It was an early departure, and I wanted to be awake and thinking about her at the moment her bus pulled out, so I could say farewell in my mind. I went to the window and looked out at the cold, wet sky. I wondered if she was thinking of us and if she was going to miss us. I'd always had mixed feelings about bringing her to New York, but I'd agreed to let her come. Once she arrived, I'd been too busy taking care of myself to look after her. "I'm sorry, Maureen," I said when the time came, "sorry for everything."

AFTER THAT, I HARDLY ever saw Mom or Dad. Neither did Brian. He had gotten married and bought a run-down Victorian house on Long Island that he restored, and he and his wife had a child, a little girl. They were his family now. Lori, who was still living in her apartment near the Port Authority, was more in touch with Mom and Dad, but she, too, had gone her own way. We hadn't gotten together since Maureen's arraignment. Something in all of us broke that day, and afterward, we no longer had the spirit for family gatherings.

About a year after Maureen took off for California, I got a call at work from Dad. He said he needed to get together to discuss something important.

"Can't we do it over the phone?"

"I need to see you in person, honey."

Dad asked me to come down to the Lower East Side that evening. "And if it's not too much trouble," he added, "could you stop on your way and pick up a bottle of vodka?"

"Oh, so that's what this is about."

"No, no, honey. I do need to talk to you. But I would appreciate some vodka. Nothing fancy, just the cheapest rotgut they have. A pint would be fine. A fifth would be great."

I was annoyed by Dad's sly request for vodka—tossing it out at the end of the conversation as if it were an afterthought, when I figured it was probably the purpose of the call. That afternoon I called Mom, who still never drank anything stronger than tea, and asked if I should indulge Dad.

"Your father is who he is," Mom said. "It's a little late in the game to try to reform him now. Humor the man."

That night I stopped in a liquor store and bought a half gallon of the cheapest rotgut on the shelf, just as Dad had requested, then took a taxi down to the Lower East Side. I climbed the dark staircase and pushed open the unlocked door. Mom and Dad were lying in their bed under a pile of thin blankets. I got the impression they'd been there all day. Mom squealed when she saw me, and Dad started apologizing for the mess, saying if Mom would let him clear out some of her crap, they might at least be able to swing a cat in here, which got Mom accusing Dad of being a bum.

"Good to see you," I said as I kissed them. "It's been a while."

Mom and Dad struggled up into sitting positions. I saw Dad eyeing the brown paper bag, and I passed it to him.

"A magnum," Dad said, his voice choked with gratitude as he eased the big bottle from the bag. He unscrewed the cap and took a long, deep pull. "Thank you, my darling," he said. "You are so good to your old man."

Mom wore a heavy cable-knit sweater. The skin of her hands was deeply cracked, and her hair was tangled, but her face had a healthy pink glow, and her eyes were clear and bright. Beside her, Dad looked gaunt. His hair, still coal black except for touches of gray at his temples, was combed back, but his cheeks were sunken, and he had a thin beard. He'd always been clean-shaven, even during those days on the streets.

"Why are you growing a beard, Dad?" I asked.

"Every man should grow one once."

"But why now?"

"It's now or never," Dad said. "The fact is, I'm dying."

I laughed nervously, then looked at Mom, who had reached for her sketch pad without saying anything.

Dad was watching me carefully. He passed me the vodka bottle. Although I almost never drank, I took a sip and felt the burn as the liquor slid down my throat.

"This stuff could grow on you," I said.

"Don't let it," Dad said.

He started telling me how he'd acquired a rare tropical disease after getting into a bloody fistfight with some Nigerian drug dealers. The doctors had examined him, pronounced the rare disease incurable, and told him he had anywhere from a few weeks to a few months to live.

It was a ridiculous yarn. The fact was that, although Dad was only fifty-nine, he had been smoking four packs of cigarettes a day since he was thirteen, and by this time he was also putting away a good two quarts of booze daily. He was, as he had put it many a time, completely pickled.

But despite all the hell-raising and destruction and chaos he had created in our lives, I could not imagine what my life would be like—what the world would be like—without him in it. As awful as he could be, I always knew he loved me in a way no one else ever had. I looked out the window.

"Now, no snot-slinging or boohooing about 'poor ol' Rex,'" Dad said. "I don't want any of that, either now or when I'm gone."

I nodded.

"But you always loved your old man, didn't you?"

"I did, Dad," I said. "And you loved me."

"Now, that's the God's honest truth." Dad chuckled. "We had some times, didn't we?"

"We did."

"Never did build that Glass Castle."

"No. But we had fun planning it."

"Those were some damn fine plans."

Mom stayed out of the conversation, sketching quietly.

"Dad," I said, "I'm sorry, I really should have asked you to my graduation."

"To hell with that." He laughed. "Ceremonies never did mean diddly to me." He took another long pull on his magnum. "I got a lot to regret about my life," he said. "But I'm goddamn proud of you, Mountain Goat, the way you turned out. Whenever I think of you, I figure I must have done something right."

"'Course you did."

"Well, all right then."

We talked about the old days some and, finally, it was time to go. I kissed them both, and at the door, I turned to look at Dad one more time.

"Hey," he said. He winked and pointed his finger at me. "Have I ever let you down?"

He started chuckling because he knew there was only one way I could ever answer that question. I just smiled. And then I closed the door.

Two weeks later, Dad had a heart attack. When I got to the hospital, he was in a bed in the emergency room, his eyes closed. Mom and Lori were standing next to him. "It's just the machines keeping him alive at his point," Mom said.

I knew Dad would have hated that, spending his final moments in a hospital hooked up to machines. He'd have wanted to be out in the wild somewhere. He always said that when he died, we should put him on a mountaintop and let the buzzards and coyotes tear his body apart. I had this crazy urge to scoop him up in my arms and charge through the doors—to check out Rex Walls–style one last time.

Instead, I took his hand. It was warm and heavy. An hour later, they turned the machines off.

In the months that followed, I found myself always wanting to be somewhere other than where I was. If I was at work, I'd wish I were at home. If I was in the apartment, I couldn't wait to get out of it. If a taxi I had hailed was stuck in traffic for over a minute, I got out and walked. I felt best when I was on the move, going someplace rather than being there. I took up ice-skating. I rose early in the morning and made my way through the quiet, dawn-lit streets to the rink, where I laced up my skates so tightly my feet throbbed. I welcomed the numbing cold and even the jolt of my falls on the hard, wet ice. The fast-paced, repetitive maneuvers distracted me, and sometimes I went back at night to skate again, returning home only when it was late and I was exhausted. It took me a while to realize that just being on the move wasn't enough; that I needed to reconsider everything.

A year after Dad died, I left Eric. He was a good man, but not the right one for me. And Park Avenue was not where I belonged.

I took a small apartment on the West Side. It had neither a doorman nor a fireplace, but there were large windows that flooded the rooms with light, and parquet floors and a small foyer, just like that first apartment Lori and I had found in the Bronx. It felt right.

I went ice-skating less often, and when my skates were stolen, I never replaced them. My compulsion to be always on the move began to fade. But I liked to go for long walks at night. I often walked west toward the river. The city lights obscured the stars, but on clear nights, I could see Venus on the horizon, up over the dark water, glowing steadily.

V

THANKSGIVING

I was standing on the platform with my second husband, John. A whistle sounded in the distance, red lights flashed, and a bell clanged as the gates were lowered across the roadway. The whistle sounded again, and then the train appeared around the bend through the trees and rumbled toward the station, its massive twin headlights pale in the bright November afternoon.

The train eased to a stop. The electric engines hummed and vibrated, and after a long pause, the doors opened. Passengers spilled out, carrying their folded newspapers and canvas weekend bags and brightly colored coats. Through the crowd, I saw Mom and Lori getting out at the back of the train, and I waved.

It had been five years since Dad died. I had seen Mom only sporadically since then, and she'd never met John nor been to the old country farmhouse we'd bought the year before. It had been John's idea to invite her and Lori and Brian out to the house for Thanksgiving, the first Walls family get-together since Dad's funeral.

Mom broke into a huge smile and started hurrying toward us. Instead of an overcoat, she was wearing what looked to be about four sweaters and a shawl, a pair of corduroy trousers, and some old sneakers. She carried bulky shopping bags in both hands. Lori, behind her, wore a black cape and a black fedora. They made quite a pair.

Mom hugged me. Her long hair was mostly gray, but her cheeks were rosy and her eyes as bright as ever. Then Lori hugged me, and I introduced John.

"Excuse my attire," Mom said, "but I plan to change out of my comfy shoes into some dress shoes for dinner." She reached into one of her shopping bags and pulled out a pair of banged-up penny loafers.

The winding road back to the house led under stone bridges, through woods and villages, and past marsh ponds where swans floated on mirrorlike water. Most of the leaves had fallen, and gusts of wind sent them spiraling along the roadside. Through the thickets of bare trees, you could see houses that were invisible during the summer.

As he drove, John told Mom and Lori about the area, about the duck farms and the flower farms and the Indian origin of our town's name. Sitting beside him, I studied his profile and couldn't help smiling. John wrote books and magazine articles. Like me, he had moved around a lot while growing up, but his mother had been raised in an Appalachian village in Tennessee, about a hundred miles southwest of Welch, so you could say our families hailed from the same neck of the woods. I'd never met a man I would rather spend time with. I loved him for all sorts of reasons: He cooked without recipes; he wrote nonsense poems for his nieces; his large, warm family had accepted me as one of their own. And when I first showed him my scar, he said it was interesting. He used the word "textured." He said "smooth" was boring but "textured" was interesting, and the scar meant that I was stronger than whatever it was that had tried to hurt me.

We pulled into the drive. Jessica, John's fifteen-year-old daughter from his first marriage, came out of the house, along with Brian and his eight-year-old daughter, Veronica, and their bull mastiff, Charlie. Brian hadn't seen much of Mom since Dad's funeral, either. He hugged her and immediately started ribbing her about the plucked-from-the-Dumpster presents she'd brought for everyone in the shopping bags: rusting silverware, old books and magazines, a few pieces of fine bone china from the twenties with only minor chips.

Brian had become a decorated sergeant detective, supervising a special unit that investigated organized crime. He and his wife had split up around the time Eric and I did, but he had consoled himself by buying and renovating a wreck of a town house in Brooklyn. He put in new wiring and plumbing, a new firebox, reinforced floor joists, and a new porch all on his own. It was the second time he'd taken on a true dump and restored it to perfection. Also, at least two women were after him to marry them. He was doing pretty darn well.

We showed Mom and Lori the gardens, which were ready for winter. John and I had done all the work ourselves: raked the leaves and shredded them in the chipper, cut back the dead perennials and mulched the beds, shoveled compost onto the vegetable garden and tilled it, and dug up the dahlia bulbs and stored them in a bucket of sand in the basement. John had also split and stacked the wood from a dead maple we'd cut down, and climbed up on the roof to replace some rotted cedar shingles.

Mom nodded at all our preparations; she'd always appreciated self-sufficiency. She admired the wisteria that wrapped around the potting shed, the trumpet vine on the arbor, and the big grove of bamboo in the back. When she saw the pool, an impulse seized her, and she ran out onto the green elastic cover to test its strength, Charlie the dog loping after her. The cover sagged beneath them, and she fell down, shrieking with laughter. John and Brian had to help pull her off as Brian's daughter, Veronica—who hadn't seen Mom since she was a toddler—stared wide-eyed.

"Grandma Walls is different from your other grandma," I told her.

"Way different," Veronica said.

John's daughter, Jessica, turned to me and said, "But she laughs just like you do."

I showed Mom and Lori the house. I still went into the office in the city once a week, but this was where John and I lived and worked, our home—the first house I'd ever owned. Mom and Lori admired the wide-planked floorboards, the big fireplaces, and the ceiling beams made from locust posts, with gouge marks from the ax that had felled them. Mom's eye settled on an Egyptian couch we'd bought at a flea market. It had carved legs and a wooden backrest inlaid with mother-of-pearl triangles. She nodded in approval. "Every household," she said, "needs one piece of furniture in really bad taste."

The kitchen was filled with the smell of the roasting turkey John had prepared, with a stuffing of sausage, mushrooms, walnuts, apples, and spiced bread crumbs. He'd also made creamed onions, wild rice, cranberry sauce, and squash casserole. I'd baked three pies with apples from a nearby orchard.

"Bonanza!" Brian shouted.

"Feast time!" I said to him.

He looked at the dishes. I knew what he was thinking, what he thought every time he saw a spread like this one. He shook his head and said, "You know, it's really not that hard to put food on the table if that's what you decide to do."

"Now, no recriminations," Lori told him.

After we sat down for dinner, Mom told us her good news. She had been a squatter for almost fifteen years, and the city had finally decided to sell the apartments to her and the other squatters for one dollar apiece. She couldn't accept our invitation to stay awhile, she said, because she had to get back for a board meeting of the squatters. Mom also said she'd been in touch with Maureen, who was still living in California, and that our kid sister, whom I hadn't spoken to since she left New York, was thinking of coming back for a visit.

We started talking about some of Dad's great escapades: letting me pet the cheetah, taking us Demon Hunting, giving us stars for Christmas.

"We should drink a toast to Rex," John said.

Mom stared at the ceiling, miming perplexed thought. "I've got it." She held up her glass. "Life with your father was never boring."

We raised our glasses. I could almost hear Dad chuckling at Mom's comment in the way he always did when he was truly enjoying something. It had grown dark outside. A wind picked up, rattling the windows, and the candle flames suddenly shifted, dancing along the border between turbulence and order.

About the Author

Jeannette Walls lives in New York City and Virginia and is married to the writer John Taylor. She is a regular contributor to MSNBC.com.

Turn the page for a preview of Jeannette Walls's new book

The Silver Star

Coming soon from Scribner

MY SISTER SAVED my life when I was just a baby. Here's what happened. After a fight with her family, Mom decided to leave home in the middle of the night, taking us with her. She put me in the infant carrier and set it on the roof of the car while she stashed some things in the trunk, then she settled Liz, who was three, in the backseat. Mom was going through a rough period at the time and had a lot on her mind—craziness, craziness, craziness, she'd say later. Completely forgetting about me—I was only a few months old—Mom drove off.

Liz shrieked my name and pointed to the roof of the car. At first Mom didn't understand what Liz was saying, then she realized what she'd done and slammed on the brakes. The carrier slid forward onto the hood, but since I was strapped in, I was all right. In fact, I wasn't even crying. In the years afterward, whenever Mom told the story, which she found hilarious and acted out in dramatic detail, she liked to say thank goodness Liz had her wits about her, otherwise that carrier would have flown right off and I'd have been a goner.

Liz remembered the whole thing vividly, but she never thought it was funny. She had saved me. That was the kind of sister Liz was. And that was why, the night the whole mess started, I wasn't worried that Mom had been gone for four days. I was more worried about the chicken potpies.

I really hated it when the crust on our chicken potpies got burned, but the timer on the toaster oven was broken, and so that night I was staring into the oven's little glass window because, once those pies began turning brown, you had to watch them the entire time.

Liz was setting the table. Mom was off in Los Angeles, at some recording studio auditioning for a role as a backup singer.

"Do you think she'll get the job?" I asked Liz.

"I have no idea," Liz said.

"I do. I have a good feeling about this one."

Mom had been going into the city a lot ever since we had moved to Lost Lake, a little town in the Colorado Desert of southern California. Usually she was gone for only a night or two, never this long. We didn't know exactly when she'd be back, and since the telephone had been turned off—Mom was arguing with the phone company about some long-distance calls she said she didn't make—she had no way of calling us.

Still, it didn't seem like a big deal. Mom's career had always taken up a sizeable chunk of her time. Even when we were younger, she'd have a sitter or a friend watch us while she flew off to some place like Nashville—so Liz and I were used to being on our own. Liz was in charge, since she was fifteen and I'd just turned twelve, but I wasn't the kind of kid who needed to be babied.

When Mom was away, all we ate was chicken potpies. I loved them and could eat them every night. Liz said that if you had a glass of milk with your chicken potpie, you were getting a dinner that included all four food groups—meat, vegetables, grain, and dairy—so it was the perfect diet.

Plus, they were fun to eat. You each got your very own pie in the nifty little tinfoil pie plate, and you could do whatever you wanted with it. I liked to break up the crust and mush it together with the bits of carrots and peas and the yellow gunk. Liz thought mushing it all together was uncouth. It also made the crust soggy, and to her, what made the chicken potpies so appealing was the contrast between the crispy crust and the goopy filling. She preferred to leave the crust intact, cutting dainty wedges with each bite.

Once the piecrusts had turned that wonderful golden brown, with the little ridged edges almost but not quite burned, I told Liz they were ready. She pulled them out of the toaster oven, and we sat down at the red Formica table.

At dinnertime, when Mom was away, we liked to play games Liz made up. One she called Chew-and-Spew, where you waited until the other person had a mouthful of food or milk, then you tried to make her laugh. Liz pretty much always won, because it was sort of easy to make me laugh. In fact, sometimes I laughed so hard the milk came shooting out of my nose.

Another game she made up was called the Lying Game. One person gave two statements, one true, the second a lie, and the other person got to ask five questions about the statements, then had to guess which one was the lie. Liz usually won the Lying Game, too, but as with Chew-and-Spew, it didn't matter who won. What was fun was playing the game. That night I was excited because I had what I thought was an unbelievable stumper: A frog's eyeballs go into its mouth when it's swallowing or a frog's blood is green.

"That's easy," Liz said. "Green blood is the lie."

"I can't believe you guessed it right away!"

"We dissected frogs in biology."

I was still talking about how hilarious and bizarre it was that a frog used its eyeballs to swallow when Mom walked through the door carrying a white box tied with red string. "Key lime pie for my girls!" she announced, holding up the box. Her face was glowing and she had a giddy smile. "It's a special occasion, because our lives are about to change."

As Mom cut the pie and passed the slices around, she told us that while she'd been at that recording studio, she'd met a man. He was a record producer named Mark Parker, and he'd told her that the reason she wasn't landing gigs as a backup singer was that her voice was too distinctive and she was upstaging the lead singers.

"Mark said I wasn't cut out to play second fiddle to anyone," Mom explained. He told her she had star quality, and that night he took her out to dinner and they talked about how to jump-start her career. "He's so smart and funny," Mom said. "You girls will adore him."

"Is he serious, or is he just a tire-kicker?" I asked.

"Watch it, Bean," Mom said.

Bean's not my real name, of course, but that's what everyone calls me. Bean.

It wasn't my idea. When I was born, Mom named me Jean, but the first time Liz laid eyes on me, she called me Jean the Bean because I was teeny like a bean and because it rhymed—Liz was always rhyming—and then simply Bean because it was shorter. But sometimes she would go and make it longer, calling me the Beaner or Bean Head, maybe Clean Bean when I'd taken a bath, Lean Bean because I was so skinny, Queen

Bean just to make me feel good, or Mean Bean if I was in a bad mood. Once, when I got food poisoning after eating a bowl of bad chili, she called me Green Bean, and then later, when I was hugging the toilet and feeling even worse, she called me Greener Beaner.

Liz couldn't resist playing with words. That was why she loved the name of our new town, Lost Lake. "Let's go look for it," she'd say, or "I wonder who lost it," or "Maybe the lake should ask for directions." We'd moved to Lost Lake from Pasadena four months ago, on New Year's Day of 1970. Mom said a change of scenery would give us a fresh start for the new decade.

Lost Lake was a pretty neat place, in my opinion. Most of the people who lived there were Mexicans who kept chickens and goats in their yards, which was where they practically lived themselves, cooking on grills and dancing to the Mexican music that blared from their radios. Dogs and cats roamed the dusty streets, and irrigation canals at the edge of town carried water to the crop fields. No one looked sideways at you if you wore your big sister's hand-me-downs or your mom drove an old brown Dart. Our neighbors lived in little adobe houses, but we rented a cinder-block bungalow. It was Mom's idea to paint the cinder blocks turquoise blue and the door and windowsills tangerine orange. "Let's not even pretend we want to blend in," she said.

Mom was a singer, songwriter, and actress. She had never actually been in a movie or made a record, but she hated to be called "aspiring," and truth be told, she was a little older than the people described that way in the movie magazines she was always buying. Mom's thirty-sixth birthday was coming up, and she complained that the singers who were getting all the attention, like Janis Joplin and Joni Mitchell, were at least ten years younger than her.

Even so, Mom always said her big break was right around the corner. Sometimes she got callbacks after auditions, but she usually came home shaking her head and saying the guys at the studio were just tire-kickers who wanted a second look at her cleavage. So while Mom had her career, it wasn't one that produced much in the way of income—yet. Mostly we lived on Mom's inheritance. It hadn't been a ton of money to begin with, and by the time we moved to Lost Lake, we were on a fairly tight budget.

When Mom wasn't taking trips into L.A.—which were draining because the drive was nearly four hours in each direction—she tended to sleep late and spend the day writing songs, playing them on one of her four guitars. Her favorite, a 1961 Zemaitis, cost about a year's rent. She also had a Gibson Southern Jumbo, a honey-colored Martin, and a Spanish guitar made from Brazilian rosewood. If she wasn't practicing her songs, she was working on a musical play based on her life, about breaking away from her stifling old-South family, jettisoning her jerk of a husband and string of deadbeat boyfriends—together with all the tire-kickers who didn't reach the boyfriend stage—and discovering her true voice in music. She called the play "Finding the Magic."

Mom always talked about how the secret to the creative process was finding the magic. That, she said, was what you needed to do in life as well. Find the magic. In musical harmony, in the rain on your face and the sun on your bare shoulders, in the morning dew that soaked your sneakers and the wildflowers you picked for free in the roadside ditch, in love at first sight and those sad memories of the one who got away. "Find the magic," Mom always said. "And if you can't find the magic," she added, "then make the magic."

The three of us were magic, Mom liked to say. She assured us that no matter how famous she became, nothing would ever be more important to her than her two girls. We were a tribe of three, she said. Three was a perfect number, she'd go on. Think of it. The holy trinity, three musketeers, three kings of Orient, three little pigs, three stooges, three blind mice, three wishes, three strikes, three cheers, three's a charm. The three of us were all we needed, Mom said.

But that didn't keep her from going out on dates with tire-kickers.

Jeannette Walls on her second book Half Broke Horses

This is a book about my grandmother, Lily Casey Smith.

It was originally meant to be about my mother's childhood growing up on a 180,000-acre cattle ranch in Arizona. But as I talked to Mom about those years, she kept insisting that her mother was the one who had led the truly interesting life and that the book should be about Lily.

My grandmother was—and I say this with all due respect—quite a character. Born in a dugout house off the Pecos River, she'd been at times a cowgirl, horse trainer, mustang breaker, jockey, airplane pilot, and Chicago flapper as well as a mother and teacher who helped her husband run that huge ranch. However, at first I resisted writing about her. While I had been close to her as a child, she died when I was eight, and most of what I knew about her came secondhand.

Still, I'd been hearing the stories about Lily Casey Smith all my life, stories she told over and over to my mother, who told them to me. Lily was a spirited woman, a passionate teacher and talker who explained in great detail what had happened to her, why it had happened, what she'd done about it, and what she'd learned from it, all with the idea of imparting life lessons to my mother. My mother—who struggles to remember my phone number—has an astonishing recall for details about her mother and father and about their parents as well as an amazing knowledge of the history and geology of Arizona. She never once told me something, whether about the Havasupai tribe or the Mogollon Rim, slaughtering cattle or breaking horses, that I could not confirm.

While interviewing my mother and other family members, I came across a couple of books about her paternal grandfather and maternal great-grandfather that confirmed some of the family stories: *Major Lot Smith, Mormon Raider,* by Ivan Barrett, and *Robert Casey and the Ranch on the Rio Hondo,* by James Shinkle.

Although those books substantiated certain events, such as the murder of Robert Casey and his children's feud over the herd, they contradicted others. Shinkle noted that while researching his book, he came across conflicting versions of events and was frequently unable to get to the ultimate truth. In telling my grandmother's story, I never aspired to that sort of historical accuracy. I saw the book more in the vein of an oral history, a retelling of stories handed down by my family through the years, and undertaken with the storyteller's traditional liberties.

I wrote my story in the first person because I wanted to capture Lily's distinctive voice, which I clearly recall. At the time I didn't think of the book as fiction. Lily Casey Smith was a very real woman, and to say that I created her or the events of her life is giving me more credit than I'm due. However, since I don't have the words from Lily herself, and since I have also drawn on my imagination to fill in details that are hazy or missing—and I've changed a few names to protect people's privacy—the only honest thing to do is call the book a novel.

Turn the page for a preview of Jeannette Walls's second book

Half Broke Horses

A True-Life Novel

Now available from Scribner

Lily Casey Smith, Ashfork, Arizona, 1934

THOSE OLD COWS KNEW trouble was coming before we did.

It was late on an August afternoon, the air hot and heavy like it usually was in the rainy season. Earlier we'd seen some thunderheads near the Burnt Spring Hills, but they'd passed way up to the north. I'd mostly finished my chores for the day and was heading down to the pasture with my brother, Buster, and my sister, Helen, to bring the cows in for their milking. But when we got there, those girls were acting all bothered. Instead of milling around at the gate, like they usually did at milking time, they were standing stiff-legged and straight-tailed, twitching their heads around, listening.

Buster and Helen looked up at me, and without a word, I knelt down and pressed my ear to the hard-packed dirt. There was a rumbling, so faint and low that you felt it more than you heard it. Then I knew what the cows knew—a flash flood was coming.

As I stood up, the cows bolted, heading for the southern fence line, and when they reached the barbed wire, they jumped over it—higher and cleaner than I'd ever seen cows jump—and then they thundered off toward higher ground.

I figured we best bolt, too, so I grabbed Helen and Buster by the hand. By then I could feel the ground rumbling through my shoes. I saw the first water sluicing through the lowest part of the pasture, and I knew we didn't have time to make it to higher ground ourselves. In the middle of the field was an old cottonwood tree, broad-branched and gnarled, and we ran for that.

Helen stumbled, so Buster grabbed her other hand, and we lifted her off the ground and carried her between us as we ran. When we reached the cottonwood, I pushed Buster up to the lowest branch, and he pulled Helen into the tree behind him. I shimmied up and wrapped my arms around Helen just as a wall of water, about six feet high and pushing rocks and tree limbs in front of it, slammed into the cottonwood, dousing all three of us. The tree shuddered and bent over so far that you could hear wood cracking, and some lower branches were torn off. I feared it might be uprooted, but the cottonwood held fast and so did we, our arms locked as a great rush of caramel-colored water, filled with bits of wood and the occasional matted gopher and tangle of snakes, surged beneath us, spreading out across the lowland and seeking its level.

We just sat there in that cottonwood tree watching for about an hour. The sun started to set over the Burnt Spring Hills, turning the high clouds crimson and sending long purple shadows eastward. The water was still flowing beneath us, and Helen said her arms were getting tired. She was only seven and was afraid she couldn't hold on much longer.

Buster, who was nine, was perched up in the big fork of the tree. I was ten, the oldest, and I took charge, telling Buster to trade places with Helen so she could sit upright without having to cling too hard. A little while later, it got dark, but a bright moon came out and we could see just fine. From time to time we all switched places so no one's arms would wear out. The bark was chafing my thighs, and Helen's, too, and when we needed to pee, we had to just wet ourselves. About halfway through the night, Helen's voice started getting weak.

"I can't hold on any longer," she said.

"Yes, you can," I told her. "You can because you have to." We were going to make it, I told them. I knew we would make it because I could see it in my mind. I could see us walking up the hill to the house tomorrow morning, and I could see Mom and Dad running out. It would happen—but it was up to us to make it happen.

To keep Helen and Buster from drifting off to sleep and falling out of the cottonwood, I grilled them on their multiplication tables. When we'd run through those, I went on to presidents and state capitals, then word definitions, word rhymes, and whatever else I could come up with, snapping at them if their voices faltered, and that was how I kept Helen and Buster awake through the night.

By first light, you could see that the water still covered the ground. In most places, a flash flood drained away after a couple of hours, but the pasture was in bottomland near the river, and sometimes the water remained for days. But it had stopped moving and had begun seeping down through the sinkholes and mudflats.

"We made it," I said.

I figured it would be safe to wade through the water, so we scrambled out of the cottonwood tree. We were so stiff from holding on all night that our joints could scarcely move, and the mud kept sucking at our shoes, but we got to dry land as the sun was coming up and climbed the hill to the house just the way I had seen it.

Dad was on the porch, pacing back and forth in that uneven stride he had on account of his gimp leg. When he saw us, he let out a yelp of delight and started hobbling down the steps toward us. Mom came running out of the house. She sank to her knees, clasped her hands in front of her, and started praying up to the heavens, thanking the Lord for delivering her children from the flood.

It was she who had saved us, she declared, by staying up all night praying. "You get down on your knees and thank your guardian angel," she said. "And you thank me, too."

Helen and Buster got down and started praying with Mom, but I just stood there looking at them. The way I saw it, I was the one who'd saved us all, not Mom and not some guardian angel. No one was up in that cottonwood tree except the three of us. Dad came alongside me and put his arm around my shoulders.

"There weren't no guardian angel, Dad," I said. I started explaining how I'd gotten us to the cottonwood tree in time, figuring out how to switch places when our arms got tired and keeping Buster and Helen awake through the long night by quizzing them.

Dad squeezed my shoulder. "Well, darling," he said, "maybe the angel was you."